Based on the Texas Essential Knowledge and Skills (TEKS)

STAAR

SUCCESS STRATEGIES
EOC English I

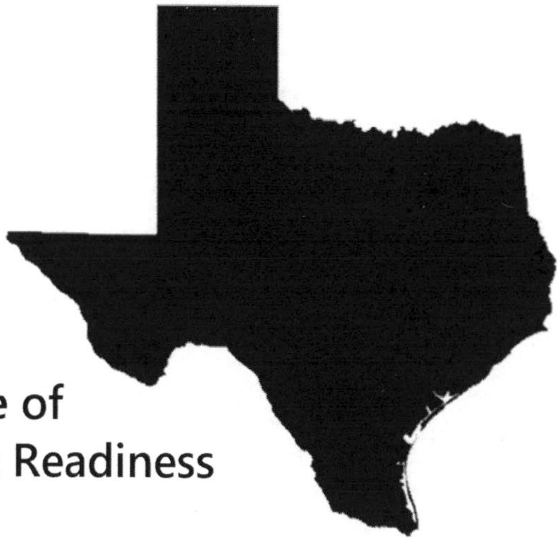

STAAR Test Review for the State of
Texas Assessments of Academic Readiness

Dear Future Exam Success Story:

First of all, **THANK YOU** for purchasing Mometrix study materials!

Second, congratulations! You are one of the few determined test-takers who are committed to doing whatever it takes to excel on your exam. **You have come to the right place.** We developed these study materials with one goal in mind: to deliver you the information you need in a format that's concise and easy to use.

In addition to optimizing your guide for the content of the test, we've outlined our recommended steps for breaking down the preparation process into small, attainable goals so you can make sure you stay on track.

We've also analyzed the entire test-taking process, identifying the most common pitfalls and showing how you can overcome them and be ready for any curveball the test throws you.

Standardized testing is one of the biggest obstacles on your road to success, which only increases the importance of doing well in the high-pressure, high-stakes environment of test day. Your results on this test could have a significant impact on your future, and this guide provides the information and practical advice to help you achieve your full potential on test day.

Your success is our success

We would love to hear from you! If you would like to share the story of your exam success or if you have any questions or comments in regard to our products, please contact us at **800-673-8175** or **support@mometrix.com**.

Thanks again for your business and we wish you continued success!

Sincerely,
The Mometrix Test Preparation Team

Need more help? Check out our flashcards at: http://MometrixFlashcards.com/STAAR

Written and edited by the Mometrix Test Preparation Team
Printed in the United States of America

TABLE OF CONTENTS

Introduction

Thank you for purchasing this resource! You have made the choice to prepare yourself for a test that could have a huge impact on your future, and this guide is designed to help you be fully ready for test day. Obviously, it's important to have a solid understanding of the test material, but you also need to be prepared for the unique environment and stressors of the test, so that you can perform to the best of your abilities.

For this purpose, the first section that appears in this guide is the **Success Strategies**. We've devoted countless hours to meticulously researching what works and what doesn't, and we've boiled down our findings to the five most impactful steps you can take to improve your performance on the test. We start at the beginning with study planning and move through the preparation process, all the way to the testing strategies that will help you get the most out of what you know when you're finally sitting in front of the test.

We recommend that you start preparing for your test as far in advance as possible. However, if you've bought this guide as a last-minute study resource and only have a few days before your test, we recommend that you skip over the first two Success Strategies since they address a long-term study plan.

If you struggle with **test anxiety**, we strongly encourage you to check out our recommendations for how you can overcome it. Test anxiety is a formidable foe, but it can be beaten, and we want to make sure you have the tools you need to defeat it.

Success Strategy #1 – Plan Big, Study Small

There's a lot riding on your performance. If you want to ace this test, you're going to need to keep your skills sharp and the material fresh in your mind. You need a plan that lets you review everything you need to know while still fitting in your schedule. We'll break this strategy down into three categories.

Information Organization

Start with the information you already have: the official test outline. From this, you can make a complete list of all the concepts you need to cover before the test. Organize these concepts into groups that can be studied together, and create a list of any related vocabulary you need to learn so you can brush up on any difficult terms. You'll want to keep this vocabulary list handy once you actually start studying since you may need to add to it along the way.

Time Management

Once you have your set of study concepts, decide how to spread them out over the time you have left before the test. Break your study plan into small, clear goals so you have a manageable task for each day and know exactly what you're doing. Then just focus on one small step at a time. When you manage your time this way, you don't need to spend hours at a time studying. Studying a small block of content for a short period each day helps you retain information better and avoid stressing over how much you have left to do. You can relax knowing that you have a plan to cover everything in time. In order for this strategy to be effective though, you have to start studying early and stick to your schedule. Avoid the exhaustion and futility that comes from last-minute cramming!

Study Environment

The environment you study in has a big impact on your learning. Studying in a coffee shop, while probably more enjoyable, is not likely to be as fruitful as studying in a quiet room. It's important to keep distractions to a minimum. You're only planning to study for a short block of time, so make the most of it. Don't pause to check your phone or get up to find a snack. It's also important to **avoid multitasking**. Research has consistently shown that multitasking will make your studying dramatically less effective. Your study area should also be comfortable and well-lit so you don't have the distraction of straining your eyes or sitting on an uncomfortable chair.

The time of day you study is also important. You want to be rested and alert. Don't wait until just before bedtime. Study when you'll be most likely to comprehend and remember. Even better, if you know what time of day your test will be, set that time aside for study. That way your brain will be used to working on that subject at that specific time and you'll have a better chance of recalling information.

Finally, it can be helpful to team up with others who are studying for the same test. Your actual studying should be done in as isolated an environment as possible, but the work of organizing the information and setting up the study plan can be divided up. In between study sessions, you can discuss with your teammates the concepts that you're all studying and quiz each other on the details. Just be sure that your teammates are as serious about the test as you are. If you find that your study time is being replaced with social time, you might need to find a new team.

Success Strategy #2 – Make Your Studying Count

You're devoting a lot of time and effort to preparing for this test, so you want to be absolutely certain it will pay off. This means doing more than just reading the content and hoping you can remember it on test day. It's important to make every minute of study count. There are two main areas you can focus on to make your studying count:

Retention

It doesn't matter how much time you study if you can't remember the material. You need to make sure you are retaining the concepts. To check your retention of the information you're learning, try recalling it at later times with minimal prompting. Try carrying around flashcards and glance at one or two from time to time or ask a friend who's also studying for the test to quiz you.

To enhance your retention, look for ways to put the information into practice so that you can apply it rather than simply recalling it. If you're using the information in practical ways, it will be much easier to remember. Similarly, it helps to solidify a concept in your mind if you're not only reading it to yourself but also explaining it to someone else. Ask a friend to let you teach them about a concept you're a little shaky on (or speak aloud to an imaginary audience if necessary). As you try to summarize, define, give examples, and answer your friend's questions, you'll understand the concepts better and they will stay with you longer. Finally, step back for a big picture view and ask yourself how each piece of information fits with the whole subject. When you link the different concepts together and see them working together as a whole, it's easier to remember the individual components.

Finally, practice showing your work on any multi-step problems, even if you're just studying. Writing out each step you take to solve a problem will help solidify the process in your mind, and you'll be more likely to remember it during the test.

Modality

Modality simply refers to the means or method by which you study. Choosing a study modality that fits your own individual learning style is crucial. No two people learn best in exactly the same way, so it's important to know your strengths and use them to your advantage.

For example, if you learn best by visualization, focus on visualizing a concept in your mind and draw an image or a diagram. Try color-coding your notes, illustrating them, or creating symbols that will trigger your mind to recall a learned concept. If you learn best by hearing or discussing information, find a study partner who learns the same way or read aloud to yourself. Think about how to put the information in your own words. Imagine that you are giving a lecture on the topic and record yourself so you can listen to it later.

For any learning style, flashcards can be helpful. Organize the information so you can take advantage of spare moments to review. Underline key words or phrases. Use different colors for different categories. Mnemonic devices (such as creating a short list in which every item starts with the same letter) can also help with retention. Find what works best for you and use it to store the information in your mind most effectively and easily.

Success Strategy #3 – Practice the Right Way

Your success on test day depends not only on how many hours you put into preparing, but also on whether you prepared the right way. It's good to check along the way to see if your studying is paying off. One of the most effective ways to do this is by taking practice tests to evaluate your progress. Practice tests are useful because they show exactly where you need to improve. Every time you take a practice test, pay special attention to these three groups of questions:

- The questions you got wrong
- The questions you had to guess on, even if you guessed right
- The questions you found difficult or slow to work through

This will show you exactly what your weak areas are, and where you need to devote more study time. Ask yourself why each of these questions gave you trouble. Was it because you didn't understand the material? Was it because you didn't remember the vocabulary? Do you need more repetitions on this type of question to build speed and confidence? Dig into those questions and figure out how you can strengthen your weak areas as you go back to review the material.

Additionally, many practice tests have a section explaining the answer choices. It can be tempting to read the explanation and think that you now have a good understanding of the concept. However, an explanation likely only covers part of the question's broader context. Even if the explanation makes sense, **go back and investigate** every concept related to the question until you're positive you have a thorough understanding.

As you go along, keep in mind that the practice test is just that: practice. Memorizing these questions and answers will not be very helpful on the actual test because it is unlikely to have any of the same exact questions. If you only know the right answers to the sample questions, you won't be prepared for the real thing. **Study the concepts** until you understand them fully, and then you'll be able to answer any question that shows up on the test.

It's important to wait on the practice tests until you're ready. If you take a test on your first day of study, you may be overwhelmed by the amount of material covered and how much you need to learn. Work up to it gradually.

On test day, you'll need to be prepared for answering questions, managing your time, and using the test-taking strategies you've learned. It's a lot to balance, like a mental marathon that will have a big impact on your future. Like training for a marathon, you'll need to start slowly and work your way up. When test day arrives, you'll be ready.

Start with what you've read in the first two Success Strategies—plan your course and study in the way that works best for you. If you have time, consider using multiple study resources to get different approaches to the same concepts. It can be helpful to see difficult concepts from more than one angle. Then find a good source for practice tests. Many times, the test website will suggest potential study resources or provide sample tests.

Practice Test Strategy

If you're able to find at least three practice tests, we recommend this strategy:

UNTIMED AND OPEN-BOOK PRACTICE

Take the first test with no time constraints and with your notes and study guide handy. Take your time and focus on applying the strategies you've learned.

TIMED AND OPEN-BOOK PRACTICE

Take the second practice test open-book as well, but set a timer and practice pacing yourself to finish in time.

TIMED AND CLOSED-BOOK PRACTICE

Take any other practice tests as if it were test day. Set a timer and put away your study materials. Sit at a table or desk in a quiet room, imagine yourself at the testing center, and answer questions as quickly and accurately as possible.

Keep repeating timed and closed-book tests on a regular basis until you run out of practice tests or it's time for the actual test. Your mind will be ready for the schedule and stress of test day, and you'll be able to focus on recalling the material you've learned.

Success Strategy #4 – Pace Yourself

Once you're fully prepared for the material on the test, your biggest challenge on test day will be managing your time. Just knowing that the clock is ticking can make you panic even if you have plenty of time left. Work on pacing yourself so you can build confidence against the time constraints of the exam. Pacing is a difficult skill to master, especially in a high-pressure environment, so **practice is vital**.

Set time expectations for your pace based on how much time is available. For example, if a section has 60 questions and the time limit is 30 minutes, you know you have to average 30 seconds or less per question in order to answer them all. Although 30 seconds is the hard limit, set 25 seconds per question as your goal, so you reserve extra time to spend on harder questions. When you budget extra time for the harder questions, you no longer have any reason to stress when those questions take longer to answer.

Don't let this time expectation distract you from working through the test at a calm, steady pace, but keep it in mind so you don't spend too much time on any one question. Recognize that taking extra time on one question you don't understand may keep you from answering two that you do understand later in the test. If your time limit for a question is up and you're still not sure of the answer, mark it and move on, and come back to it later if the time and the test format allow. If the testing format doesn't allow you to return to earlier questions, just make an educated guess; then put it out of your mind and move on.

On the easier questions, be careful not to rush. It may seem wise to hurry through them so you have more time for the challenging ones, but it's not worth missing one if you know the concept and just didn't take the time to read the question fully. Work efficiently but make sure you understand the question and have looked at all of the answer choices, since more than one may seem right at first.

Even if you're paying attention to the time, you may find yourself a little behind at some point. You should speed up to get back on track, but do so wisely. Don't panic; just take a few seconds less on each question until you're caught up. Don't guess without thinking, but do look through the answer choices and eliminate any you know are wrong. If you can get down to two choices, it is often worthwhile to guess from those. Once you've chosen an answer, move on and don't dwell on any that you skipped or had to hurry through. If a question was taking too long, chances are it was one of the harder ones, so you weren't as likely to get it right anyway.

On the other hand, if you find yourself getting ahead of schedule, it may be beneficial to slow down a little. The more quickly you work, the more likely you are to make a careless mistake that will affect your score. You've budgeted time for each question, so don't be afraid to spend that time. Practice an efficient but careful pace to get the most out of the time you have.

Test-Taking Strategies

This section contains a list of test-taking strategies that you may find helpful as you work through the test. By taking what you know and applying logical thought, you can maximize your chances of answering any question correctly!

It is very important to realize that every question is different and every person is different: no single strategy will work on every question, and no single strategy will work for every person. That's why we've included all of them here, so you can try them out and determine which ones work best for different types of questions and which ones work best for you.

Question Strategies

Read Carefully

Read the question and answer choices carefully. Don't miss the question because you misread the terms. You have plenty of time to read each question thoroughly and make sure you understand what is being asked. Yet a happy medium must be attained, so don't waste too much time. You must read carefully, but efficiently.

Contextual Clues

Look for contextual clues. If the question includes a word you are not familiar with, look at the immediate context for some indication of what the word might mean. Contextual clues can often give you all the information you need to decipher the meaning of an unfamiliar word. Even if you can't determine the meaning, you may be able to narrow down the possibilities enough to make a solid guess at the answer to the question.

Prefixes

If you're having trouble with a word in the question or answer choices, try dissecting it. Take advantage of every clue that the word might include. Prefixes and suffixes can be a huge help. Usually they allow you to determine a basic meaning. Pre- means before, post- means after, pro - is positive, de- is negative. From prefixes and suffixes, you can get an idea of the general meaning of the word and try to put it into context.

Hedge Words

Watch out for critical hedge words, such as *likely, may, can, sometimes, often, almost, mostly, usually, generally, rarely,* and *sometimes.* Question writers insert these hedge phrases to cover every possibility. Often an answer choice will be wrong simply because it leaves no room for exception. Be on guard for answer choices that have definitive words such as *exactly* and *always.*

Switchback Words

Stay alert for *switchbacks.* These are the words and phrases frequently used to alert you to shifts in thought. The most common switchback words are *but, although,* and *however.* Others include *nevertheless, on the other hand, even though, while, in spite of, despite, regardless of.* Switchback words are important to catch because they can change the direction of the question or an answer choice.

Face Value

When in doubt, use common sense. Accept the situation in the problem at face value. Don't read too much into it. These problems will not require you to make wild assumptions. If you have to go beyond creativity and warp time or space in order to have an answer choice fit the question, then you should move on and consider the other answer choices. These are normal problems rooted in reality. The applicable relationship or explanation may not be readily apparent, but it is there for you to figure out. Use your common sense to interpret anything that isn't clear.

Answer Choice Strategies

Answer Selection

The most thorough way to pick an answer choice is to identify and eliminate wrong answers until only one is left, then confirm it is the correct answer. Sometimes an answer choice may immediately seem right, but be careful. The test writers will usually put more than one reasonable answer choice on each question, so take a second to read all of them and make sure that the other choices are not equally obvious. As long as you have time left, it is better to read every answer choice than to pick the first one that looks right without checking the others.

Answer Choice Families

An answer choice family consists of two (in rare cases, three) answer choices that are very similar in construction and cannot all be true at the same time. If you see two answer choices that are direct opposites or parallels, one of them is usually the correct answer. For instance, if one answer choice says that quantity *x* increases and another either says that quantity *x* decreases (opposite) or says that quantity *y* increases (parallel), then those answer choices would fall into the same family. An answer choice that doesn't match the construction of the answer choice family is more likely to be incorrect. Most questions will not have answer choice families, but when they do appear, you should be prepared to recognize them.

Eliminate Answers

Eliminate answer choices as soon as you realize they are wrong, but make sure you consider all possibilities. If you are eliminating answer choices and realize that the last one you are left with is also wrong, don't panic. Start over and consider each choice again. There may be something you missed the first time that you will realize on the second pass.

Avoid Fact Traps

Don't be distracted by an answer choice that is factually true but doesn't answer the question. You are looking for the choice that answers the question. Stay focused on what the question is asking for so you don't accidentally pick an answer that is true but incorrect. Always go back to the question and make sure the answer choice you've selected actually answers the question and is not merely a true statement.

Extreme Statements

In general, you should avoid answers that put forth extreme actions as standard practice or proclaim controversial ideas as established fact. An answer choice that states the "process should be used in certain situations, if…" is much more likely to be correct than one that states the "process should be discontinued completely." The first is a calm rational statement and doesn't even make a definitive, uncompromising stance, using a hedge word *if* to provide wiggle room, whereas the second choice is a radical idea and far more extreme.

BENCHMARK

As you read through the answer choices and you come across one that seems to answer the question well, mentally select that answer choice. This is not your final answer, but it's the one that will help you evaluate the other answer choices. The one that you selected is your benchmark or standard for judging each of the other answer choices. Every other answer choice must be compared to your benchmark. That choice is correct until proven otherwise by another answer choice beating it. If you find a better answer, then that one becomes your new benchmark. Once you've decided that no other choice answers the question as well as your benchmark, you have your final answer.

PREDICT THE ANSWER

Before you even start looking at the answer choices, it is often best to try to predict the answer. When you come up with the answer on your own, it is easier to avoid distractions and traps because you will know exactly what to look for. The right answer choice is unlikely to be word-for-word what you came up with, but it should be a close match. Even if you are confident that you have the right answer, you should still take the time to read each option before moving on.

General Strategies

TOUGH QUESTIONS

If you are stumped on a problem or it appears too hard or too difficult, don't waste time. Move on! Remember though, if you can quickly check for obviously incorrect answer choices, your chances of guessing correctly are greatly improved. Before you completely give up, at least try to knock out a couple of possible answers. Eliminate what you can and then guess at the remaining answer choices before moving on.

CHECK YOUR WORK

Since you will probably not know every term listed and the answer to every question, it is important that you get credit for the ones that you do know. Don't miss any questions through careless mistakes. If at all possible, try to take a second to look back over your answer selection and make sure you've selected the correct answer choice and haven't made a costly careless mistake (such as marking an answer choice that you didn't mean to mark). This quick double check should more than pay for itself in caught mistakes for the time it costs.

PACE YOURSELF

It's easy to be overwhelmed when you're looking at a page full of questions; your mind is confused and full of random thoughts, and the clock is ticking down faster than you would like. Calm down and maintain the pace that you have set for yourself. Especially as you get down to the last few minutes of the test, don't let the small numbers on the clock make you panic. As long as you are on track by monitoring your pace, you are guaranteed to have time for each question.

DON'T RUSH

It is very easy to make errors when you are in a hurry. Maintaining a fast pace in answering questions is pointless if it makes you miss questions that you would have gotten right otherwise. Test writers like to include distracting information and wrong answers that seem right. Taking a little extra time to avoid careless mistakes can make all the difference in your test score. Find a pace that allows you to be confident in the answers that you select.

KEEP MOVING

Panicking will not help you pass the test, so do your best to stay calm and keep moving. Taking deep breaths and going through the answer elimination steps you practiced can help to break through a stress barrier and keep your pace.

Final Notes

The combination of a solid foundation of content knowledge and the confidence that comes from practicing your plan for applying that knowledge is the key to maximizing your performance on test day. As your foundation of content knowledge is built up and strengthened, you'll find that the strategies included in this chapter become more and more effective in helping you quickly sift through the distractions and traps of the test to isolate the correct answer.

Now it's time to move on to the test content chapters of this book, but be sure to keep your goal in mind. As you read, think about how you will be able to apply this information on the test. If you've already seen sample questions for the test and you have an idea of the question format and style, try to come up with questions of your own that you can answer based on what you're reading. This will give you valuable practice applying your knowledge in the same ways you can expect to on test day.

Good luck and good studying!

Reading

Prose

Common Forms of Prose Fiction

Historical Fiction

Historical fiction is set in particular historical periods, including prehistoric and mythological. Examples include Walter Scott's *Rob Roy* and *Ivanhoe*; Leo Tolstoy's *War and Peace;* Robert Graves' *I, Claudius;* Mary Renault's *The King Must Die* and *The Bull from the Sea* (an historical novel using Greek mythology); Virginia Woolf's *Orlando* and *Between the Acts;* and John Dos Passos's *U.S.A* trilogy. **Picaresque** novels recount episodic adventures of a rogue protagonist or *pícaro,* like Miguel de Cervantes' *Don Quixote* or Henry Fielding's *Tom Jones.* **Gothic** novels originated as a reaction against 18th-century Enlightenment rationalism, featuring horror, mystery, superstition, madness, supernatural elements, and revenge. Early examples include Horace Walpole's *Castle of Otranto,* Matthew Gregory Lewis' *Monk,* Mary Shelley's *Frankenstein,* and Bram Stoker's *Dracula.* In America, Edgar Allan Poe wrote many Gothic works. Contemporary novelist Anne Rice has penned many Gothic novels under the pseudonym A. N. Roquelaure. **Psychological** novels, originating in 17th-century France, explore characters' motivations. Examples include Abbé Prévost's *Manon Lescaut;* George Eliot's novels; Fyodor Dostoyevsky's *Crime and Punishment;* Tolstoy's *Anna Karenina;* Gustave Flaubert's *Madame Bovary;* and the novels of Henry James, James Joyce, and Vladimir Nabokov.

Novels of Manners

Novels of manners are fictional stories that observe, explore, and analyze the social behaviors of a specific time and place. While deep psychological themes are more universal across different historical periods and countries, the manners of a particular society are shorter-lived and more varied; the novel of manners captures these societal details. Novels of manners can also be regarded as symbolically representing, in artistic form, certain established and secure social orders. Characteristics of novels of manners include descriptions of a society with defined behavioral codes; language that uses standardized, impersonal formulas; and inhibition of emotional expression, as contrasted with the strong emotions expressed in romantic or sentimental novels. Jane Austen's detailed descriptions of English society and characters struggling with the definitions and restrictions placed on them by society are excellent models of the novel of manners. In the 20th century, Evelyn Waugh's *Handful of Dust* is a novel of social manners, and his *Sword of Honour* trilogy contains novels of military manners. Another 20th-century example is *The Unbearable Bassington* by Saki (the pen name of writer H. H. Munro), focusing on Edwardian society.

Western-World Sentimental Novels

Sentimental love novels originated in the movement of Romanticism. Eighteenth-century examples of novels that emphasize the emotional aspect of love include Samuel Richardson's *Pamela* (1740) and Jean-Jacques Rousseau's *Nouvelle Héloïse* (1761). Also in the 18th century, Laurence Sterne's novel *Tristram Shandy* (1760-1767) is an example of a novel with elements of sentimentality. The Victorian era's rejection of emotionalism caused the term "sentimental" to have undesirable connotations. However, even non-sentimental novelists such as William Makepeace Thackeray and Charles Dickens incorporated sentimental elements in their writing. A 19th-century author of genuinely sentimental novels was Mrs. Henry Wood (e.g., *East Lynne,* 1861). In the 20th century, Erich Segal's sentimental novel *Love Story* (1970) was a popular bestseller.

EPISTOLARY NOVELS

Epistolary novels are told in the form of letters written by their characters rather than in typical narrative form. Samuel Richardson, the best-known author of epistolary novels like *Pamela* (1740) and *Clarissa* (1748), widely influenced early Romantic epistolary novels throughout Europe that freely expressed emotions. Richardson, a printer, published technical manuals on letter-writing for young gentlewomen; his epistolary novels were fictional extensions of those nonfictional instructional books. Nineteenth-century English author Wilkie Collins' *The Moonstone* (1868) was a mystery written in epistolary form. By the 20th century, the format of well-composed written letters came to be regarded as artificial and outmoded. A 20th-century evolution of letters was tape-recording transcripts, such as in French playwright Samuel Beckett's drama *Krapp's Last Tape.* Though evoking modern alienation, Beckett still created a sense of fictional characters' direct communication without author intervention as Richardson had.

PASTORAL NOVELS

Pastoral novels lyrically idealize country life as idyllic and utopian, akin to the Garden of Eden. *Daphnis and Chloe*, written by Greek novelist Longus around the second or third century, influenced Elizabethan pastoral romances like Thomas Lodge's *Rosalynde* (1590), which inspired Shakespeare's *As You Like It*, and Philip Sidney's *Arcadia* (1590). Jacques-Henri Bernardin de St. Pierre's French work *Paul et Virginie* (1787) demonstrated the early Romantic view of the innocence and goodness of nature. Though the style lost popularity by the 20th century, pastoral elements can still be seen in novels like *The Rainbow* (1915) and *Lady Chatterley's Lover* (1928), both by D. H. Lawrence. Growing realism transformed pastoral writing into less ideal and more dystopian, distasteful and ironic depictions of country life in George Eliot's and Thomas Hardy's novels. Saul Bellow's novel *Herzog* (1964) may demonstrate how urban ills highlight an alternative pastoral ideal. The pastoral style is commonly thought to be overly idealized and outdated today, as seen in Stella Gibbons' pastoral satire, Cold Comfort Farm (1932).

BILDUNGSROMAN

Bildungsroman is German for "education novel." This term is also used in English to describe "apprenticeship" novels focusing on coming-of-age stories, including youth's struggles and searches for things such as identity, spiritual understanding, or the meaning in life. Johann Wolfgang von Goethe's *Wilhelm Meisters Lehrjahre* (1796) is credited as the origin of this genre. Two of Charles Dickens' novels, *David Copperfield* (1850) and *Great Expectations* (1861), also fit this form. H. G. Wells wrote *bildungsromans* about questing for apprenticeships to address the complications of modern life in *Joan and Peter* (1918) and from a Utopian perspective in *The Dream* (1924). School *bildungsromans* include Thomas Hughes' *Tom Brown's School Days* (1857) and Alain-Fournier's *Le Grand Meaulnes* (1913). Many Hermann Hesse novels, including *Demian, Steppenwolf, Siddhartha, Magister Ludi,* and *Beneath the Wheel* are *bildungsromans* about a struggling, searching youth. Samuel Butler's *The Way of All Flesh* (1903) and James Joyce's *A Portrait of the Artist as a Young Man* (1916) are two modern examples. Variations include J. D. Salinger's *The Catcher in the Rye* (1951), set both within and beyond school, and William Golding's *Lord of the Flies* (1955), a novel not set in a school but one that is a coming-of-age story nonetheless.

ROMAN À CLEF

Roman à clef, French for "novel with a key," refers to books that require a real-life frame of reference, or key, for full comprehension. In Geoffrey Chaucer's *Canterbury Tales,* the Nun's Priest's Tale contains details that confuse readers unaware of history about the Earl of Bolingbroke's involvement in an assassination plot. Other literary works fitting this form include John Dryden's political satirical poem "Absalom and Achitophel" (1681), Jonathan Swift's satire "A Tale of a Tub" (1704), and George Orwell's political allegory *Animal Farm* (1945), all of which cannot be understood completely without knowing their camouflaged historical contents. *Roman à clefs* disguise truths too dangerous for authors to state directly. Readers must know about the enemies of D. H. Lawrence and Aldous Huxley to appreciate their respective novels: *Aaron's Rod* (1922) and *Point Counter Point* (1928). Marcel Proust's *Remembrance of Things Past (À la recherché du temps perdu,* 1871-1922) is informed by his social context. James Joyce's *Finnegans Wake* is an enormous *roman à clef* containing multitudinous personal references.

Review Video: Major Forms of Prose
Visit mometrix.com/academy and enter code: 565543

OTHER COMMON TYPES OF PROSE

- A **narrative** is any composition that tells a story. Narratives have characters, settings, and a structure. Narratives may be fiction or nonfiction stories and may follow a linear or nonlinear structure. The purpose of a narrative is generally to entertain, but nonfiction narratives can be informative, as well. Narratives also appear in a variety of structures and formats.
- **Biographies** are books written about another person's life. Biographies can be valuable historical resources. Though they provide a narrow view of the relevant time period and culture, their specificity can also provide a unique context for that period or culture. Biographies, especially those whose subject was a well-known and influential figure, can provide a more complete picture of the figure's life or contributions. Biographies can also serve as a source of inspiration or communicate a moral because of their focus on one person over an extended period of time.
- **Myths**, or stories from mythology, exist in most ancient cultures and continue to influence modern cultures. Mythology is so influential that it has even inspired numerous pieces of modern literature and media in popular culture. While popular culture most clearly references mythology from the Ancient Greek and Roman cultures, literature has been influenced by mythologies from around the entire world. Since mythology is so prevalent in ancient literature, it makes sense that universal themes and morals often appear in mythology and even drive some myths. This suggests connections between cultures through the stories they pass down.
- **Fables** are short, didactic stories that typically feature imaginary creatures or talking animals. The famous story "The Tortoise and the Hare" is a fable. Fables are still told and used today because of their universally understandable morals and characters, making them suitable for children's literature and media.
- **Fairy tales** are stories that involve fictional creatures or realistic characters with fantastical traits and abilities. Fairy tales often end happily and depict the victory of good over evil. The plots and characters in fairy tales are often far-fetched and whimsical.
- **Folk Tales** are stories that have withstood time and are usually popular in a particular region or culture. Folk tales often depict the clever success of a common person, though the story may, alternatively, end poorly for the protagonist. Folk tales are easily confused with fairytales because fairytales can be a type of folk tale.
- **Legends** are stories that typically focus on one character and highlight their victory over a particular enemy or obstacle. Legends often feature some facts or are inspired by true events, but are still understood to be either exaggerated or partially fictional. Heroes are often the protagonists of legends as they often save or protect others as they conquer enemies and obstacles.

- A **short story** is a fictional narrative that is shorter than a novel. However, there is not a definite page or word count that defines the short story category. Short stories tend to focus on one or few elements of a story in order to efficiently tell the story. Though they are often brief, short stories may still contain a moral or impact their readers.

Common Genres in Prose

- The **mystery** genre includes stories with plots that follow a protagonist as they work to solve an unexplained situation, such as a murder, disappearance, or robbery. Protagonists of mysteries may be hired professionals or amateurs who solve the mystery despite their lack of experience and resources. Mysteries allow the reader to solve the case along with the protagonist, and often grant the reader an advantageous perspective, creating dramatic irony. The *Sherlock Holmes* novels by Sir Arthur Conan Doyle are examples of mystery novels.
- **Science Fiction** is a genre that is based on the manipulation and exaggeration of real scientific discoveries and processes. These works are speculative and frequently depict a world where scientific discoveries and society have progressed beyond the point reached at the time of the work's creation. Works of science fiction often take place in a distant location or time, allowing for the dramatic advancements and conveniences they often depict. *Dune,* written by Frank Herbert, is an example of a science-fiction novel.
- The **fantasy** genre includes stories that feature imaginary creatures and supernatural abilities, but often take place in settings that resemble real places and cultures in history. Fantasy novels usually follow a gifted protagonist from humble beginnings as they embark on a quest, journey, or adventure and encounter mystical beings and personally challenging obstacles. Common themes in the fantasy genre include personal growth, good versus evil, and the value of the journey. J.R.R. Tolkien's *The Lord of the Rings* trilogy belongs to the fantasy genre.
- **Realistic fiction** describes fictional narratives that include events and characters that do not exist, but could appear in reality. Within the narrative, these characters and events may be depicted in real places. For example, Pip, the protagonist of Charles Dickens's *Great Expectations*, was not a real person, but the novel shows him living in London, England for much of his young adulthood. Realistic fiction contains no far-fetched or impossible elements and presents situations that can or do occur in real life. A contemporary example of realistic fiction is *Wonder* by R.J. Palacio.
- **Historical fiction** includes works that take place in the past and model their setting after real historical cultures, societies, and time periods. These works may include real historical figures and events, but they also may not. Works of historical fiction must be fully informed by the period and location they are set in, meaning both the major and minor details of the work must be historically compatible with the work's setting. Examples of historical fiction include Kathryn Stockett's *The Help* and Markus Zusak's *The Book Thief.*
- The phrase **Literary Nonfiction** describes nonfiction narratives that present true facts and events in a way that entertains readers and displays creativity. Literary nonfiction, also called creative nonfiction, may resemble fiction in its style and flow, but the truth of the events it describes sets it apart from fictional literature. Different types of books may be considered literary nonfiction, such as biographies, if they appear to employ creativity in their writing. An example of literary nonfiction is *The Immortal Life of Henrietta Lacks* by Rebecca Skloot.

Realism and Satire

Realism

Realism is a literary form with the goal of representing reality as faithfully as possible. Its genesis in Western literature was a reaction against the sentimentality and extreme emotionalism of the works written during the Romantic literary movement, which championed feelings and emotional expression. Realists focused in great detail on immediacy of time and place, on specific actions of their characters, and the justifiable consequences of those actions. Some techniques of realism include writing in vernacular (conversational language), using specific dialects, and placing an emphasis on character rather than plot. Realistic literature also often addresses ethical issues. Historically, realistic works have often concentrated on the middle classes of the authors' societies. Realists eschew treatments that are too dramatic or sensationalistic as exaggerations of the reality that they strive to portray as closely as they are able. Influenced by his own bleak past, Fyodor Dostoevsky wrote several novels, such as *Crime and Punishment* (1866) that shunned romantic ideals and sought to portray a stark reality. Henry James was a prominent writer of realism in novels such as *Daisy Miller* (1879). Samuel Clemens (Mark Twain) skillfully represented the language and culture of lower-class Mississippi in his novel *The Adventures of Huckleberry Finn* (1885).

Satire

Satire uses sarcasm, irony, and humor as social criticism to lampoon human folly. Unlike realism, which intends to depict reality as it exists without exaggeration, satire often involves creating situations or ideas that deliberately exaggerate reality to appear ridiculous to illuminate flawed behaviors. Ancient Roman satirists included Horace and Juvenal. Alexander Pope's poem "The Rape of the Lock" satirized the values of fashionable members of the 18th-century upper-middle class, which Pope found shallow and trivial. The theft of a lock of hair from a young woman is blown out of proportion: the poem's characters regard it as seriously as they would a rape. Irishman Jonathan Swift satirized British society, politics, and religion in works like "A Modest Proposal" and *Gulliver's Travels.* In "A Modest Proposal," Swift used essay form and mock-serious tone, satirically "proposing" cannibalism of babies and children as a solution to poverty and overpopulation. He satirized petty political disputes in *Gulliver's Travels.*

Poetry

Poetry Terminology

Unlike prose, which traditionally (except in forms like stream of consciousness) consists of complete sentences connected into paragraphs, poetry is written in **verses**. These may form complete sentences, clauses, or phrases. Poetry may be written with or without rhyme. It can be metered, following a particular rhythmic pattern such as iambic, dactylic, spondaic, trochaic, or **anapestic**, or may be without regular meter. The terms **iamb** and **trochee**, among others, identify stressed and unstressed syllables in each verse. Meter is also described by the number of beats or stressed syllables per verse: **dimeter** (2), **trimeter** (3), **tetrameter** (4), **pentameter** (5), and so forth. Using the symbol ᴗ to denote unstressed and / to denote stressed syllables, **iambic** = ᴗ/; **trochaic** = /ᴗ; **spondaic** =//; **dactylic** =/ᴗᴗ; **anapestic** =ᴗᴗ/. **Rhyme schemes** identify which lines rhyme, such as ABAB, ABCA, AABA, and so on. Poetry with neither rhyme nor meter is called **free verse**. Poems may be in free verse, metered but unrhymed, rhymed but without meter, or using both rhyme and meter. In English, the most common meter is iambic pentameter. Unrhymed iambic pentameter is called **blank verse**.

MAJOR FORMS OF POETRY

From man's earliest days, he expressed himself with poetry. A large percentage of the surviving literature from ancient times is in **epic poetry**, utilized by Homer and other Greco-Roman poets. Epic poems typically recount heroic deeds and adventures, using stylized language and combining dramatic and lyrical conventions. **Epistolary poems**, poems that are written and read as letters, also developed in ancient times. In the fourteenth and fifteenth centuries, the **ballad** became a popular convention. Ballads often follow a rhyme scheme and meter and focus on subjects such as love, death, and religion. Many ballads tell stories, and several modern ballads are put to music. From these early conventions, numerous other poetic forms developed, such as **elegies**, **odes**, and **pastoral poems**. Elegies are mourning poems written in three parts: lament, praise of the deceased, and solace for loss. Odes evolved from songs to the typical poem of the Romantic time period, expressing strong feelings and contemplative thoughts. Pastoral poems idealize nature and country living. Poetry can also be used to make short, pithy statements. **Epigrams** (memorable rhymes with one or two lines) and **limericks** (two lines of iambic dimeter followed by two lines of iambic dimeter and another of iambic trimeter) are known for humor and wit.

HAIKU

Haiku was originally a Japanese poetry form. In the 13th century, haiku was the opening phrase of renga, a 100-stanza oral poem. By the 16th century, haiku diverged into a separate short poem. When Western writers discovered haiku, the form became popular in English, as well as other languages. A haiku has 17 syllables, traditionally distributed across three lines as 5/7/5, with a pause after the first or second line. Haiku are syllabic and unrhymed. Haiku philosophy and technique are that brevity's compression forces writers to express images concisely, depict a moment in time, and evoke illumination and enlightenment. An example is 17th-century haiku master Matsuo Basho's classic: "An old silent pond... / A frog jumps into the pond, / splash! Silence again." Modern American poet Ezra Pound revealed the influence of haiku in his two-line poem "In a Station of the Metro." In this poem, line 1 has 12 syllables (combining the syllable count of the first two lines of a haiku) and line 2 has 7, but it still preserves haiku's philosophy and imagistic technique: "The apparition of these faces in the crowd; / Petals on a wet, black bough."

SONNETS

The sonnet traditionally has 14 lines of iambic pentameter, tightly organized around a theme. The Petrarchan sonnet, named for 14th-century Italian poet Petrarch, has an eight-line stanza, the octave, and a six-line stanza, the sestet. There is a change or turn, known as the volta, between the eighth and ninth verses, setting up the sestet's answer or summary. The rhyme scheme is ABBA/ABBA/CDECDE or CDCDCD. The English or Shakespearean sonnet has three quatrains and one couplet, with the rhyme scheme ABAB/CDCD/EFEF/GG. This format better suits English, which has fewer rhymes than Italian. The final couplet often contrasts sharply with the preceding quatrains, as in Shakespeare's sonnets—for example, Sonnet 130, "My mistress' eyes are nothing like the sun...And yet, by heaven, I think my love as rare / As any she belied with false compare." Variations on the sonnet form include Edmund Spenser's Spenserian sonnet in the 16th century, John Milton's Miltonic sonnet in the 17th century, and sonnet sequences. Sonnet sequences are seen in works such as John Donne's *La Corona* and Elizabeth Barrett Browning's *Sonnets from the Portuguese*.

Review Video: Structural Elements of Poetry
Visit mometrix.com/academy and enter code: 265216

Poetic Themes and Devices

Carpe Diem Tradition in Poetry

Carpe diem is Latin for "seize the day." A long poetic tradition, it advocates making the most of time because it passes swiftly and life is short. It is found in multiple languages, including Latin, Torquato Tasso's Italian, Pierre de Ronsard's French, and Edmund Spenser's English, and is often used in seduction to argue for indulging in earthly pleasures. Roman poet Horace's Ode 1.11 tells a younger woman, Leuconoe, to enjoy the present, not worrying about inevitable aging. Two Renaissance Metaphysical Poets, Andrew Marvell and Robert Herrick, treated *carpe diem* more as a call to action. In "To His Coy Mistress," Marvell points out that time is fleeting, arguing for love, and concluding that because they cannot stop time, they may as well defy it, getting the most out of the short time they have. In "To the Virgins, to Make Much of Time," Herrick advises young women to take advantage of their good fortune in being young by getting married before they become too old to attract men and have babies.

"To His Coy Mistress" begins, "Had we but world enough, and time, / This coyness, lady, were no crime." Using imagery, Andrew Marvell describes leisure they could enjoy if time were unlimited. Arguing for seduction, he continues famously, "But at my back I always hear/Time's winged chariot hurrying near; / And yonder all before us lie / Deserts of vast eternity." He depicts time as turning beauty to death and decay. Contradictory images in "amorous birds of prey" and "tear our pleasures with rough strife / Through the iron gates of life" overshadow romance with impending death, linking present pleasure with mortality and spiritual values with moral considerations. Marvell's concluding couplet summarizes *carpe diem*: "Thus, though we cannot make our sun / Stand still, yet we will make him run." "To the Virgins, to Make Much of Time" begins with the famous "Gather ye rosebuds while ye may." Rather than seduction to live for the present, Robert Herrick's experienced persona advises young women's future planning: "Old time is still a-flying / And this same flower that smiles today, / Tomorrow will be dying."

Effect of Structure on Meaning in Poetry

The way a poem is structured can affect its meaning. Different structural choices can change the way a reader understands a poem, so poets are careful to ensure that the form they use reflects the message they want to convey. The main structural elements in poetry include lines and stanzas. The number of lines within a stanza and the number of stanzas vary between different poems, but some poetic forms require a poem to have a certain number of lines and stanzas. Some of these forms also require each line to conform to a certain meter, or number and pattern of syllables. Many forms are associated with a certain topic or tone because of their meter. Poetic forms include sonnets, concrete poems, haiku, and villanelles. Another popular form of poetry is free verse, which is poetry that does not conform to a particular meter or rhyme scheme.

The arrangement of lines and stanzas determines the speed at which a poem is read. Long lines are generally read more quickly since the reader is often eager to reach the end of the line and does not have to stop to find the next word. Short lines cause the reader to briefly pause and look to the next line, so their reading is slowed. These effects often contribute to the meaning a reader gleans from a poem, so poets aim to make the line length compatible with the tone of their message.

For example, Edgar Allan Poe's poem "The Raven" is written with mostly long lines. The poem's speaker experiences troubling events and becomes paranoid throughout the poem, and he narrates his racing thoughts. Poe's use of long lines leads the reader to read each line quickly, allowing their reading experience to resemble the thoughts of the narrator:

Deep into that darkness peering, long I stood there wondering, fearing,
Doubting, dreaming dreams no mortal ever dared to dream before;
   But the silence was unbroken, and the stillness gave no token,
   And the only word there spoken was the whispered word, "Lenore?"
This I whispered, and an echo murmured back the word, "Lenore!"—
         Merely this and nothing more.

The poem's meter also contributes to its tone, but consider the same stanza written using shorter lines:

Deep into that darkness peering,
long I stood there wondering, fearing,
Doubting, dreaming dreams no mortal
ever dared to dream before;
   But the silence was unbroken,
and the stillness gave no token,
   And the only word there spoken
was the whispered word, "Lenore?"
This I whispered, and an echo
murmured back the word, "Lenore!"—
         Merely this and nothing more.

Breaking the lines apart creates longer pauses and a slower, more suspenseful experience for the reader. While the tone of the poem is dark and suspense is appropriate, the longer lines allow Poe to emphasize and show the narrator's emotions. The narrator's emotions are more important to the poem's meaning than the creation of suspense, making longer lines more suitable in this case.

Concrete Poetry

A less common form of poetry is concrete poetry, also called shape poetry. **Concrete poems** are arranged so the full poem takes a shape that is relevant to the poem's message. For example, a concrete poem about the beach may be arranged to look like a palm tree. This contributes to a poem's meaning by influencing which aspect of the poem or message that the reader focuses on. In the beach poem example, the image of the palm tree leads the reader to focus on the poem's setting and visual imagery. The reader may also look for or anticipate the mention of a palm tree in the poem. This technique allows the poet to direct the reader's attention and emphasize a certain element of their work.

Free Verse

Free verse is a very common form of poetry. Because **free verse** poetry does not always incorporate meter or rhyme, it relies more heavily on punctuation and structure to influence the reader's experience and create emphasis. Free verse poetry makes strategic use of the length and number of both lines and stanzas. While meter and rhyme direct the flow and tone of other types of poems, poets of free verse pieces use the characteristics of lines and stanzas to establish flow and tone, instead.

Free verse also uses punctuation in each line to create flow and tone. The punctuation in each line directs the reader to pause after certain words, allowing the poet to emphasize specific ideas or images to clearly communicate their message. Similar to the effects of line length, the presence of punctuation at the end of a line can create pauses that affect a reader's pace. **End-stopped** lines, or lines with a punctuation mark at the end, create a pause that can contribute to the poem's flow or create emphasis. **Enjambed** lines, or lines that do not end with a punctuation mark, carry a sentence to the next line and create an effect similar to long lines. The use of enjambment can speed up a poem's flow and reflect an idea within the poem or contribute to tone.

Poetic Structure to Enhance Meaning

The opening stanza of Romantic English poet, artist and printmaker William Blake's famous poem "The Tyger" demonstrates how a poet can create tension by using line length and punctuation independently of one another: "Tyger! Tyger! burning bright / In the forests of the night, / What immortal hand or eye / Could frame thy fearful symmetry?" The first three lines of this stanza are **trochaic** (/ᴗ), with "masculine" endings—that is, strongly stressed syllables at the ends of each of the lines. But Blake's punctuation contradicts this rhythmic regularity by not providing any divisions between the words "bright" and "In" or between "eye" and "Could." This irregular punctuation foreshadows how Blake disrupts the meter at the end of this first stanza by using a contrasting **dactyl** (/ᴗᴗ), with a "feminine" (unstressed) ending syllable in the last word, "sýmmetry." Thus Blake uses structural contrasts to heighten the intrigue of his work.

In enjambment, one sentence or clause in a poem does not end at the end of its line or verse, but runs over into the next line or verse. Clause endings coinciding with line endings give readers a feeling of completion, but enjambment influences readers to hurry to the next line to finish and understand the sentence. In his blank-verse epic religious poem "Paradise Lost," John Milton wrote: "Anon out of the earth a fabric huge / Rose like an exhalation, with the sound / Of dulcet symphonies and voices sweet, / Built like a temple, where pilasters round / Were set, and Doric pillars overlaid / With golden architrave." Only the third line is end-stopped. Milton, describing the palace of Pandemonium bursting from Hell up through the ground, reinforced this idea through phrases and clauses bursting through the boundaries of the lines. A **caesura** is a pause in mid-verse. Milton's commas in the third and fourth lines signal caesuras. They interrupt flow, making the narration jerky to imply that Satan's glorious-seeming palace has a shaky and unsound foundation.

Couplets and Meter to Enhance Meaning in Poetry

When a poet uses a couplet—a stanza of two lines, rhymed or unrhymed—it can function as the answer to a question asked earlier in the poem, or the solution to a problem or riddle. Couplets can also enhance the establishment of a poem's mood, or clarify the development of a poem's theme. Another device to enhance thematic development is irony, which also communicates the poet's tone and draws the reader's attention to a point the poet is making. The use of meter gives a poem a rhythmic context, contributes to the poem's flow, makes it more appealing to the reader, can represent natural speech rhythms, and produces specific effects. For example, in "The Song of Hiawatha," Henry Wadsworth Longfellow uses trochaic (/ ᴗ) tetrameter (four beats per line) to evoke for readers the rhythms of Native American chanting: "*By* the *shores* of *Gitch*e *Gum*ee, / *By* the *shin*ing *Big*-Sea-*Wat*er / *Stood* the *wig*wam *of* No*ko*mis." (Italicized syllables are stressed; non-italicized syllables are unstressed.)

Reflection of Content Through Structure

Wallace Stevens' short yet profound poem "The Snow Man" is reductionist: the snow man is a figure without human biases or emotions. Stevens begins, "One must have a mind of winter," the criterion for realizing nature and life does not inherently possess subjective qualities; we only invest it with these. Things are not as we see them; they simply are. The entire poem is one long sentence of clauses connected by conjunctions and commas, and modified by relative clauses and phrases. The successive phrases lead readers continually to reconsider as they read. Stevens' construction of the poem mirrors the meaning he conveys. With a mind of winter, the snow man, Stevens concludes, "nothing himself, beholds nothing that is not there, and the nothing that is."

Contrast of Content and Structure

Robert Frost's poem "Stopping by Woods on a Snowy Evening" (1923) is deceptively short and simple, with only four stanzas, each of only four lines, and short and simple words. Reinforcing this is Frost's use of regular rhyme and meter. The rhythm is iambic tetrameter throughout; the rhyme scheme is AABA in the first three stanzas and AAAA in the fourth. In an additional internal subtlety, B ending "here" in the first stanza is rhymed with A endings "queer," "near," and "year" of the second; B ending "lake" in the second is rhymed in A endings "shake", "mistake," and "flake" of the third. The final stanza's AAAA endings reinforce the ultimate darker theme. Though the first three stanzas seem to describe quietly watching snow fill the woods, the last stanza evokes the seductive pull of mysterious death: "The woods are lovely, dark and deep," countered by the obligations of living life: "But I have promises to keep, / And miles to go before I sleep, / And miles to go before I sleep." The last line's repetition strengthens Frost's message that despite death's temptation, life's course must precede it.

Effects of Figurative Devices on Meaning in Poetry

Through exaggeration, hyperbole communicates the strength of a poet's or persona's feelings and enhances the mood of the poem. Imagery appeals to the reader's senses, creating vivid mental pictures, evoking reader emotions and responses, and helping to develop themes. Irony also aids thematic development by drawing the reader's attention to the poet's point and communicating the poem's tone. Thematic development is additionally supported by the comparisons of metaphors and similes, which emphasize similarities, enhance imagery, and affect readers' perceptions. The use of mood communicates the atmosphere of a poem, builds a sense of tension, and evokes the reader's emotions. Onomatopoeia appeals to the reader's auditory sense and enhances sound imagery even when the poem is visual (read silently) rather than auditory (read aloud). Rhyme connects and unites verses, gives the rhyming words emphasis, and makes poems more fluent. Symbolism communicates themes, develops imagery, evokes readers' emotions, and elicits a response from the reader.

Repetition to Enhance Meaning

A **villanelle** is a nineteen-line poem composed of five tercets and one quatrain. The defining characteristic is the repetition: two lines appear repeatedly throughout the poem. In Theodore Roethke's "The Waking," the two repeated lines are "I wake to sleep, and take my waking slow," and "I learn by going where I have to go." At first these sound paradoxical, but the meaning is gradually revealed through the poem. The repetition also fits with the theme of cycle: the paradoxes of waking to sleep, learning by going, and thinking by feeling represent a constant cycle through life. They also symbolize abandoning conscious rationalism to embrace spiritual vision. We wake from the vision to "Great Nature," and "take the lively air." "This shaking keeps me steady"—another paradox—juxtaposes and balances fear of mortality with ecstasy in embracing experience. The transcendent vision of all life's interrelationship demonstrates, "What falls away is always. And is near." Readers experience the poem holistically, like music, through Roethke's integration of theme, motion, and sound.

Sylvia Plath's villanelle "Mad Girl's Love Song" narrows the scope from universal to personal but keeps the theme of cycle. The two repeated lines, "I shut my eyes and all the world drops dead" and "(I think I made you up inside my head.)" reflect the existential viewpoint that nothing exists in any absolute reality outside of our own perceptions. In the first stanza, the middle line, "I lift my lids and all is born again," in its recreating the world, bridges between the repeated refrain statements—one of obliterating reality, the other of having constructed her lover's existence. Unlike other villanelles wherein key lines are subtly altered in their repetitions, Plath repeats these exactly each time. This reflects the young woman's love, constant throughout the poem as it neither fades nor progresses.

Drama

Early Development

English **drama** originally developed from religious ritual. Early Christians established traditions of presenting pageants or mystery plays, traveling on wagons and carts through the streets to depict Biblical events. Medieval tradition assigned responsibility for performing specific plays to the different guilds. In Middle English, "mystery" referred to craft, or trade, and religious ritual and truth. Historically, mystery plays were to be reproduced exactly the same every time they were performed, like religious rituals. However, some performers introduced individual interpretations of roles and even improvised. Thus, drama was born. Narrative detail and nuanced acting were evident in mystery cycles by the Middle Ages. As individualized performance evolved, plays on other subjects also developed. Middle English mystery plays extant include the York Cycle, Coventry Cycle, Chester Mystery Plays, N-Town Plays, and Towneley/Wakefield Plays. In recent times, these plays began to draw interest again, and several modern actors such as Dame Judi Dench began their careers with mystery plays.

Review Video: Dramas
Visit mometrix.com/academy and enter code: 216060

Defining Characteristics

In the Middle Ages, plays were commonly composed in **verse**. By the time of the Renaissance, Shakespeare and other dramatists wrote plays that mixed **prose**, **rhymed verse**, and **blank verse**. The traditions of costumes and masks were seen in ancient Greek drama, medieval mystery plays, and Renaissance drama. Conventions like **asides**, in which actors make comments directly to the audience unheard by other characters, and **soliloquies** were also common during Shakespeare's Elizabethan dramatic period. **Monologues** date back to ancient Greek drama. Elizabethan dialogue tended to use colloquial prose for lower-class characters' speech and stylized verse for upper-class characters. Another Elizabethan convention was the play-within-a-play, as in *Hamlet.* As drama moved toward realism, dialogue became less poetic and more conversational, as in most modern English-language plays. Contemporary drama, both onstage and onscreen, includes a convention of **breaking the fourth wall**, as actors directly face and address audiences.

Comedy

Today, most people equate the idea of **comedy** with something funny, and of **tragedy** with something sad. However, the ancient Greeks defined these differently. Comedy needed not be humorous or amusing; it needed only a happy ending. The classical definition of comedy, as included in Aristotle's works, is any work that tells the story of a sympathetic main character's rise in fortune. According to Aristotle, protagonists need not be heroic or exemplary, nor evil or worthless, but ordinary people of unremarkable morality. Comic figures who were sympathetic were usually of humble origins, proving their "natural nobility" through their actions as they were tested. Characters born into nobility were often satirized as self-important or pompous.

Shakespearean Comedy

William Shakespeare lived in England from 1564-1616. He was a poet and playwright of the Renaissance period in Western culture. He is generally considered the foremost dramatist in world literature and the greatest author to write in the English language. He wrote many poems, particularly sonnets, of which 154 survive today, and approximately 38 plays. Though his sonnets are greater in number and are very famous, he is best known for his plays, including comedies, tragedies, tragicomedies and historical plays. His play titles include: *All's Well That Ends Well, As You Like It, The Comedy of Errors, Love's Labour's Lost, Measure for Measure, The Merchant of Venice, The Merry Wives of Windsor, A Midsummer Night's Dream, Much Ado About Nothing, The Taming of the Shrew, The Tempest, Twelfth Night, The Two Gentlemen of Verona, The Winter's Tale, King John, Richard II, Henry IV, Henry V, Richard III, Romeo and Juliet, Coriolanus, Titus Andronicus, Julius Caesar, Macbeth, Hamlet, Troilus and Cressida, King Lear, Othello, Antony and Cleopatra,* and *Cymbeline.* Some scholars have suggested that Christopher Marlowe wrote several of Shakespeare's works. While most scholars reject this theory, Shakespeare did pay homage to Marlowe, alluding to several of his characters, themes, or verbiage, as well as borrowing themes from several of his plays (e.g., Marlowe's *Jew of Malta* influenced Shakespeare's *Merchant of Venice*).

When Shakespeare was writing, during the Elizabethan period of the Renaissance, Aristotle's version of comedies was popular. While some of Shakespeare's comedies were humorous and others were not, all had happy endings. *A Comedy of Errors* is a farce. Based and expanding on a Classical Roman comedy, it is lighthearted and includes slapstick humor and mistaken identity. *Much Ado About Nothing* is a romantic comedy. It incorporates some more serious themes, including social mores, perceived infidelity, marriage's duality as both trap and ideal, honor and its loss, public shame, and deception, but also much witty dialogue and a happy ending.

Dramatic Comedy

Three types of dramas classified as comedy include the farce, the romantic comedy, and the satirical comedy.

Farce

The **farce** is a zany, goofy type of comedy that includes pratfalls and other forms of slapstick humor. The characters in a farce tend to be ridiculous or fantastical in nature. The plot also tends to contain highly improbable events, featuring complications and twists that continue throughout, and incredible coincidences that would likely never occur in reality. Mistaken identity, deceptions, and disguises are common devices used in farcical comedies. Shakespeare's play *The Comedy of Errors,* with its cases of accidental mistaken identity and slapstick, is an example of farce. Contemporary examples of farce include the Marx Brothers' movies, the Three Stooges movies and TV episodes, and the *Pink Panther* movie series.

Romantic Comedy

Romantic comedies are probably the most popular of the types of comedy, in both live theater performances and movies. They include not only humor and a happy ending, but also love. In the typical plot of a romantic comedy, two people well suited to one another are either brought together for the first time, or reconciled after being separated. They are usually both sympathetic characters and seem destined to be together, yet they are separated by some intervening complication, such as ex-lovers, interfering parents or friends, or differences in social class. The happy ending is achieved through the lovers overcoming all these obstacles. William Shakespeare's *Much Ado About Nothing*, Walt Disney's version of *Cinderella* (1950), and Broadway musical *Guys and Dolls* (1955) are example of romantic comedies. Many live-action movies are also examples of romantic comedies, such as *The Princess Bride* (1987), *Sleepless in Seattle* (1993), *You've Got Mail* (1998), and *Forget Paris* (1995).

Satirical Comedy and Black Comedy

Satires generally mock and lampoon human foolishness and vices. **Satirical comedies** fit the classical definition of comedy by depicting a main character's rise in fortune, but they also fit the definition of satire by making that main character either a fool, morally corrupt, or cynical in attitude. All or most of the other characters in the satirical comedy display similar foibles. These include cuckolded spouses, dupes, and other gullible types; tricksters, con artists, and criminals; hypocrites; fortune seekers; and other deceptive types who prey on the gullible, who are their willing and unwitting victims. Some classical examples of satirical comedies include *The Birds* by ancient Greek comedic playwright Aristophanes, and *Volpone* by 17th-century poet and playwright Ben Jonson, who made the comedy of humors popular. When satirical comedy is extended to extremes, it becomes **black comedy**, wherein the comedic occurrences are grotesque or terrible.

Tragedy

The opposite of comedy is tragedy, portraying a hero's fall in fortune. While by classical definitions, tragedies could be sad, Aristotle went further, requiring that they depict suffering and pain to cause "terror and pity" in audiences. Additionally, he decreed that tragic heroes can be basically good, admirable, or noble, and that their downfalls result from personal action, choice, or error, not by bad luck or accident.

Aristotle's Criteria for Tragedy

In his *Poetics,* Aristotle defined five critical terms relative to tragedy:

- ***Anagnorisis:*** Meaning tragic insight or recognition, this is a moment of realization by a tragic hero or heroine that he or she has become enmeshed in a "web of fate."
- ***Hamartia:*** This is often called a "tragic flaw," but is better described as a tragic error. *Hamartia* is an archery term meaning a shot missing the bull's eye, used here as a metaphor for a mistake—often a simple one—which results in catastrophe.
- ***Hubris:*** While often called "pride," this is actually translated as "violent transgression," and signifies an arrogant overstepping of moral or cultural bounds—the sin of the tragic hero who over-presumes or over-aspires.
- ***Nemesis:*** translated as "retribution," this represents the cosmic punishment or payback that the tragic hero ultimately receives for committing hubristic acts.
- ***Peripateia:*** Literally "turning," this is a plot reversal consisting of a tragic hero's pivotal action, which changes his or her status from safe to endangered.

Hegel's Theory of Tragedy

Georg Wilhelm Friedrich Hegel (1770-1831) proposed a different theory of tragedy than Aristotle (384-322 BCE), which was also very influential. Whereas Aristotle's criteria involved character and plot, Hegel defined tragedy as a dynamic conflict of opposite forces or rights. For example, if an individual believes in the moral philosophy of the conscientious objector (i.e., that fighting in wars is morally wrong, but is confronted with being drafted into military service), this conflict would fit Hegel's definition of a tragic plot premise. Hegel theorized that a tragedy must involve some circumstance in which two values, or two rights, are fatally at odds with one another and conflict directly. Hegel did not view this as good triumphing over evil, or evil winning out over good, but rather as one good fighting against another good unto death. He saw this conflict of two goods as truly tragic. In ancient Greek playwright Sophocles' tragedy *Antigone,* the main character experiences this tragic conflict between her public duties and her family and religious responsibilities.

Revenge Tragedy

Along with Aristotelian definitions of comedy and tragedy, ancient Greece was the origin of the **revenge tragedy**. This genre became highly popular in Renaissance England, and is still popular today in contemporary movies. In a revenge tragedy, the protagonist has suffered a serious wrong, such as the murder of a family member. However, the wrongdoer has not been punished. In contemporary plots, this often occurs when some legal technicality has interfered with the miscreant's conviction and sentencing, or when authorities are unable to locate and apprehend the criminal. The protagonist then faces the conflict of suffering this injustice, or exacting his or her own justice by seeking revenge. Greek revenge tragedies include *Agamemnon* and *Medea.* Playwright Thomas Kyd's *The Spanish Tragedy* (1582-1592) is credited with beginning the Elizabethan genre of revenge tragedies. Shakespearean revenge tragedies include *Hamlet* (1599-1602) and *Titus Andronicus* (1588-1593). A Jacobean example is Thomas Middleton's *The Revenger's Tragedy* (1606, 1607).

Hamlet's "Tragic Flaw"

Despite virtually limitless interpretations, one way to view Hamlet's tragic error generally is as indecision. He suffers the classic revenge tragedy's conflict of whether to suffer with his knowledge of his mother's and uncle's assassination of his father, or to exact his own revenge and justice against Claudius, who has assumed the throne after his crime went unknown and unpunished. Hamlet's famous soliloquy, "To be or not to be" reflects this dilemma. Hamlet muses "Whether 'tis nobler in the mind to suffer the slings and arrows of outrageous fortune, / Or to take arms against a sea of troubles, / And by opposing end them?" Hamlet both longs for and fears death, as "the dread of something after death ... makes us rather bear those ills we have / Than fly to others that we know not ... Thus, conscience does make cowards of us all." For most of the play, Hamlet struggles with his responsibility to avenge his father, who was killed by Hamlet's uncle, Claudius. So, Hamlet's tragic error at first might be considered a lack of action. But he then makes several attempts at revenge, each of which end in worse tragedy, until his efforts are ended by the final tragedy – Hamlet's own death.

Informational Texts

Text Features in Informational Texts

The **title of a text** gives readers some idea of its content. The **table of contents** is a list near the beginning of a text, showing the book's sections and chapters and their coinciding page numbers. This gives readers an overview of the whole text, and helps them find specific chapters easily. An **appendix**, at the back of the book or document, includes important information that is not present in the main text. Also at the back, an **index** lists the book's important topics alphabetically with their page numbers to help readers find them easily. **Glossaries**, usually found at the backs of books, list technical terms alphabetically with their definitions to aid vocabulary learning and comprehension. Boldface print is used to emphasize certain words, often identifying words included in the text's glossary where readers can look up their definitions. **Headings** separate sections of text and show the topic of each. **Subheadings** divide subject headings into smaller, more specific categories to help readers organize information. **Footnotes**, at the bottom of the page, give readers more information, such as citations or links. **Bullet points** list items separately, making facts and ideas easier to see and understand. A **sidebar** is a box of information to one side of the main text giving additional information, often on a more focused or in-depth example of a topic.

Illustrations and **photographs** are pictures that visually emphasize important points in text. The captions below the illustrations explain what those images show. Charts and tables are visual forms of information that make something easier to understand quickly. Diagrams are drawings that show relationships or explain a process. Graphs visually show the relationships among multiple sets of information plotted along vertical and horizontal axes. Maps show geographical information visually to help readers understand the relative locations of places covered in the text. Timelines are visual graphics that show historical events in chronological order to help readers see their sequence.

Review Video: Informative Text
Visit mometrix.com/academy and enter code: 924964

Language Use

Literal and Figurative Language

As in fictional literature, informational text also uses both **literal language**, which means just what it says, and **figurative language**, which imparts more than literal meaning. For example, an informational text author might use a simile or direct comparison, such as writing that a racehorse "ran like the wind." Informational text authors also use metaphors or implied comparisons, such as "the cloud of the Great Depression." Imagery may also appear in informational texts to increase the reader's understanding of ideas and concepts discussed in the text.

Review Video: Figurative Language
Visit mometrix.com/academy and enter code: 584902

Explicit and Implicit Information

When informational text states something explicitly, the reader is told by the author exactly what is meant, which can include the author's interpretation or perspective of events. For example, a professor writes, "I have seen students go into an absolute panic just because they weren't able to complete the exam in the time they were allotted." This explicitly tells the reader that the students were afraid, and by using the words "just because," the writer indicates their fear was exaggerated out of proportion relative to what happened. However, another professor writes, "I have had students come to me, their faces drained of all color, saying 'We weren't able to finish the exam.'" This is an example of implicit meaning: the second writer did not state explicitly that the students were panicked. Instead, he wrote a description of their faces being "drained of all color." From this description, the reader can infer that the students were so frightened that their faces paled.

Review Video: Explicit and Implicit Information
Visit mometrix.com/academy and enter code: 735771

Technical Language

Technical language is more impersonal than literary and vernacular language. Passive voice makes the tone impersonal. For example, instead of writing, "We found this a central component of protein metabolism," scientists write, "This was found a central component of protein metabolism." While science professors have traditionally instructed students to avoid active voice because it leads to first-person ("I" and "we") usage, science editors today find passive voice dull and weak. Many journal articles combine both. Tone in technical science writing should be detached, concise, and professional. While one may normally write, "This chemical has to be available for proteins to be digested," professionals write technically, "The presence of this chemical is required for the enzyme to break the covalent bonds of proteins." The use of technical language appeals to both technical and non-technical audiences by displaying the author or speaker's understanding of the subject and suggesting their credibility regarding the message they are communicating.

Technical Material for Non-Technical Readers

Writing about **technical subjects** for **non-technical readers** differs from writing for colleagues because authors place more importance on delivering a critical message than on imparting the maximum technical content possible. Technical authors also must assume that non-technical audiences do not have the expertise to comprehend extremely scientific or technical messages, concepts, and terminology. They must resist the temptation to impress audiences with their scientific knowledge and expertise and remember that their primary purpose is to communicate a message that non-technical readers will understand, feel, and respond to. Non-technical and technical styles include similarities. Both should formally cite any references or other authors' work utilized in the text. Both must follow intellectual property and copyright regulations. This includes the author's protecting his or her own rights, or a public domain statement, as he or she chooses.

Non-Technical Audiences

Writers of technical or scientific material may need to write for many non-technical audiences. Some readers have no technical or scientific background, and those who do may not be in the same field as the authors. Government and corporate policymakers and budget managers need technical information they can understand for decision-making. Citizens affected by technology or science are a different audience. Non-governmental organizations can encompass many of the preceding groups. Elementary and secondary school programs also need non-technical language for presenting technical subject matter. Additionally, technical authors will need to use non-technical language when collecting consumer responses to surveys, presenting scientific or para-scientific material to the public, writing about the history of science, and writing about science and technology in developing countries.

Use of Everyday Language

Authors of technical information sometimes must write using non-technical language that readers outside their disciplinary fields can comprehend. They should use not only non-technical terms, but also use normal, everyday language to accommodate readers whose native language is different than the language the text is written in. For example, instead of writing that "eustatic changes like thermal expansion are causing hazardous conditions in the littoral zone," an author would do better to write that "a rising sea level is threatening the coast." When technical terms cannot be avoided, authors should also define or explain them using non-technical language. Although authors must cite references and acknowledge their use of others' work, they should avoid the kinds of references or citations that they would use in scientific journals—unless they reinforce author messages. They should not use endnotes, footnotes, or any other complicated referential techniques because non-technical journal publishers usually do not accept them. Including high-resolution illustrations, photos, maps, or satellite images and incorporating multimedia into digital publications will enhance non-technical writing about technical subjects. Technical authors may publish using non-technical language in e-journals, trade journals, specialty newsletters, and daily newspapers.

Making Inferences About Informational Text

With informational text, reader comprehension depends not only on recalling important statements and details, but also on reader inferences based on examples and details. Readers add information from the text to what they already know to draw inferences about the text. These inferences help the readers to fill in the information that the text does not explicitly state, enabling them to understand the text better. When reading a nonfictional autobiography or biography, for example, the most appropriate inferences might concern the events in the book, the actions of the subject of the autobiography or biography, and the message the author means to convey. When reading a nonfictional expository (informational) text, the reader would best draw inferences about problems and their solutions, and causes and their effects. When reading a nonfictional persuasive text, the reader will want to infer ideas supporting the author's message and intent.

Structures or Organizational Patterns in Informational Texts

Informational text can be descriptive, appealing to the five senses and answering the questions what, who, when, where, and why. Another method of structuring informational text is sequence and order. Chronological texts relate events in the sequence that they occurred, from start to finish, while how-to texts organize information into a series of instructions in the sequence in which the steps should be followed. Comparison-contrast structures of informational text describe various ideas to their readers by pointing out how things or ideas are similar and how they are different. Cause and effect structures of informational text describe events that occurred and identify the causes or reasons that those events occurred. Problem and solution structures of informational text introduce and describe problems and offer one or more solutions for each problem described.

Review Video: Organizational Methods to Structure Text
Visit mometrix.com/academy and enter code: 606263

Determining an Informational Author's Purpose

Informational authors' purposes are why they write texts. Readers must determine authors' motivations and goals. Readers gain greater insight into a text by considering the author's motivation. This develops critical reading skills. Readers perceive writing as a person's voice, not simply printed words. Uncovering author motivations and purposes empowers readers to know what to expect from the text, read for relevant details, evaluate authors and their work critically, and respond effectively to the motivations and persuasions of the text. The main idea of a text is what the reader is supposed to understand from reading it; the purpose of the text is why the author has written it and what the author wants readers to do with its information. Authors state some purposes clearly, while other purposes may be unstated but equally significant. When stated purposes contradict other parts of a text, the author may have a hidden agenda. Readers can better evaluate a text's effectiveness, whether they agree or disagree with it, and why they agree or disagree through identifying unstated author purposes.

Identifying Author's Point of View or Purpose

In some informational texts, readers find it easy to identify the author's point of view and purpose, such as when the author explicitly states his or her position and reason for writing. But other texts are more difficult, either because of the content or because the authors give neutral or balanced viewpoints. This is particularly true in scientific texts, in which authors may state the purpose of their research in the report, but never state their point of view except by interpreting evidence or data.

To analyze text and identify point of view or purpose, readers should ask themselves the following four questions:

1. With what main point or idea does this author want to persuade readers to agree?
2. How does this author's word choice affect the way that readers consider this subject?
3. How do this author's choices of examples and facts affect the way that readers consider this subject?
4. What is it that this author wants to accomplish by writing this text?

Review Video: Purpose
Visit mometrix.com/academy and enter code: 511819

Evaluating Arguments Made by Informational Text Writers

When evaluating an informational text, the first step is to identify the argument's conclusion. Then identify the author's premises that support the conclusion. Try to paraphrase premises for clarification and make the conclusion and premises fit. List all premises first, sequentially numbered, then finish with the conclusion. Identify any premises or assumptions not stated by the author but required for the stated premises to support the conclusion. Read word assumptions sympathetically, as the author might. Evaluate whether premises reasonably support the conclusion. For inductive reasoning, the reader should ask if the premises are true, if they support the conclusion, and if so, how strongly. For deductive reasoning, the reader should ask if the argument is valid or invalid. If all premises are true, then the argument is valid unless the conclusion can be false. If it can, then the argument is invalid. An invalid argument be made valid through alterations such as the addition of needed premises.

Use of Rhetoric in Informational Texts

There are many ways authors can support their claims, arguments, beliefs, ideas, and reasons for writing in informational texts. For example, authors can appeal to readers' sense of **logic** by communicating their reasoning through a carefully sequenced series of logical steps to help "prove" the points made. Authors can appeal to readers' **emotions** by using descriptions and words that evoke feelings of sympathy, sadness, anger, righteous indignation, hope, happiness, or any other emotion to reinforce what they express and share with their audience. Authors may appeal to the **moral** or **ethical values** of readers by using words and descriptions that can convince readers that something is right or wrong. By relating personal anecdotes, authors can supply readers with more accessible, realistic examples of points they make, as well as appealing to their emotions. They can provide supporting evidence by reporting case studies. They can also illustrate their points by making analogies to which readers can better relate.

Persuasive Techniques

Persuasive Techniques

To **appeal using reason**, writers present logical arguments, such as using "If... then... because" statements. To **appeal to emotions**, authors may ask readers how they would feel about something or to put themselves in another's place, present their argument as one that will make the audience feel good, or tell readers how they should feel. To **appeal to character**, **morality**, or **ethics**, authors present their points to readers as the right or most moral choices. Authors cite expert opinions to show readers that someone very knowledgeable about the subject or viewpoint agrees with the author's claims. **Testimonials**, usually via anecdotes or quotations regarding the author's subject, help build the audience's trust in an author's message through positive support from ordinary people. **Bandwagon appeals** claim that everybody else agrees with the author's argument and persuade readers to conform and agree, also. Authors **appeal to greed** by presenting their choice as cheaper, free, or more valuable for less cost. They **appeal to laziness** by presenting their views as more convenient, easy, or relaxing. Authors also anticipate potential objections and argue against them before audiences think of them, thereby depicting those objections as weak.

Authors can use **comparisons** like analogies, similes, and metaphors to persuade audiences. For example, a writer might represent excessive expenses as "hemorrhaging" money, which the author's recommended solution will stop. Authors can use negative word connotations to make some choices unappealing to readers, and positive word connotations to make others more appealing. Using **humor** can relax readers and garner their agreement. However, writers must take care: ridiculing opponents can be a successful strategy for appealing to readers who already agree with the author, but can backfire by angering other readers. **Rhetorical questions** need no answer, but create effect that can force agreement, such as asking the question, "Wouldn't you rather be paid more than less?" **Generalizations** persuade readers by being impossible to disagree with; writers can make these appear to support their viewpoints, like saying, "We all want peace, not war" regarding more specific political arguments. **Transfer** and **association** persuade by example: if advertisements show attractive actors enjoying their products, audiences imagine they will experience the same. **Repetition** can also sometimes effectively persuade audiences.

Review Video: Using Rhetorical Strategies for Persuasion
Visit mometrix.com/academy and enter code: 302658

Classical Author Appeals

In his *On Rhetoric,* ancient Greek philosopher Aristotle defined three basic types of appeal used in writing, which he called *pathos*, *ethos*, and *logos*. ***Pathos*** means suffering or experience and refers to appeals to the emotions (the English word *pathetic* comes from this root). Writing that is meant to entertain audiences, by making them either happy, as with comedy, or sad, as with tragedy, uses *pathos*. Aristotle's *Poetics* states that evoking the emotions of terror and pity is one of the criteria for writing tragedy. ***Ethos*** means character and connotes ideology (the English word *ethics* comes from this root). Writing that appeals to credibility, based on academic, professional, or personal merit uses *ethos*. ***Logos*** means "I say" and refers to a plea, opinion, expectation, word or speech, account, opinion, or reason (the English word *logic* comes from this root.) Aristotle used it to mean persuasion that appeals to the audience through reasoning and logic to influence their opinions.

Critical Evaluation of Effectiveness of Persuasive Methods

First, readers should identify the author's **thesis**—what he or she argues for or against. They should consider the argument's content and the author's reason for presenting it. Does the author offer **solutions** to problems raised? If so, are they realistic? Note all central ideas and evidence supporting the author's thesis. Research any unfamiliar subjects or vocabulary. Readers should then outline or summarize the work in their own words. Identify which types of appeals the author uses. Readers should evaluate how well the author communicated meaning from the reader's perspective: Did they respond to emotional appeals with anger, concern, happiness, etc.? If so, why? Decide if the author's reasoning sufficed for changing the reader's mind. Determine whether the content and presentation were accurate, cohesive, and clear. Readers should also ask themselves whether they found the author believable or not, and why or why not.

Evaluating an Argument

Argumentative and persuasive passages take a stand on a debatable issue, seek to explore all sides of the issue, and find the best possible solution. Argumentative and persuasive passages should not be combative or abusive. The word *argument* may remind you of two or more people shouting at each other and walking away in anger. However, an argumentative or persuasive passage should be a calm and reasonable presentation of an author's ideas for others to consider. When an author writes reasonable arguments, his or her goal is not to win or have the last word. Instead, authors want to reveal current understanding of the question at hand and suggest a solution to a problem. The purpose of argument and persuasion in a free society is to reach the best solution.

Evidence

The term **text evidence** refers to information that supports a main point or minor points and can help lead the reader to a conclusion about the text's credibility. Information used as text evidence is precise, descriptive, and factual. A main point is often followed by supporting details that provide evidence to back up a claim. For example, a passage may include the claim that winter occurs during opposite months in the Northern and Southern hemispheres. Text evidence for this claim may include examples of countries where winter occurs in opposite months. Stating that the tilt of the Earth as it rotates around the sun causes winter to occur at different times in separate hemispheres is another example of text evidence. Text evidence can come from common knowledge, but it is also valuable to include text evidence from credible, relevant outside sources.

Review Video: Text Evidence
Visit mometrix.com/academy and enter code: 486236

Evidence that supports the thesis and additional arguments needs to be provided. Most arguments must be supported by facts or statistics. A fact is something that is known with certainty, has been verified by several independent individuals, and can be proven to be true. In addition to facts, examples and illustrations can support an argument by adding an emotional component. With this component, you persuade readers in ways that facts and statistics cannot. The emotional component is effective when used alongside objective information that can be confirmed.

Credibility

The text used to support an argument can be the argument's downfall if the text is not credible. A text is **credible**, or believable, when its author is knowledgeable and objective, or unbiased. The author's motivations for writing the text play a critical role in determining the credibility of the text and must be evaluated when assessing that credibility. Reports written about the ozone layer by an environmental scientist and a hairdresser will have a different level of credibility.

Review Video: Credible
Visit mometrix.com/academy and enter code: 827257

Appeal to Emotion

Sometimes, authors will appeal to the reader's emotion in an attempt to persuade or to distract the reader from the weakness of the argument. For instance, the author may try to inspire the pity of the reader by delivering a heart-rending story. An author also might use the bandwagon approach, in which he suggests that his opinion is correct because it is held by the majority. Some authors resort to name-calling, in which insults and harsh words are delivered to the opponent in an attempt to distract. In advertising, a common appeal is the celebrity testimonial, in which a famous person endorses a product. Of course, the fact that a famous person likes something should not really mean anything to the reader. These and other emotional appeals are usually evidence of poor reasoning and a weak argument.

Counter Arguments

When authors give both sides to the argument, they build trust with their readers. As a reader, you should start with an undecided or neutral position. If an author presents only his or her side to the argument, then they are not exhibiting credibility and are weakening their argument.

Building common ground with readers can be effective for persuading neutral, skeptical, or opposed readers. Sharing values with undecided readers can allow people to switch positions without giving up what they feel is important. People who may oppose a position need to feel that they can change their minds without betraying who they are as a person. This appeal to having an open mind can be a powerful tool in arguing a position without antagonizing other views. Objections can be countered on a point-by-point basis or in a summary paragraph. Be mindful of how an author points out flaws in counter arguments. If they are unfair to the other side of the argument, then you should lose trust with the author.

Rhetorical Devices

- An **anecdote** is a brief story authors may relate to their argument, which can illustrate their points in a more real and relatable way.
- **Aphorisms** concisely state common beliefs and may rhyme. For example, Benjamin Franklin's "Early to bed and early to rise / Makes a man healthy, wealthy, and wise" is an aphorism.
- **Allusions** refer to literary or historical figures to impart symbolism to a thing or person and to create reader resonance. In John Steinbeck's *Of Mice and Men,* protagonist George's last name is Milton. This alludes to John Milton, who wrote *Paradise Lost*, and symbolizes George's eventual loss of his dream.
- **Satire** exaggerates, ridicules, or pokes fun at human flaws or ideas, as in the works of Jonathan Swift and Mark Twain.
- A **parody** is a form of satire that imitates another work to ridicule its topic or style.
- A **paradox** is a statement that is true despite appearing contradictory.
- **Hyperbole** is overstatement using exaggerated language.
- An **oxymoron** combines seeming contradictions, such as "deafening silence."
- **Analogies** compare two things that share common elements.
- **Similes** (stated comparisons using the words *like* or *as*) and **metaphors** (stated comparisons that do not use *like* or *as*) are considered forms of analogy.
- When using logic to reason with audiences, **syllogism** refers either to deductive reasoning or a deceptive, very sophisticated, or subtle argument.
- **Deductive reasoning** moves from general to specific, **inductive reasoning** from specific to general.
- **Diction** is author word choice that establishes tone and effect.
- **Understatement** achieves effects like contrast or irony by downplaying or describing something more subtly than warranted.
- **Chiasmus** uses parallel clauses, the second reversing the order of the first. Examples include T. S. Eliot's "Has the Church failed mankind, or has mankind failed the Church?" and John F. Kennedy's "Ask not what your country can do for you; ask what you can do for your country."
- **Anaphora** regularly repeats a word or phrase at the beginnings of consecutive clauses or phrases to add emphasis to an idea. A classic example of anaphora was Winston Churchill's emphasis of determination: "We shall fight in the trenches. We shall fight on the oceans. We shall fight in the sky."

Arguments and Logical Errors

Author's Argument in Argumentative Writing

When an author writes in an argumentative mode, the argument is a belief, position, or opinion that the author wants to convince readers to believe as well. For the first step, readers should identify the **issue**. Some issues are controversial, meaning people disagree about them. Gun control, foreign policy, and the death penalty are all controversial issues. The next step is to determine the **author's position** on the issue. That position or viewpoint constitutes the author's argument. Readers should then identify the **author's assumptions**: things he or she accepts, believes, or takes for granted without needing proof. Inaccurate or illogical assumptions produce flawed arguments and can mislead readers. Readers should identify what kinds of **supporting evidence** the author offers, such as research results, personal observations or experiences, case studies, facts, examples, expert testimony and opinions, and comparisons. Readers should decide how relevant this support is to the argument.

Review Video: Argumentative Writing
Visit mometrix.com/academy and enter code: 561544

Evaluating an Author's Argument

The first three reader steps to **evaluate an author's argument** are to identify the **author's assumptions**, identify the **supporting evidence**, and decide **whether the evidence is relevant**. For example, if an author is not an expert on a particular topic, then that author's personal experience or opinion might not be relevant. The fourth step is to assess the **author's objectivity**. For example, consider whether the author introduces clear, understandable supporting evidence and facts to support the argument. The fifth step is evaluating whether the author's **argument is complete**. When authors give sufficient support for their arguments and also anticipate and respond effectively to opposing arguments or objections to their points, their arguments are complete. However, some authors omit information that could detract from their arguments. If instead they stated this information and refuted it, it would strengthen their arguments. The sixth step in evaluating an author's argumentative writing is to assess whether the **argument is valid**. Providing clear, logical reasoning makes an author's argument valid. Readers should ask themselves whether the author's points follow a sequence that makes sense, and whether each point leads to the next. The seventh step is to determine whether the author's **argument is credible**, meaning that it is convincing and believable. Arguments that are not valid are not credible, so step seven depends on step six. Readers should be mindful of their own biases as they evaluate and should not expect authors to conclusively prove their arguments, but rather to provide effective support and reason.

Evaluating an Author's Method of Appeal

To evaluate the effectiveness of an appeal, it is important to consider the author's purpose for writing. Any appeals an author uses in their argument must be relevant to the argument's goal. For example, a writer that argues for the reclassification of Pluto, but primarily uses appeals to emotion, will not have an effective argument. This writer should focus on using appeals to logic and support their argument with provable facts. While most arguments should include appeals to logic, emotion, and credibility, some arguments only call for one or two of these types of appeal. Evidence can support an appeal, but the evidence must be relevant to truly strengthen the appeal's effectiveness. If the writer arguing for Pluto's reclassification uses the reasons for Jupiter's classification as evidence, their argument would be weak. This information may seem relevant because it is related to the classification of planets. However, this classification is highly dependent on the size of the celestial object, and Jupiter is significantly bigger than Pluto. This use of evidence is illogical and does not support the appeal. Even when appropriate evidence and appeals are used, appeals and arguments lose their effectiveness when they create logical fallacies.

Opinions, Facts, and Fallacies

Critical thinking skills are mastered through understanding various types of writing and the different purposes of authors can have for writing different passages. Every author writes for a purpose. When you understand their purpose and how they accomplish their goal, you will be able to analyze their writing and determine whether or not you agree with their conclusions.

Readers must always be aware of the difference between fact and opinion. A **fact** can be subjected to analysis and proven to be true. An **opinion**, on the other hand, is the author's personal thoughts or feelings and may not be altered by research or evidence. If the author writes that the distance from New York City to Boston is about two hundred miles, then he or she is stating a fact. If the author writes that New York City is too crowded, then he or she is giving an opinion because there is no objective standard for overpopulation. Opinions are often supported by facts. For instance, an author might use a comparison between the population density of New York City and that of other major American cities as evidence of an overcrowded population. An opinion supported by facts tends to be more convincing. On the other hand, when authors support their opinions with other opinions, readers should employ critical thinking and approach the argument with skepticism.

Review Video: Fact or Opinion
Visit mometrix.com/academy and enter code: 870899

Reliable Sources

When you have an argumentative passage, you need to be sure that facts are presented to the reader from **reliable sources**. An opinion is what the author thinks about a given topic. An opinion is not common knowledge or proven by expert sources, instead the information is the personal beliefs and thoughts of the author. To distinguish between fact and opinion, a reader needs to consider the type of source that is presenting information, the information that backs-up a claim, and the author's motivation to have a certain point-of-view on a given topic. For example, if a panel of scientists has conducted multiple studies on the effectiveness of taking a certain vitamin, then the results are more likely to be factual than those of a company that is selling a vitamin and simply claims that taking the vitamin can produce positive effects. The company is motivated to sell their product, and the scientists are using the scientific method to prove a theory. Remember, if you find sentences that contain phrases such as "I think...", then the statement is an opinion.

Biases

In their attempts to persuade, writers often make mistakes in their thought processes and writing choices. These processes and choices are important to understand so you can make an informed decision about the author's credibility. Every author has a point of view, but authors demonstrate a **bias** when they ignore reasonable counterarguments or distort opposing viewpoints. A bias is evident whenever the author's claims are presented in a way that is unfair or inaccurate. Bias can be intentional or unintentional, but readers should be skeptical of the author's argument in either case. Remember that a biased author may still be correct. However, the author will be correct in spite of, not because of, his or her bias.

A **stereotype** is a bias applied specifically to a group of people or a place. Stereotyping is considered to be particularly abhorrent because it promotes negative, misleading generalizations about people. Readers should be very cautious of authors who use stereotypes in their writing. These faulty assumptions typically reveal the author's ignorance and lack of curiosity.

Review Video: Bias and Stereotype
Visit mometrix.com/academy and enter code: 644829

Figurative Language

Literal and Figurative Meaning

When language is used **literally**, the words mean exactly what they say and nothing more. When language is used **figuratively**, the words mean something beyond their literal meaning. For example, "The weeping willow tree has long, trailing branches and leaves" is a literal description. But "The weeping willow tree looks as if it is bending over and crying" is a figurative description—specifically, a **simile** or stated comparison. Another figurative language form is **metaphor**, or an implied comparison. A good example is the metaphor of a city, state, or city-state as a ship, and its governance as sailing that ship. Ancient Greek lyrical poet Alcaeus is credited with first using this metaphor, and ancient Greek tragedian Aeschylus then used it in *Seven Against Thebes,* and then Plato used it in the *Republic.*

Figures of Speech

A figure of speech is a verbal expression whose meaning is figurative rather than literal. For example, the phrase "butterflies in the stomach" does not refer to actual butterflies in a person's stomach. It is a metaphor representing the fluttery feelings experienced when a person is nervous or excited—or when one "falls in love," which does not mean physically falling. "Hitting a sales target" does not mean physically hitting a target with arrows as in archery; it is a metaphor for meeting a sales quota. "Climbing the ladder of success" metaphorically likens advancing in one's career to ascending ladder rungs. Similes, such as "light as a feather" (meaning very light, not a feather's actual weight), and hyperbole, like "I'm starving/freezing/roasting," are also figures of speech. Figures of speech are often used and crafted for emphasis, freshness of expression, or clarity.

Review Video: Figure of Speech
Visit mometrix.com/academy and enter code: 111295

Figurative Language

Figurative language extends past the literal meanings of words. It offers readers new insight into the people, things, events, and subjects covered in a work of literature. Figurative language also enables readers to feel they are sharing the authors' experiences. It can stimulate the reader's senses, make comparisons that readers find intriguing or even startling, and enable readers to view the world in different ways. When looking for figurative language, it is important to consider the context of the sentence or situation. Phrases that appear out of place or make little sense when read literally are likely instances of figurative language. Once figurative language has been recognized, context is also important to determining the type of figurative language being used and its function. For example, when a comparison is being made, a metaphor or simile is likely being used. This means the comparison may emphasize or create irony through the things being compared. Seven specific types of figurative language include: alliteration, onomatopoeia, personification, imagery, similes, metaphors, and hyperbole.

Review Video: Figurative Language
Visit mometrix.com/academy and enter code: 584902

Alliteration and Onomatopoeia

Alliteration describes a series of words beginning with the same sounds. **Onomatopoeia** uses words imitating the sounds of things they name or describe. For example, in his poem "Come Down, O Maid," Alfred Tennyson writes of "The moan of doves in immemorial elms, / And murmuring of innumerable bees." The word "moan" sounds like some sounds doves make, "murmuring" represents the sounds of bees buzzing. Onomatopoeia also includes words that are simply meant to represent sounds, such as "meow," "kaboom," and "whoosh."

Review Video: Alliteration
Visit mometrix.com/academy and enter code: 462837

Personification

Another type of figurative language is **personification**. This is describing a non-human thing, like an animal or an object, as if it were human. The general intent of personification is to describe things in a manner that will be comprehensible to readers. When an author states that a tree *groans* in the wind, he or she does not mean that the tree is emitting a low, pained sound from a mouth. Instead, the author means that the tree is making a noise similar to a human groan. Of course, this personification establishes a tone of sadness or suffering. A different tone would be established if the author said that the tree was *swaying* or *dancing*. Alfred Tennyson's poem "The Eagle" uses all of these types of figurative language: "He clasps the crag with crooked hands." Tennyson used alliteration, repeating /k/ and /kr/ sounds. These hard-sounding consonants reinforce the imagery giving visual and tactile impressions of the eagle.

Review Video: Personification
Visit mometrix.com/academy and enter code: 260066

Similes and Metaphors

Similes are stated comparisons using "like" or "as." Similes can be used to stimulate readers' imaginations and appeal to their senses. Because a simile includes *like* or *as,* the device creates more space between the description and the thing being described than a metaphor does. If an author says that *a house was like a shoebox*, then the tone is different than the author saying that the house *was* a shoebox. Authors will choose between a metaphor and a simile depending on their intended tone.

Similes also help compare fictional characters to well-known objects or experiences, so the reader can better relate to them. William Wordsworth's poem about "Daffodils" begins, "I wandered lonely as a cloud." This simile compares his loneliness to that of a cloud. It is also personification, giving a cloud the human quality loneliness. In his novel *Lord Jim* (1900), Joseph Conrad writes in Chapter 33, "I would have given anything for the power to soothe her frail soul, tormenting itself in its invincible ignorance like a small bird beating about the cruel wires of a cage." Conrad uses the word "like" to compare the girl's soul to a small bird. His description of the bird beating at the cage shows the similar helplessness of the girl's soul to gain freedom.

Review Video: Simile
Visit mometrix.com/academy and enter code: 642949

A **metaphor** is a type of figurative language in which the writer equates something with another thing that is not particularly similar, instead of using *like* or *as*. For instance, *the bird was an arrow arcing through the sky*. In this sentence, the arrow is serving as a metaphor for the bird. The point of a metaphor is to encourage the reader to consider the item being described in a *different way*. Let's continue with this metaphor for a flying bird. You are asked to envision the bird's flight as being similar to the arc of an arrow. So, you imagine the flight to be swift and bending. Metaphors are a way for the author to describe an item *without being direct and obvious*. This literary device is a lyrical and suggestive way of providing information. Note that the reference for a metaphor will not always be mentioned explicitly by the author. Consider the following description of a forest in winter: *Swaying skeletons reached for the sky and groaned as the wind blew through them.* In this example, the author is using *skeletons* as a metaphor for leafless trees. This metaphor creates a spooky tone while inspiring the reader's imagination.

LITERARY EXAMPLES OF METAPHOR

A **metaphor** is an implied comparison, i.e. it compares something to something else without using "like", "as", or other comparative words. For example, in "The Tyger" (1794), William Blake writes, "Tyger Tyger, burning bright, / In the forests of the night." Blake compares the tiger to a flame not by saying it is like a fire, but by simply describing it as "burning." Henry Wadsworth Longfellow's poem "O Ship of State" (1850) uses an extended metaphor by referring consistently throughout the entire poem to the state, union, or republic as a seagoing vessel, referring to its keel, mast, sail, rope, anchors, and to its braving waves, rocks, gale, tempest, and "false lights on the shore". Within the extended metaphor, Wordsworth uses a specific metaphor: "the anchors of thy hope!"

TED HUGHES' ANIMAL METAPHORS

Ted Hughes frequently used animal metaphors in his poetry. In "The Thought Fox," a model of concise, structured beauty, Hughes characterizes the poet's creative process with succinct, striking imagery of an idea entering his head like a wild fox. Repeating "loneliness" in the first two stanzas emphasizes the poet's lonely work: "Something else is alive / Beside the clock's loneliness." He treats an idea's arrival as separate from himself. Three stanzas detail in vivid images a fox's approach from the outside winter forest at starless midnight —its nose, "Cold, delicately" touching twigs and leaves; "neat" paw prints in snow; "bold" body; brilliant green eyes; and self-contained, focused progress—"Till, with a sudden sharp hot stink of fox," he metaphorically depicts poetic inspiration as the fox's physical entry into "the dark hole of the head." Hughes ends by summarizing his vision of a poet as an interior, passive idea recipient, with the outside world unchanged: "The window is starless still; the clock ticks, / The page is printed."

Review Video: Metaphor
Visit mometrix.com/academy and enter code: 133295

HYPERBOLE

Hyperbole is excessive exaggeration used for humor or emphasis rather than for literal meaning. For example, in *To Kill a Mockingbird*, Harper Lee wrote, "People moved slowly then. There was no hurry, for there was nowhere to go, nothing to buy and no money to buy it with, nothing to see outside the boundaries of Maycomb County." This was not literally true; Lee exaggerates the scarcity of these things for emphasis. In "Old Times on the Mississippi," Mark Twain wrote, "I... could have hung my hat on my eyes, they stuck out so far." This is not literal, but makes his description vivid and funny. In his poem "As I Walked Out One Evening", W. H. Auden wrote, "I'll love you, dear, I'll love you / Till China and Africa meet, / And the river jumps over the mountain / And the salmon sing in the street." He used things not literally possible to emphasize the duration of his love.

Review Video: Hyperbole and Understatement
Visit mometrix.com/academy and enter code: 308470

LITERARY IRONY

In literature, irony demonstrates the opposite of what is said or done. The three types of irony are **verbal irony**, **situational irony**, and **dramatic irony**. Verbal irony uses words opposite to the meaning. Sarcasm may use verbal irony. One common example is describing something that is confusing as "clear as mud." For example, in his 1986 movie *Hannah and Her Sisters,* author, director, and actor Woody Allen says to his character's date, "I had a great evening; it was like the

Nuremburg Trials." Notice these employ similes. In situational irony, what happens contrasts with what was expected. O. Henry's short story *The Gift of the Magi* uses situational irony: a husband and wife each sacrifice their most prized possession to buy each other a Christmas present. The irony is that she sells her long hair to buy him a watch fob, while he sells his heirloom pocket-watch to buy her the jeweled combs for her hair she had long wanted; in the end, neither of them can use their gifts. In dramatic irony, narrative informs audiences of more than its characters know. For example, in *Romeo and Juliet,* the audience is made aware that Juliet is only asleep, while Romeo believes her to be dead, which then leads to Romeo's death.

Review Video: Irony
Visit mometrix.com/academy and enter code: 374204

Idioms

Idioms create comparisons, and often take the form of similes or metaphors. Idioms are always phrases and are understood to have a meaning that is different from its individual words' literal meaning. For example, "break a leg" is a common idiom that is used to wish someone luck or tell them to perform well. Literally, the phrase "break a leg" means to injure a person's leg, but the phrase takes on a different meaning when used as an idiom. Another example is "call it a day," which means to temporarily stop working on a task, or find a stopping point, rather than literally referring to something as "a day." Many idioms are associated with a region or group. For example, an idiom commonly used in the American South is "'til the cows come home." This phrase is often used to indicate that something will take or may last for a very long time, but not that it will literally last until the cows return to where they reside.

Literary Analysis

Literary Terminology

In works of prose such as novels, a group of connected sentences covering one main topic is termed a **paragraph**. In works of poetry, a group of verses similarly connected is called a **stanza**. In drama, when early works used verse, these were also divided into stanzas or **couplets**. Drama evolved to use predominantly prose. Overall, whether prose or verse, the conversation in a play is called **dialogue**. Large sections of dialogue spoken by one actor are called **soliloquies** or **monologues**. Dialogue that informs audiences but is unheard by other characters is called an **aside**. Novels and plays share certain common elements, such as **characters**, the people in the story; **plot**, the action of the story; **climax** when action or dramatic tension reaches its highest point; and **denouement**, the resolution following the climax. Sections dividing novels are called **chapters**, while sections of plays are called **acts**. Subsections of plays' acts are called **scenes**. Novel chapters usually do not have subsections. However, some novels do include groups of chapters that form different sections.

Literary Analysis

The best literary analysis shows special insight into at least one important aspect of a text. When analyzing literary texts, it can be difficult to find a starting place. Many texts can be analyzed several different ways, often leaving an overwhelming number of options for writers to consider. However, narrowing the focus to a particular element of literature can be helpful when preparing to analyze a text. Symbolism, themes, and motifs are common starting points for literary analysis. These three methods of analysis can lead to a holistic analysis of a text, since they involve elements that are often distributed throughout the text. However, not all texts feature these elements in a way that facilitates a strong analysis, if they are present at all. It is also common to focus on character or plot development for analysis. These elements are compatible with theme, symbolism, and allusion.

Setting and imagery, figurative language, and any external contexts can also contribute to analysis or complement one of these other elements. The application of a critical, or literary, theory to a text can also provide a thorough and strong analysis.

SETTING AND TIME FRAME

A literary text has both a setting and time frame. A **setting** is the place in which the story as a whole is set. The **time frame** is the period in which the story is set. This may refer to the historical period the story takes place in or if the story takes place over a single day. Both setting and time frame are relevant to a text's meaning because they help the reader place the story in time and space. An author uses setting and time frame to anchor a text, create a mood, and enhance its meaning. This helps a reader understand why a character acts the way he does, or why certain events in the story are important. The setting impacts the **plot** and character **motivations**, while the time frame helps place the story in **chronological context**.

EXAMPLE

Read the following excerpt from The Adventures of Huckleberry Finn by Mark Twain and analyze the relevance of setting to the text's meaning:

> We said there warn't no home like a raft, after all. Other places do seem so cramped up and smothery, but a raft don't. You feel mighty free and easy and comfortable on a raft.

This excerpt from *The Adventures of Huckleberry Finn* by Mark Twain reveals information about the **setting** of the book. By understanding that the main character, Huckleberry Finn, lives on a raft, the reader can place the story on a river, in this case, the Mississippi River in the South before the Civil War. The information about the setting also gives the reader clues about the **character** of Huck Finn: he clearly values independence and freedom, and he likes the outdoors. The information about the setting in the quote helps the reader to better understand the rest of the text.

THEME

The **theme** of a passage is what the reader learns from the text or the passage. It is the lesson or **moral** contained in the passage. It also is a unifying idea that is used throughout the text; it can take the form of a common setting, idea, symbol, design, or recurring event. A passage can have two or more themes that convey its overall idea. The theme or themes of a passage are often based on **universal themes**. They can frequently be expressed using well-known sayings about life, society, or human nature, such as "Hard work pays off" or "Good triumphs over evil." Themes are not usually stated **explicitly**. The reader must figure them out by carefully reading the passage. Themes are often the reason why passages are written; they give a passage unity and meaning. Themes are created through **plot development**. The events of a story help shape the themes of a passage.

EXAMPLE

Explain why "Take care of what you care about" accurately describes the theme of the following excerpt.

> Luca collected baseball cards, but he wasn't very careful with them. He left them around the house. His dog liked to chew. One day, Luca and his friend Bart were looking at his collection. Then they went outside. When Luca got home, he saw his dog chewing on his cards. They were ruined.

This excerpt tells the story of a boy who is careless with his baseball cards and leaves them lying around. His dog ends up chewing them and ruining them. The lesson is that if you care about something, you need to take care of it. This is the theme, or point, of the story. Some stories have more than one theme, but this is not really true of this excerpt. The reader needs to figure out the theme based on what happens in the story. Sometimes, as in the case of fables, the theme is stated directly in the text. However, this is not usually the case.

Review Video: Theme
Visit mometrix.com/academy and enter code: 732074

Conflict

A **conflict** is a problem to be solved. Literary plots typically include one conflict or more. Characters' attempts to resolve conflicts drive the narrative's forward movement. **Conflict resolution** is often the protagonist's primary occupation. Physical conflicts like exploring, wars, and escapes tend to make plots most suspenseful and exciting. Emotional, mental, or moral conflicts tend to make stories more personally gratifying or rewarding for many audiences. Conflicts can be external or internal. A major type of internal conflict is some inner personal battle, or **man versus self**. Major types of external conflicts include **man versus nature**, **man versus man**, and **man versus society**. Readers can identify conflicts in literary plots by identifying the protagonist and antagonist and asking why they conflict, what events develop the conflict, where the climax occurs, and how they identify with the characters.

Read the following paragraph and discuss the type of conflict present:

> Timothy was shocked out of sleep by the appearance of a bear just outside his tent. After panicking for a moment, he remembered some advice he had read in preparation for this trip: he should make noise so the bear would not be startled. As Timothy started to hum and sing, the bear wandered away.

There are three main types of conflict in literature: **man versus man**, **man versus nature**, and **man versus self**. This paragraph is an example of man versus nature. Timothy is in conflict with the bear. Even though no physical conflict like an attack exists, Timothy is pitted against the bear. Timothy uses his knowledge to "defeat" the bear and keep himself safe. The solution to the conflict is that Timothy makes noise, the bear wanders away, and Timothy is safe.

Review Video: Conflict
Visit mometrix.com/academy and enter code: 559550

Conflict Resolution

The way the conflict is **resolved** depends on the type of conflict. The plot of any book starts with the lead up to the conflict, then the conflict itself, and finally the solution, or **resolution**, to the conflict. In **man-versus-man** conflicts, the conflict is often resolved by two parties coming to some sort of agreement or by one party triumphing over the other party. In **man-versus-nature** conflicts, the conflict is often resolved by man coming to some realization about some aspect of nature. In **man-versus-self** conflicts, the conflict is often resolved by the character growing or coming to an understanding about part of himself.

Syntax and Word Choice

Authors use words and **syntax**, or sentence structure, to make their texts unique, convey their own writing style, and sometimes to make a point or emphasis. They know that word choice and syntax contribute to the reader's understanding of the text as well as to the tone and mood of a text.

Review Video: Syntax
Visit mometrix.com/academy and enter code: 242280

Allusion

An allusion is an uncited but recognizable reference to something else. Authors use language to make allusions to places, events, artwork, and other books in order to make their own text richer. For example, an author may allude to a very important text in order to make his own text seem more important. Martin Luther King, Jr. started his "I Have a Dream" speech by saying "Five score years ago…" This is a clear allusion to President Abraham Lincoln's "Gettysburg Address" and served to remind people of the significance of the event. An author may allude to a place to ground his text or make a cultural reference to make readers feel included. There are many reasons that authors make allusions.

Review Video: Allusion
Visit mometrix.com/academy and enter code: 294065

Comic Relief

Comic relief is the use of comedy by an author to break up a dramatic or tragic scene and infuse it with a bit of **lightheartedness**. In William Shakespeare's *Hamlet*, two gravediggers digging the grave for Ophelia share a joke while they work. The death and burial of Ophelia are tragic moments that directly follow each other. Shakespeare uses an instance of comedy to break up the tragedy and give his audience a bit of a break from the tragic drama. Authors sometimes use comic relief so that their work will be less depressing; other times they use it to create irony or contrast between the darkness of the situation and the lightness of the joke. Often, authors will use comedy to parallel what is happening in the tragic scenes.

Mood and Tone

Mood is a story's atmosphere, or the feelings the reader gets from reading it. The way authors set the mood in writing is comparable to the way filmmakers use music to set the mood in movies. Instead of music, though, writers judiciously select descriptive words to evoke certain moods. The mood of a work may convey joy, anger, bitterness, hope, gloom, fear, apprehension, or any other emotion the author wants the reader to feel. In addition to vocabulary choices, authors also use figurative expressions, particular sentence structures, and choices of diction that project and reinforce the moods they want to create. Whereas mood is the reader's emotions evoked by reading what is written, **tone** is the emotions and attitudes of the writer that she or he expresses in the writing. Authors use the same literary techniques to establish tone as they do to establish mood. An author may use a humorous tone, an angry or sad tone, a sentimental or unsentimental tone, or something else entirely.

Mood and Tone in The Great Gatsby

To understand the difference between mood and tone, look at this excerpt from F. Scott Fitzgerald's *The Great Gatsby*. In this passage, Nick Caraway, the novel's narrator, is decribing his afforfable house, which sits in a neighborhood full of expensive mansions.

> "I lived at West Egg, the—well the less fashionable of the two, though this is a most superficial tag to express the bizarre and not a little sinister contrast betweeen them. My house was at the very tip of the egg, only fifty yard from the Sound, and squeezed between two huge places that rented for twelve or fifteen thousand a season ... My own house was an eyesore, but it was a small eyesore, and it had been overlooked, so I had a view of the water, a partial view of my neighbor's lawn, and the consoling proximity of millionaires—all for eighty dollars a month."

In this description, the mood created for the reader does not match the tone created through the narrator. The mood in this passage is one of disatisfaction and inferiority. Nick compares his home to his neighbors', saying he lives in the "less fashionable" neighborhood and that his house is "overlooked," an "eyesore," and "squeezed between two huge" mansions. He also adds that his placement allows him the "consoling proximity of millionaires." A literal reading of these details leads the reader to have negative feelings toward Nick's house and his economic inferiority to his neighbors, creating the mood.

However, Fitzgerald also conveys an opposing attitude, or tone, through Nick's description. Nick calls the distinction between the neighboorhoods "superficial," showing a suspicion of the value suggested by the neighborhoods' titles, properties, and residents. Nick also undermines his critique of his own home by calling it "a small eyesore" and claiming it has "been overlooked." However, he follows these statements with a description of his surroundings, claiming that he has "a view of the water" and can see some of his wealthy neighbor's property from his home, and a comparison between the properties' rent. While the mental image created for the reader depicts a small house shoved between looming mansions, the tone suggests that Nick enjoys these qualities about his home, or at least finds it charming. He acknowledges its shortcomings, but includes the benefits of his home's unassuming appearance.

Review Video: Style, Tone, and Mood
Visit mometrix.com/academy and enter code: 416961

Character Development

When depicting characters or figures in a written text, authors generally use actions, dialogue, and descriptions as characterization techniques. Characterization can occur in both fiction and nonfiction and is used to show a character or figure's personality, demeanor, and thoughts. This helps create a more engaging experience for the reader by providing a more concrete picture of a character or figure's tendencies and features. Characterizations also gives authors the opportunity to integrate elements such as dialects, activities, attire, and attitudes into their writing.

To understand the meaning of a story, it is vital to understand the characters as the author describes them. We can look for contradictions in what a character thinks, says, and does. We can notice whether the author's observations about a character differ from what other characters in the story say about that character. A character may be dynamic, meaning they change significantly during the story, or static, meaning they remain the same from beginning to end. Characters may be two-dimensional, not fully developed, or may be well developed with characteristics that stand out vividly. Characters may also symbolize universal properties. Additionally, readers can compare and contrast characters to analyze how each one developed.

A well-known example of character development can be found in Charles Dickens's *Great Expectations*. The novel's main character, Pip, is introduced as a young boy, and he is depicted as innocent, kind, and humble. However, as Pip grows up and is confronted with the social hierarchy of Victorian England, he becomes arrogant and rejects his loved ones in pursuit of his own social advancement. Once he achieves his social goals, he realizes the merits of his former lifestyle, and lives with the wisdom he gained in both environments and life stages. Dickens shows Pip's ever-changing character through his interactions with others and his inner thoughts, which evolve as his personal values and personality shift.

Review Video: Character Changes
Visit mometrix.com/academy and enter code: 408719

Dialogue

Effectively written **dialogue** serves at least one, but usually several, purposes. It advances the story and moves the plot, develops the characters, sheds light on the work's theme or meaning, and can, often subtly, account for the passage of time not otherwise indicated. It can alter the direction that the plot is taking, typically by introducing some new conflict or changing existing ones. Dialogue can establish a work's narrative voice and the characters' voices and set the tone of the story or of particular characters. When fictional characters display enlightenment or realization, dialogue can give readers an understanding of what those characters have discovered and how. Dialogue can illuminate the motivations and wishes of the story's characters. By using consistent thoughts and syntax, dialogue can support character development. Skillfully created, it can also represent real-life speech rhythms in written form. Via conflicts and ensuing action, dialogue also provides drama.

Dialogue in Fiction

In fictional works, effectively written dialogue does more than just break up or interrupt sections of narrative. While dialogue may supply exposition for readers, it must nonetheless be believable. Dialogue should be dynamic, not static, and it should not resemble regular prose. Authors should not use dialogue to write clever similes or metaphors, or to inject their own opinions. Nor should they use dialogue at all when narrative would be better. Most importantly, dialogue should not slow the plot movement. Dialogue must seem natural, which means careful construction of phrases rather than actually duplicating natural speech, which does not necessarily translate well to the written word. Finally, all dialogue must be pertinent to the story, rather than just added conversation.

Point of View

Another element that impacts a text is the author's point of view. The **point of view** of a text is the perspective from which a passage is told. An author will always have a point of view about a story before he or she draws up a plot line. The author will know what events they want to take place, how they want the characters to interact, and how they want the story to resolve. An author will also have an opinion on the topic or series of events which is presented in the story that is based on their prior experience and beliefs.

The two main points of view that authors use, especially in a work of fiction, are first person and third person. If the narrator of the story is also the main character, or *protagonist*, the text is written in first-person point of view. In first person, the author writes from the perspective of *I*. Third-person point of view is probably the most common that authors use in their passages. Using third person, authors refer to each character by using *he* or *she.* In third-person omniscient, the narrator is not a character in the story and tells the story of all of the characters at the same time.

Review Video: Point of View
Visit mometrix.com/academy and enter code: 383336

First-Person Narration

First-person narratives let narrators express inner feelings and thoughts, especially when the narrator is the protagonist as Lemuel Gulliver is in Jonathan Swift's *Gulliver's Travels.* The narrator may be a close friend of the protagonist, like Dr. Watson in Sir Arthur Conan Doyle's *Sherlock Holmes.* Or, the narrator can be less involved with the main characters and plot, like Nick Carraway in F. Scott Fitzgerald's *The Great Gatsby.* When a narrator reports others' narratives, she or he is a "**frame narrator**," like the nameless narrator of Joseph Conrad's *Heart of Darkness* or Mr. Lockwood in Emily Brontë's *Wuthering Heights.* **First-person plural** is unusual but can be effective. Isaac Asimov's *I, Robot*, William Faulkner's *A Rose for Emily*, Maxim Gorky's *Twenty-Six Men and a Girl*, and Jeffrey Eugenides' *The Virgin Suicides* all use first-person plural narration. Author Kurt Vonnegut is the first-person narrator in his semi-autobiographical novel *Timequake.* Also unusual, but effective, is a **first-person omniscient** (rather than the more common third-person omniscient) narrator, like Death in Markus Zusak's *The Book Thief* and the ghost in Alice Sebold's *The Lovely Bones.*

Second-Person Narration

While **second-person** address is very commonplace in popular song lyrics, it is the least used form of narrative voice in literary works. Popular serial books of the 1980s like *Fighting Fantasy* or *Choose Your Own Adventure* employed second-person narratives. In some cases, a narrative combines both second-person and first-person voices, using the pronouns *you* and *I.* This can draw readers into the story, and it can also enable the authors to compare directly "your" and "my" feelings, thoughts, and actions. When the narrator is also a character in the story, as in Edgar Allan Poe's short story "The Tell-Tale Heart" or Jay McInerney's novel *Bright Lights, Big City,* the narrative is better defined as first-person despite its also addressing "you."

Third-Person Narration

Narration in the **third person** is the most prevalent type, as it allows authors the most flexibility. It is so common that readers simply assume without needing to be informed that the narrator is not a character in the story, or involved in its events. **Third-person singular** is used more frequently than **third-person plural**, though some authors have also effectively used plural. However, both singular and plural are most often included in stories according to which characters are being described. The third-person narrator may be either objective or subjective, and either omniscient or limited. **Objective third-person** narration does not include what the characters described are thinking or feeling, while **subjective third-person** narration does. The **third-person omniscient** narrator knows everything about all characters, including their thoughts and emotions, and all related places, times, and events. However, the **third-person limited** narrator may know everything about a particular character, but is limited to that character. In other words, the narrator cannot speak about anything that character does not know.

Alternating-Person Narration

Although authors more commonly write stories from one point of view, there are also instances wherein they alternate the narrative voice within the same book. For example, they may sometimes use an omniscient third-person narrator and a more intimate first-person narrator at other times.

In J. K. Rowling's series of *Harry Potter* novels, she often writes in a third-person limited narrative, but sometimes changes to narration by characters other than the protagonist. George R. R. Martin's series *A Song of Ice and Fire* changes the point of view to coincide with divisions between chapters. The same technique is used by Erin Hunter (a pseudonym for several authors of the *Warriors, Seekers,* and *Survivors* book series). Authors using first-person narrative sometimes switch to third-person to describe significant action scenes, especially those where the narrator was absent or uninvolved, as Barbara Kingsolver does in her novel *The Poisonwood Bible.*

Historical and Social Context

Fiction that is heavily influenced by a historical or social context cannot be comprehended as the author intended if the reader does not keep this context in mind. Many important elements of the text will be influenced by any context, including symbols, allusions, settings, and plot events. These contexts, as well as the identity of the work's author, can help to inform the reader about the author's concerns and intended meanings. For example, George Orwell published his novel *1984* in the year 1949, soon after the end of World War II. At that time, following the defeat of the Nazis, the Cold War began between the Western Allied nations and the Eastern Soviet Communists. People were therefore concerned about the conflict between the freedoms afforded by Western democracies versus the oppression represented by Communism. Orwell had also previously fought in the Spanish Civil War against a Spanish regime that he and his fellows viewed as oppressive. From this information, readers can infer that Orwell was concerned about oppression by totalitarian governments. This informs *1984*'s story of Winston Smith's rebellion against the oppressive "Big Brother" government, of the fictional dictatorial state of Oceania, and his capture, torture, and ultimate conversion by that government. Some literary theories also seek to use historical and social contexts to reveal deeper meanings and implications in a text.

Textual Evidence

No literary analysis is complete without textual evidence. Summaries, paraphrases, and quotes are all forms of textual evidence, but direct quotes from the text are the most effective form of evidence. The best textual evidence is relevant, accurate, and clearly supports the writer's claim. This can include pieces of descriptions, dialogue, or exposition that shows the applicability of the analysis to the text. Analysis that is average, or sufficient, shows an understanding of the text; contains supporting textual evidence that is relevant and accurate, if not strong; and shows a specific and clear response. Analysis that partially meets criteria also shows understanding, but the textual evidence is generalized, incomplete, only partly relevant or accurate, or connected only weakly. Inadequate analysis is vague, too general, or incorrect. It may give irrelevant or incomplete textual evidence, or may simply summarize the plot rather than analyzing the work. It is important to incorporate textual evidence from the work being analyzed and any supplemental materials and to provide appropriate attribution for these sources.

Theme and Plot

Themes in Literature

When we read parables, their themes are the lessons they aim to teach. When we read fables, the moral of each story is its theme. When we read fictional works, the authors' perspectives regarding life and human behavior are their themes. Unlike in parables and fables, themes in literary fiction are usually not meant to preach or teach the readers a lesson. Hence, themes in fiction are not as explicit as they are in parables or fables. Instead, they are implicit, and the reader only infers them. By analyzing the fictional characters through thinking about their actions and behavior, understanding the setting of the story, and reflecting on how its plot develops, the reader comes to infer the main theme of the work. When writers succeed, they communicate with their readers such that common ground is established between author and audience. While a reader's individual experience may differ in its details from the author's written story, both may share universal underlying truths which allow author and audience to connect.

Determining Theme

In well-crafted literature, theme, structure, and plot are interdependent and inextricable: each element informs and reflects the others. The structure of a work is how it is organized. The theme is the central idea or meaning found in it. The plot is what happens in the story. Titles can also inform us of a work's theme. For instance, the title of Edgar Allan Poe's "The Tell-Tale Heart" informs readers of the story's theme of guilt before they even read about the repeated heartbeat the protagonist hears immediately before and constantly after committing and hiding a murder. Repetitive patterns of events or behaviors also give clues to themes. The same is true of symbols. For example, in F. Scott Fitzgerald's *The Great Gatsby,* for Jay Gatsby the green light at the end of the dock symbolizes Daisy Buchanan and his own dreams for the future. More generally, it is also understood as a symbol of the American Dream, and narrator Nick Carraway explicitly compares it to early settlers' sight of America rising from the ocean.

Thematic Development

Theme in The Great Gatsby

In *The Great Gatsby*, F. Scott Fitzgerald portrayed 1920s America as greedy, cynical, and rife with moral decay. Jay Gatsby's lavish weekly parties symbolize the reckless excesses of the Jazz Age. The growth of bootlegging and organized crime in reaction to Prohibition is symbolized by the character of Meyer Wolfsheim and by Gatsby's own ill-gotten wealth. Fitzgerald symbolized social divisions using geography. The "old money" aristocrats like the Buchanans lived on East Egg, while the "new money" bourgeois like Gatsby lived on West Egg. Fitzgerald also used weather, as many authors have, to reinforce narrative and emotional tones in the novel. Just as in *Romeo and Juliet,* where William Shakespeare set the confrontation of Tybalt and Mercutio and its deadly consequences on the hottest summer day under a burning sun, in *The Great Gatsby*, Fitzgerald did the same with Tom Wilson's deadly confrontation with Gatsby. Both works are ostensible love stories carrying socially critical themes about the destructiveness of pointless and misguided behaviors—family feuds in the former, pursuit of money in the latter.

Review Video: Thematic Development
Visit mometrix.com/academy and enter code: 576507

Theme in Les Misérables

In Victor Hugo's novel *Les Misérables*, the overall metamorphosis of protagonist Jean Valjean from a cynical ex-convict into a noble benefactor demonstrates Hugo's theme of the importance of love and compassion for others. Hugo also reflects this in more specific plot events. For example, Valjean's love for Cosette sustains him through many difficult periods and trying events. Hugo illustrates how love and compassion for others beget the same in them: Bishop Myriel's kindness to Valjean eventually inspires him to become honest. Years later, Valjean, as M. Madeleine, has rescued Fauchelevent from under a fallen carriage, Fauchelevent returns the compassionate act by giving Valjean sanctuary in the convent. M. Myriel's kindness also ultimately enables Valjean to rescue Cosette from the Thénardiers. Receiving Valjean's father-like love enables Cosette to fall in love with and marry Marius, and the love between Cosette and Marius enables the couple to forgive Valjean for his past crimes when they are revealed.

THEME IN "THE TELL-TALE HEART"

In one of his shortest stories, "The Tell-Tale Heart," Poe used economy of language to emphasize the murderer-narrator's obsessive focus on bare details like the victim's cataract-milky eye, the sound of a heartbeat, and insistence he is sane. The narrator begins by denying he is crazy, even citing his extreme agitation as proof of sanity. Contradiction is then extended: the narrator loves the old man, yet kills him. His motives are irrational—not greed or revenge, but to relieve the victim of his "evil eye." Because "eye" and "I" are homonyms, readers may infer that eye/I symbolizes the old man's identity, contradicting the killer's delusion that he can separate them. The narrator distances himself from the old man by perceiving his eye as separate, and dismembering his dead body. This backfires when he imagines the victim's heartbeat, which is really his own, just before he kills him and frequently afterward. Guilty and paranoid, he gives himself away. Poe predated Freud in exploring the paradox of killing those we love and the concept of projecting our own processes onto others.

THEME IN THE WORKS OF WILLIAM FAULKNER AND CHARLES DICKENS

William Faulkner contrasts the traditions of the antebellum South with the rapid changes of post-Civil War industrialization in his short story "A Rose for Emily." Living inside the isolated world of her house, Emily Grierson denies the reality of modern progress. Contradictorily, she is both a testament to time-honored history and a mysterious, eccentric, unfathomable burden. Faulkner portrays her with deathlike imagery even in life, comparing her to a drowned woman and referring to her skeleton. Emily symbolizes the Old South; as her social status is degraded, so is the antebellum social order. Like Miss Havisham in Charles Dickens' *Great Expectations,* Emily preserves her bridal bedroom, denying change and time's passage. Emily tries to control death through denial, shown in her necrophilia with her father's corpse and her killing of Homer Barron to stop him from leaving her, then also denying his death. Faulkner uses the motif of dust throughout to represent not only the decay of Emily, her house, and Old Southern traditions, but also how her secrets are obscured from others.

THEME IN MOBY-DICK

The great White Whale in *Moby-Dick* plays various roles to different characters. In Captain Ahab's obsessive, monomaniacal quest to kill it, the whale represents all evil, and Ahab believes it his duty and destiny to rid the world of it. Ishmael attempts through multiple scientific disciplines to understand the whale objectively, but fails—it is hidden underwater and mysterious to humans—reinforcing Melville's theme that humans can never know everything; here the whale represents the unknowable. Melville reverses white's usual connotation of purity in Ishmael's dread of white, associated with crashing waves, polar animals, albinos—all frightening and unnatural. White is often viewed as an absence of color, yet white light is the sum total of all colors in the spectrum. In the same way, white can signify both absence of meaning, and totality of meaning incomprehensible to humans. As a creature of nature, the whale also symbolizes how 19th-century white men's exploitative expansionistic actions were destroying the natural environment.

THEME IN THE OLD MAN AND THE SEA

Because of the old fisherman Santiago's struggle to capture a giant marlin, some people characterize Ernest Hemingway's *The Old Man and the Sea* as telling of man against nature. However, it can more properly be interpreted as telling of man's role as part of nature. Both man and fish are portrayed as brave, proud, and honorable. In Hemingway's world, all creatures, including humans, must either kill or be killed. Santiago reflects, "man can be destroyed but not defeated," following this principle in his life. As heroes are often created through their own deaths, Hemingway seems to believe that while being destroyed is inevitable, destruction enables living beings to transcend it by fighting bravely with honor and dignity. Hemingway echoes Romantic poet John Keats' contention that only immediately before death can we understand beauty as it is about to be destroyed. He also echoes ancient Greek and Roman myths and the Old Testament with the tragic flaw of overweening pride or overreaching. Like Icarus, Prometheus, and Adam and Eve, the old man "went out too far."

Universal Themes

The Old Testament book of Genesis, the Quran, and the Epic of Gilgamesh all contain flood stories. Versions differ somewhat: Genesis describes a worldwide flood, attributing it to God's decision that mankind, his creation, had become incontrovertibly wicked in spirit and must be destroyed for the world to start anew. The Quran describes the flood as regional, caused by Allah after sending Nuh (notice the similarity in name to Noah) as a messenger to his people to cease their evil. The Quran stipulates that Allah only destroys those who deny or ignore messages from his messengers. Marked similarities also exist: in the Gilgamesh poems Utnapishtim, like Noah, is instructed to build a ship to survive the flood. Both men also send out birds afterward as tests, using doves and a raven, though with different outcomes. Many historians and archeologists believe a Middle Eastern tidal wave was a real basis for these stories. However, their universal themes remain the same: the flood was seen as God's way of wiping out humans whose behavior had become ungodly.

Theme of Overreaching

A popular theme throughout literature is the human trait of **reaching too far** or **presuming** too much. In Greek mythology, Daedalus constructed wings of feathers and wax that men might fly like birds. He permitted his son Icarus to try them, but cautioned the boy not to fly too close to the sun. The impetuous youth (in what psychologist David Elkind later named adolescence's myth of invincibility) ignored this, flying too close to the sun. The wax melted, the wings disintegrated, and Icarus fell into the sea and perished. In the Old Testament, God warned Adam and Eve not to eat fruit from the tree of knowledge of good and evil. Because they ignored this command, they were banished from Eden's eternal perfection, condemning them to mortality and suffering. The Romans were themselves examples of overreaching in their conquest and assimilation of most of the then-known world and ultimate demise. In Christopher Marlowe's *Dr. Faustus* and Johann Wolfgang von Goethe's *Faust,* the protagonist sells his soul to the Devil for unlimited knowledge and success, ultimately leading to his own tragic end.

Story Vs. Discourse

In terms of plot, "story" is the characters, places, and events originating in the author's mind, while "discourse" is how the author arranges and sequences events—which may be chronological or not. Story is imaginary; discourse is words on the page. Discourse allows story to be told in different ways. One element of plot structure is relating events differently from the order in which they occurred. This is easily done with cause-and-effect; for example, in the sentence, "He died following a long illness," we know the illness preceded the death, but the death precedes the illness in words. In Kate Chopin's short story "The Story of an Hour" (1894), she tells some of the events out of chronological order, which has the effect of amplifying the surprise of the ending for the reader. Another element of plot structure is selection. Chopin omits some details, such as Mr. Mallard's trip home; this allows readers to be as surprised at his arrival as Mrs. Mallard is.

Plot and Meaning

Novelist E. M. Forster has made the distinction between story as relating a series of events, such as a king dying and then his queen dying, versus plot as establishing motivations for actions and causes for events, such as a king dying and then his queen dying from grief over his death. Thus, plot fulfills the function of helping readers understand cause-and-effect in events and underlying motivations in characters' actions, which in turn helps them understand life. This affects a work's meaning by supporting its ability to explain why things happen, why people do things, and ultimately the meaning of life. Some authors find that while story events convey meaning, they do not tell readers there is any one meaning in life or way of living, but rather are mental experiments with various meanings, enabling readers to explore. Hence stories may not necessarily be constructed to impose one definitive meaning, but rather to find some shape, direction, and meaning within otherwise random events.

CLASSIC ANALYSIS OF PLOT STRUCTURE

In *Poetics,* Aristotle defined plot as "the arrangement of the incidents." He meant not the story, but how it is structured for presentation. In tragedies, Aristotle found results driven by chains of cause and effect preferable to those driven by the protagonist's personality or character. He identified "unity of action" as necessary for a plot's wholeness, meaning its events must be internally connected, not episodic or relying on *deus ex machina* or other external intervention. A plot must have a beginning, middle, and end. Gustav Freytag adapted Aristotle's ideas into his Pyramid (1863). The beginning, today called the exposition, incentive, or inciting moment, emphasizes causes and de-emphasizes effects. Aristotle called the ensuing cause and effect *desis*, or tying up, today called complications which occur during the rising action. These culminate in a crisis or climax, Aristotle's *peripateia.* This occurs at the plot's middle, where cause and effect are both emphasized. The falling action, which Aristotle called the *lusis* or unraveling, is today called the dénouement. The resolution comes at the catastrophe, outcome, or end, when causes are emphasized and effects de-emphasized.

Review Video: Plot Line
Visit mometrix.com/academy and enter code: 944011

ANALYSIS OF PLOT STRUCTURES THROUGH RECURRING PATTERNS

Authors of fiction select characters, places, and events from their imaginations and arrange them to create a story that will affect their readers. One way to analyze plot structure is to compare and contrast different events in a story. For example, in Kate Chopin's "The Story of an Hour," a very simple but key pattern of repetition is the husband's leaving and then returning. Such patterns fulfill the symmetrical aspect that Aristotle said was required of sound plot structure. In James Baldwin's short story, "Sonny's Blues," the narrator is Sonny's brother. In an encounter with one of Sonny's old friends early in the story, the brother initially disregards his communication. In a subsequent flashback, Baldwin informs us that this was the same way he had treated Sonny. In Nathaniel Hawthorne's "Young Goodman Brown," a pattern is created by the protagonist's recurrent efforts not to go farther into the wood. In Herman Melville's "Bartleby the Scrivener" and in William Faulkner's "Barn Burning," patterns are also created by repetition such as Bartleby's repeated refusals and the history of barn-burning episodes, respectively.

LITERARY THEORIES AND CRITICISM AND INTERPRETATION

Literary theory includes ideas that guide readers through the process of interpreting literature. Literary theory, as a subject, encompasses several specific, focused theories that lead readers to interpret or analyze literature through the context of the theory using the subjects and elements it involves. Some commonly used and discussed literary theories include **postcolonial theory**, **gender and feminist theory**, **structuralism**, **new historicism**, **reader-response theory**, and **sociological criticism**.

- **Postcolonial theory** involves the historical and geographical context of a work and leads readers to consider how colonization informs the plot, characters, setting, and other elements in the work.

- **Gender and feminist theory** invites readers to interpret by looking at its treatment of and suggestions about women and a culture's treatment of women. As with most literary theories, this information can be clearly stated or strongly implied in a work, but it may also be gleaned through looking closely at symbols, characters, and plot elements in a work.
- **Structuralism** uses the structure and organization of a work and the foundations of language to examine how and what a text conveys about the human experience and how those findings connect to common human experiences.
- **New historicism** heavily relies on the cultural and historical context of a work, including when it was written, where the author lives or lived, the culture and history of that location, and other works from the same culture. New historical readings seek to examine these details to expose the ideologies of the location and culture that influenced the work.
- **Reader-response theory** uses the individual reader's response to the text and experience while reading the text to examine the meaning of the reader's relationship with the text and what that relationship suggests about the reader or the factors impacting their experience.
- **Sociological criticism** considers the societies that are relevant to a text. The author's society and any reader's society are important to the text, as sociological criticism seeks to uncover what the text implies or reveals about those societies. This method of criticism can also involve studying the presentation of a society within the text and applying it to the author's society or their other writings.

Language and Communication

Diversity and Situational Nature of Language

Language is a diverse tool that allows people to communicate. However, language is often impacted and molded by the culture that uses it. This can make it difficult to learn and use a new language, since not all native speakers of the language will use it or interpret it the same way. For example, English is spoken all over America, but Americans in various regions of the country speak using different **dialects**. Other differences in speech include **accents** and **rhythm of speech**. Language is also manipulated by situations. Some terms and phrases have multiple meanings. A word's meaning often depends on the **context** in which the word or phrase is used, meaning that non-native speakers must learn to interpret situations to understand messages.

Factors of Language and Communication

Influences on Language

While dialect and diction are heavily influenced by an individual's culture and the location and history of the place they live, other personal factors can also impact language. A person' s ethnicity, religious beliefs or background, and gender can influence the way they use and understand language. **Ethnicity** impacts language by incorporating a group's communication norms into an individual's speech and behavior. These norms may affect a speaker's tone, volume, or pace. These factors may lead others outside of that group to misinterpret the speaker's message, depending on their understanding of how those factors are used in speech. A person's **religious beliefs** can also affect their use of language. Religious beliefs and practices may lead an individual to abstain from using certain terms and may change the context in which a speaker uses specific words, or change their understanding of the word's usage. Additionally, a person may use language differently depending on their gender. **Gender's** influence on communication varies by region and industry. A region or industry's treatment of gender roles often impacts language use among its members. This can lead members of one gender group to be more assertive or submissive or to use different terms and phrases.

Culture and Communication

Individuals from different countries and cultures communicate differently. Not only do many people speak different languages, but they also speak using different inflections, volumes, tones, and dialects. These factors can have a significant impact on communication, even if the communicators speak the same language. In different cultures, certain behaviors are associated with different meanings and implications. When communicators from different cultures have a conversation, these expectations and associations may lead to misunderstanding. For example, Americans are considered to be louder and more demonstrative than people from other countries. Someone from a country where people speak more quietly who is not aware of this characterization may perceive an American's volume or large gestures as an indication of anger, when in reality, the American speaker is calm. The American may similarly perceive the other person as sad or shy due to their quiet voice, when the speaker is actually happy and comfortable in the conversation. Awareness of these factors and effects promotes respect for others and helps speakers understand the reasons for differences in communication, rather than allowing these differences to create division or conflict.

Dialect

Language vs. Dialect

Languages are distinct and structured forms of verbal communication. Languages have cohesive sets of rules and words that are shared between the majority of that language's users. The main identifier of a language is that members of other languages are incapable of communicating fluently with members of another language group. New languages are formed as different dialects grow further apart until the members of each dialect can no longer innately communicate with each other.

Dialects are subsets of languages that do not violate the rules of the language as a whole, but which vary from other dialects in vocabulary usage, grammar forms, pronunciation, and spelling. Two major groupings of dialects are American and British English. Most American English and British English speakers can communicate with relative ease with one another, though the pronunciation, vocabulary (torch vs. flashlight; trunk vs. boot), spelling (meter vs. metre; color vs. colour), and grammar (in American English, collective nouns are always considered singular, but can be singular or plural in British English).

Development of Dialects over Time

Dialects are formed primarily through the influences of location and time, but can be the result of other elements of **social stratification** as well (economic, ethnic, religious, etc.). As one group of a language's speakers is separated from another, in British and American English speakers for example, the language develops in isolated locations at the same time, resulting in distinct dialects. Language changes continuously over time as new words and phrases are adopted and others are phased out. Eventually, these small changes result culminate into enough grammar and vocabulary changes that the speakers of the distinct dialects cannot easily communicate with one another and the dialects can then be recognized as distinct languages.

Use of Dialect in Media

Literary authors often use dialect when writing dialogue to illustrate the social and geographical backgrounds of specific characters, which supports character development. For example, in *The Adventures of Huckleberry Finn* (1885), Mark Twain's novel is written in the dialect of a young, uneducated, white, Southern character, opening with this sentence: "You don't know about me without you have read a book by the name of The Adventures of Tom Sawyer, but that ain't no matter." Twain uses a different and exaggerated dialect to represent the speech of the African-American slave Jim: "We's safe, Huck, we's safe! Jump up and crack yo' heels. Dat's de good ole Cairo at las', I jis knows it."

In *To Kill a Mockingbird,* author Harper Lee used dialect in the characters' dialogue to portray an uneducated boy in the American South: "Reckon I have. Almost died the first year I come to school and et them pecans—folks say he pizened 'em." Lee also uses many Southern regional expressions, such as "right stove up," "What in the sam holy hill?", "sit a spell," "fess" (meaning "confess"), "jim-dandy," and "hush your fussing." These contribute to Lee's characterization of the people she describes, who live in a small town in Alabama circa the 1930s. In *Wuthering Heights* (1847), Emily Bronte reproduces Britain's 18th-19th-century Yorkshire dialect in the speech of servant Joseph: "Running after t'lads, as usuald!... If I war yah, maister, I'd just slam t'boards i' their faces all on 'em, gentle and simple! Never a day ut yah're off, but yon cat o' Linton comes sneaking hither; and Miss Nelly, shoo's a fine lass!"

Dialect vs. Diction

When written as characters' dialogue in literary works, dialect represents the particular pronunciation, grammar, and figurative expressions used by certain groups of people based on their geographic region, social class, and cultural background. For example, when a character says, "There's gold up in them thar hills," the author is using dialect to add to the characterization of that individual. Diction is more related to individual characters than to groups of people. The way in which a specific character speaks, including his or her choice of words, manner of expressing himself or herself, and use of grammar all represent individual types of diction. For example, two characters in the same novel might describe the same action or event using different diction: One says "I'm heading uptown for the evening," and the other says "I'm going out for a night on the town." These convey the same literal meaning, but due to their variations in diction they are expressed in different ways.

Review Video: Dialogue, Paradox, and Dialect
Visit mometrix.com/academy and enter code: 684341

Influences on Regional Dialect

Linguistic researchers have identified regional variations in vocabulary choices, which have evolved because of differences in local climates and how they influence human behaviors. For example, in the Southern United States, the Linguistic Atlas of the Gulf States (LAGS) Project by Dr. Lee Pederson of Emory University discovered and documented that people living in the northern or Upland section of the Piedmont plateau region call the fungal infection commonly known as athlete's foot "toe itch," but people living in the southern or Lowland section call it "ground itch." The explanation for this difference is that in the north, temperatures are cooler and people wear shoes accordingly, so they associate the itching with the feet in their description, but in the south, temperatures are hotter and people often went barefoot, so they associated the itching with the ground that presumably transmitted the infection.

Using Dialect in Writing

Dialect is most appropriate for informal or creative writing. Using dialectal writing when communicating casually or informally, such as in a text message or a quick email to a peer, is acceptable. However, in academic and professional contexts, writing using indications of dialect is inappropriate and often unacceptable. If the audience includes individuals who have a higher rank than the author, or authority over the author, it is best not to write in a way that suggests a dialect.

World Literature

American Literary Periods

Dark Romantics

In American literature, a group of late Romantic writers are recognized as **Dark Romantics**. These authors' works may be associated with both the Romantic and Gothic movements. These works emphasize nature and emotion, aligning them with Romanticism, and include dark themes and tones, aligning them with Gothic literature. However, these works do not all feature the historically inspired characteristics of Gothic literature, and their morals or outcomes more closely resemble those of Romantic literature. The Dark Romantics include writers such as Edgar Allan Poe, Nathaniel Hawthorne, Emily Dickinson, and Herman Melville.

Transcendentalism

Transcendentalism was a smaller movement that occurred alongside the American Romantic movement. The **transcendentalists** shared the Romantic emphasis on emotion and also focused heavily on how a person experiences life through their senses. They extended these sentiments to suggest that through embracing one's senses, an individual could transcend, or experience a state of being above physical humanity. They also extended the Romantic emphasis on subjectivity through their praise of self-sufficiency, as exemplified through Ralph Waldo Emerson's *Self-Reliance*. Emerson was a prominent transcendentalist. His writings included an essay titled *Nature*, which explains a progression from the use of the senses to the achievement of transcendence. Transcendentalist literature includes several essays that discuss the value of the senses and emotions or the process of transcendence. Transcendentalists also wrote poetry that includes the frequent use of imagery, metaphors, and references to nature. These elements reflect the ideas of transcendentalism and create a resemblance to the alleged experience of transcendence. Ralph Waldo Emerson, Henry David Thoreau, and Walt Whitman were all prominent writers in this movement.

Colonial America

The **colonial era** in America was influenced by immigration from England to what is now New England. These immigrants were mainly Puritans who centered their society in New England on their religious beliefs, allowing those beliefs to inform all aspects of their lives. This is apparent in the literature of the time, as much of it includes essays and sermons that discuss religion or the way the Puritans believed one should live and conduct themselves. Colonial literature also includes many poems, and these works also discuss or reference religious ideas and themes. There was not much fiction written in Colonial America, as most of the literature was written to inform or persuade.

Romantic Period

The **American Romantic** movement is also known as the American Renaissance. This movement yielded several notable American writers and works that began characterizing American literature and differentiating it from British literature. This literature, written after the American Revolutionary War and until the end of the Civil War, praised individualism and featured an expression of national pride and patriotism. The transcendentalists' extreme ideas about self-sufficiency and subjectivity reiterated this individualism, and their recommendations about society and its structure furthered the separation of American literature from British literature. While this period shaped the definition of American literature, it is criticized for featuring a narrow view of American politics and social issues at the time, as well as promoting a small group of similar writers.

Harlem Renaissance

The **Harlem Renaissance** took place in America during the 1920s and 1930s. The changing economy and opportunities led African Americans in the south to seek new lifestyles in other parts of America at the beginning of the 20th century. Many moved to Harlem, a small area in New York City. This group of African Americans yielded highly influential scholarly and artistic works, including poetry, fiction, music, and plays. The Harlem Renaissance marked an opportunity for these intellectuals and artists, who were largely ignored in the aftermath of the Civil War, to use their talents and express themselves through their works. While artists often featured personal expression in their works, the Harlem Renaissance was unique in its volume of culturally expressive works. This cultural expression and the movement's main ideas also contributed to the Civil Rights movement by promoting a spirit of unity among African Americans. The Harlem Renaissance eventually ended in the wake of the stock market crash in 1929. As the Great Depression began, financial support for the arts dwindled, making it difficult for many artists to succeed financially. Some members of the Harlem Renaissance who influenced American literature include Langston Hughes, Zora Neale Hurston, and Paul Robeson.

British Literary Periods

Neoclassical

The **British Neoclassical** period began in the middle of the 17th century and ended in the late 18th century. The latter part of the movement also took place alongside the Enlightenment, a period of scientific discovery and study that influenced many Western cultures. The Enlightenment's concern with intellectual pursuits and improvement increased discussions of introspection, or an individual's analysis of their own behavior, thoughts, and self. These ideas also affected society in England, as they contributed to a general attitude of complacency and a desire to ignore the past. The period saw a slightly increased acceptance of female writers, as their works were viewed as a method of self-reflection and improvement. The changes in the British society allowed several new forms of literature to gain popularity and acceptance, usually for their introspective qualities. Essays, diaries, and letters all displayed the author's thoughts and experience, aligning them with the culture's values. Novels also gained popularity, as many were fictional diaries or epistolary novels. Journalism flourished during the Neoclassical period, leading to the creation of the newspaper. Literary criticism also gained popularity, though it was used to criticize an author and their style rather than examine or analyze the content of the work.

Victorian

The **Victorian Era** in England was influenced by variety of events and ideas, many of which were influenced by the Victorians' economy. The Industrial Revolution in England changed the circumstances of work for the Victorians. The changing industries and lack of labor laws led to several problems and a wide division between Victorian social classes. These factors inspired and saturated much of Victorian literature. Many novels' plots and characters were heavily influenced by social and economic issues, and many poems referenced and criticized specific events that occurred during this period.

While the structure of Victorian society was a major influence on literature, there were other popular topics that appeared in literature. Topics like evolution, psychology, and colonization frequently appeared in Victorian literature, reflecting the concerns and interests of the Victorian culture. The Victorian society was also characterized by a strict moral code that supported the view of women as homemakers and criticized the idea of female writers. Not only did this affect the portrayal of women in literature, but it also led some female novelists, such as the Bronte sisters, to write under a pseudonym and present their works as having been written by a man. Victorian literature also popularized forms of literature, including the novel and the dramatic monologue, a poetic form developed by Robert Browning. Victorian writers include Charles Dickens, Oscar Wilde, Elizabeth Barrett Browning, Emily Bronte, Matthew Arnold, and Thomas Hardy.

WORLD LITERARY CHARACTERISTICS AND PERIODS

While many other nations shared literary movements with America and England, there are numerous literary movements that are unique to other countries and cultures. Some of these literary movements can be understood as variations of movements like Romanticism or modernism, since they occurred at similar times and feature similar elements, but the political and cultural events of each country shaped their version of each movement. Most regions also have some type of mythology, and while different mythologies have similar characters and events, each region's mythology is unique and significant to the region's literature. Another common feature of world literature is colonialism. Many nations are former colonies of European countries, and the effects of colonization are present in modern literature from countries worldwide, making it a key feature of many regions' body of literature.

AFRICAN LITERATURE

Literature from some cultures was not recorded until the 19th century, causing any movements and trends to be informed by ideas told aloud. This is true of African literature, where stories and ideas were spoken and passed down through the generations. Early African poetry was often metaphorical, structured or written to form a paradox, and included a riddle or puzzling statement. Proverbs and didactic tales were also told frequently, reflecting the dominant religions in a given region and time period. These poems and stories also reflect the variety of languages spoken in Africa and the shifts in each language's usage. Early African literature, once people began writing it down, included stories and proverbs that had been passed down, translations of religious texts, and descriptions of the way of life in different African cultures or groups. These cultures and the events specific to each culture produce a unique body of literature that places emphasis on certain topics and ideas. For example, much of the modern literature written in South Africa discusses politics and issues of race, since the country's history is characterized by events and movements that revolved around these topics.

ASIAN LITERATURE

Asian literature features writings from several different countries and languages and has spanned many centuries. Popular forms of writing have come from Asia, such as the haiku. A couple of significant literary movements include The Hungry Generation in South Asia and the Misty Poets in China. The Hungry Generation is a literary movement involving literature written in the Bengali language, spoken mainly in West Bengal and Bangladesh. The literature is characterized by unique and innovative writing, which impacted the use of figurative language in the region. The Hungry Generation also discussed cultural issues, particularly colonization in the region, and many participants were arrested for their work. The Misty Poets in China were characterized by their expressive use of abstractions. Their name, Misty Poets, comes from their writings, which were difficult to interpret due to their use of abstract language and ambiguity. This movement was partly inspired by the Misty Poets' distaste for literary realism, though its influence is detectable within their poetry. Many of the Misty Poets were punished for their poetry, since the poetry of this movement was also politically critical.

LATIN AMERICAN LITERATURE

Latin American literature has several literary movements, many of which occurred near the same time as American and British literary movements and share ideas and trends with their English counterparts. Despite these similarities, each of these movements is distinguishable as its own movement with unique impacts of Latin American literature. By the 17th century, written language was in use in Mexico, and Latin American literary trends and figures had been recognized. During the 18th century, Latin American literature featured a variety of ideas and themes within each form of literature. By the 19th century, literary themes were more unified throughout popular Latin American literature. In the early 19th century, Latin American literature embraced the Romantic movement as it came to an end in England and the United States. Several Latin American countries were also fighting for independence during this time, amplifying the Romantic idea of national pride and identity.

In the wake of the Romantic movement, Latin American literature introduced the unique Modernismo movement, which yielded a large volume of poetry and is characterized by the use of whimsical imagery and discussions of spiritual ideas. Following Modernismo was the Vanguardia movement, which was created to introduce diversity within Latin American literature after modernism permeated the literature of the time. Vanguardia involved writers taking risks in their writing and breaking the mold from typical Latin American literature. In the 20th century, Estridentismo followed the Vanguardia movement, marrying the Vanguardia movement with the European Avant-Garde movement. Other 20th century movements function similarly by adapting literary movements from other regions to suit the themes and trends in Latin American literature, reflect Latin American cultures, and set their literature apart from other cultures.

Literary Periods and Movements

Old English

The English language developed over a long period of time through interactions between different groups in Europe, including the Romans, the Germans, and the Celtics. The Anglo-Saxons, a group that left what is now Germany and settled in England, further established the English language by using what is now called **Old English**. While Old English laid foundations for modern English, its usage fundamentally differs from the way English is used today. For example, Old English relied on inflections to create meaning, placing little importance on the order of the words in the sentence. Its use of verbs and tenses also differs from modern English grammar. The Anglo-Saxons also used kennings, or compound words that functioned as figurative language.

Old English, as a language influenced by several cultures, had dialects from its inception. Differences in usage also came from the division between secular and religious cultures. This division heavily influenced Old English literature, as most of the literature from the time is categorized according to the set of beliefs it reflects. Most of the influential literature of the time includes riddles, poems, or translations of religious texts. Surviving Old English poetry mainly discusses real heroes and battles or provides a narrative about a fictional hero. Many of these fictional poems are considered lays, or lais, which are narrative poems that are structured using couplets of lines containing eight syllables each. The translations were often of passages from the Christian Bible, adaptations of Biblical passages, or copies of Christian hymns. Old English persisted until the 12th century, where it was eventually replaced with Middle English. Influential literature from this period includes *Beowulf*, "The Wanderer," "The Wife's Lament," and "The Seafarer."

Middle English

Old English was replaced by **Middle English**, which was used from the 12th century to the 16th century. Old English was not governed by a consistent set of grammatical rules until the Norse people, their language, and its structure influenced the integration of grammar into English, leading to Middle English. Middle English relied less on inflections than Old English, instead creating variations by using affixes and synonyms. The development of grammar was further facilitated by the printing press, which made it easier for writers to comply with grammar rules since the printing of identical copies reduced variation between texts.

Old English's evolution into Middle English can be narrowed down to three stages: Early, Central, and Late Middle English. Early Middle English, though it showed a change in the language, maintained the writing style of Old English. Central Middle English is characterized by the development of dialects within written communication, which is partly due to scribes who translated texts or parts of texts using terms from their own dialect, rather than the source. Late Middle English includes numerous developments that created the foundation for Modern English. *The Canterbury Tales*, "Sir Gawain and the Green Knight," and "Le Morte d'Arthur" are all Middle English texts that are still read and studied today.

The Renaissance

The **Renaissance** swept through Europe and lasted for multiple centuries, bringing many developments in culture, the arts, education, and philosophy. The Renaissance in England did not begin until the late 15th century. Though ideas and cultures of the past, especially those of the ancient Greeks and Romans, inspired the Renaissance, the period saw innumerable developments in the English language and literature. The Renaissance was characterized by a focus on the humanities, allowing the arts, including literature, to flourish. At the time, drama was the possibly the most popular form of literature, as the popularity of plays and theatrical performances greatly increased. Much of Renaissance literature is still studied today, maintaining its influence on Western literature. Poetry was also popular, and the period saw the development of new forms of poetry, such as the sonnet. Sonnets are often recognized according to one of four styles, each of which was popularized by a Renaissance writer. Lyrical poetry, which discusses emotions and is often written using first-person point of view, was also popular during the Renaissance.

In addition to new forms and literary trends, the Renaissance period also impacted English literature by facilitating discussion over the translation of the Bible. Education at the time often included instruction in Greek and Latin, allowing those with an education to read ancient texts in their original language. However, this instruction did not reach the majority of the public. The Protestant Reformation encouraged discussions about translating the Bible to make it accessible to more people. This suggestion was challenged by those who doubted the ability of the English language to fully reflect the original text. Eventually, the Bible was translated to English, and William Tyndale's partial translation became especially influential for later translations and the continuing development of the English language. Influential writers of the English Renaissance include William Shakespeare, John Donne, John Milton, Edmund Spenser, and Christopher Marlowe.

Gothic

The Gothic literary movement, beginning in the 18th century and persisting through the 19th century, took inspiration from the architecture and cultures of the Late Middle Ages in Europe. The Late Middle Ages saw the popularity of Gothic architecture, most prominently in places of worship. These structures inspired many of the settings in **Gothic literature**, as a large volume of Gothic literature takes place in an impressive location, such as a castle or ornate mansion. Gothic works also are often set in the past, long before the time the story was written. This aligns with prominent themes in Gothic literature, as several pieces are informed by an event that occurred before the story begins or a character who died before the plot's first event.

Another common characteristic of Gothic literature is its eerie, dark, suspenseful tone. Authors of Gothic literature often created this tone by setting their works in secluded and strange locations and incorporating intense, unsettling, or even supernatural events and scenarios into the plot. This tone is also created through the theme of death or mortality that often appears in Gothic literature. These characteristics support the aim of many Gothic writers to create fiction that evokes a certain emotion from the reader or shapes their reading experience. Well-known authors of Gothic literature include Horace Watpole, Ann Radcliffe, Edgar Allan Poe, and Nathaniel Hawthorne. While the Gothic literary movement took place in the 18th and 19th centuries, many works have been published in more recent centuries that have several characteristics of Gothic literature and may be included within the overall Gothic genre.

Naturalism

Naturalism was an active literary movement in the late 19th century, taking place alongside movements such as realism and modernism. Naturalism's development in America was delayed and appeared in various ways, obscuring the true American naturalist genre. **Naturalism**, like realism, rejected the emotional focus and sentimentality of Romanticism and provided a type of social commentary. However, the naturalist movement stretched the ideas of realism, promoting literature that authentically depicts the life of the common man and criticizing the influence of morality on such literature. Naturalist literature often includes characters who belong to a lower class and experience circumstances beyond their own control and takes place in urban settings. Prominent themes in naturalist literature include nature as an apathetic force, the influence of heredity, and life as something to be endured and survived. One of the most influential naturalist writers is French writer Emile Zola. Influential American Naturalists include Stephen Crane, Hamlin Garland, and Theodore Dreiser.

Modernism

The Modernist literary movement was largely influenced by industrialization, which heavily impacted both the Unites States and England, primarily in the 19th century. **Modernism** in literature was characterized by an attempt to turn away from the norms and traditions of literature and use new techniques and methods. Modernist literature was often written in first person and used devices and techniques to reveal problems within society. For the American modernists, these societal changes came from industrialization and the first World War, which effected the general view of human nature and reliability. In England, there were additional factors contributing to this shift. Modernism began during Queen Victoria's reign, which defined the period known as the Victorian Era. The Victorian society was characterized by a strict moral code that permeated England's society at the time. This moral code was incompatible with the Modernist's desire to turn away from tradition, but the changes that accompanied Victoria's death in 1901 enabled the Modernist movement to grow in England. American Modernist writers include Ezra Pound, William Carlos Williams, and Gertrude Stein. British Modernist writers include Matthew Arnold, William Butler Yeats, T. S. Eliot, and Joseph Conrad.

Postmodernism

Postmodernism grew out of Modernism's reliance on science and universal assertions, but emphasized the individual's subjective perception of reality, as it is often more authentic to an individual's experience than a universally applied statement. Postmodernism asserts that since each person creates their own version of reality, fully and accurately defining reality is futile and impossible. Due to this skepticism, postmodern writers use many concrete details, rather than abstract details, because they can be objectively observed and are not left up to the individual. The postmodernist literary movement began around the 1960s. The literary movement included a variety of new genres and techniques, reflecting the postmodernist idea that things like art cannot be truly defined or simplified. Notable American writers of the postmodernist movement include Kurt Vonnegut, John Barth, and Thomas Pynchon. British postmodernist writers include John Fowles and Julian Barnes.

Public Speaking

Speeches

Speeches are written to be delivered in spoken language in public, to various groups of people, at formal or informal events. Some generic types include welcome speeches, thank-you speeches, keynote addresses, position papers, commemorative and dedication speeches, and farewell speeches. Speeches are commonly written in present tense and usually begin with an introduction greeting the audience. At official functions, specific audience members are named ("Chairperson [name]," "Principal [name], teachers, and students," etc.) and when audiences include a distinguished guest, he or she is often named as well. Then the speaker introduces him or herself by name, position, and department or organization as applicable. After the greeting, the speaker then introduces the topic and states the purpose of the speech. The body of the speech follows, similarly to the body of an essay, stating its main points, an explanation of each point, and supporting evidence. Finally, in the conclusion, the speaker states his or her hope for accomplishing the speech's purpose and thanks the audience for attending and listening to the speech.

Clearly Written Prose and Speeches

To achieve **clarity**, a writer or speaker must first define his or her purpose carefully. The speech should be organized logically, so that sentences make sense and follow each other in an understandable order. Sentences must also be constructed well, with carefully chosen words and structure. Organizing a speech in advance using an outline provides the writer or speaker with a blueprint, directing and focusing the composition to meet its intended purpose. Organized speeches enable audiences to comprehend and retain the presented information more easily. Humans naturally seek to impose order on the world by seeking patterns. Hence, when ideas in a speech are well-organized and adhere to a consistent pattern, the speaker communicates better with listeners and is more convincing. Speechwriters can use chronological patterns to organize events, sequential patterns to organize processes by their steps, and spatial patterns to help audiences visualize geographical locations and movements or physical scenarios. Also, comparison-contrast patterns give audiences insight about similarities and differences between and among topics, especially when listeners are more familiar with one than the other.

Evaluating Speeches for Concise Information

To convince or persuade listeners or reinforce a message, speeches must be succinct. Audiences can become confused by excessive anecdotes and details. If a speaker takes three minutes or more to get to the point, audience members' attention will start to fade and will only worsen when details deviate from the main subject. When answering a question, the asker and speaker may even forget the original question if the speaker takes too long. Speakers should practice not only rehearsing written speeches, but also developing skill for spontaneous question-and-answer sessions after speeches. Speakers should differentiate necessary from simply interesting information because audiences can become overwhelmed by too much information. Speakers should know what points they wish to make. They should not be afraid to pause before responding to questions, which indicates thoughtfulness and control rather than lack of knowledge. Restating questions increases comprehension and appropriate responses, and allows time to form answers mentally.

Organizational Patterns for Speeches

A speechwriter who uses an **advantages-disadvantages** pattern of organization presents the audience with the pros and cons of a topic. This aids writers in discussing two sides of an issue objectively without an argumentative position, enabling listeners to weigh both aspects. When a speechwriter uses a **cause-and-effect** pattern, it can help to persuade audiences to agree with an action or solution by showing significant relationships between factors. Writers may separate an outline into two main "cause" and "effect" sections or into separate sections for each cause, including the effect for each. Persuasive writing also benefits from **problem-solution** patterns: by establishing the existence of a problem, writers induce audiences to realize a need for change. By supplying a solution and supporting its superiority above other solutions, the writer convinces audiences of the value of that solution. When none of these patterns—or **chronological**, **sequential**, **spatial**, or **comparison-contrast** patterns—applies, speechwriters often use topical patterns. These organize information by various subtopics and types within the main topic or category.

Effective Speech Delivery

Speakers should deliver speeches in a natural, conversational manner rather than being rigidly formal or theatrical. Effective delivery is also supported by confidence. Speakers should be direct, building audience rapport through personal connection and vivid imagery. Speakers should be mindful of the occasion, subject, and audience of their speeches and take care to use appropriate language. Good speakers learn vocal control, including volume, speed, pitch, use of pauses, tonal variety, correct pronunciation, and clear articulation. They can express enthusiasm and emphasize important points with their voices. Nonverbal behaviors, such as eye contact, facial expressions, gestures, good posture, and body movements clarify communication, stress important ideas, and influence perceptions that the speaker is trustworthy, competent, and credible. Nonverbal communications should seem as spontaneous and natural as vocal or verbal ones. Speakers should know their speeches well and practice frequently, taking care to avoid nervous or irrelevant movements such as tapping or pacing.

Media

Media and Format Choices

Effective communication depends on choosing the correct method. Media and format choices are influenced by the target audience, the budget, and the needs of the audience.

Instructional Videos

Instructional videos have potential for excellent two-way communication because questions and feedback can be built in. Videos can be targeted to particular audiences, and they can be paused for discussion or replayed to reinforce concepts. Viewers can see processes, including "before," "during," and "after" phases. Videos are accessible because most communities have at least one DVD player or computer. Moreover, video players and computers are continually becoming less expensive to buy and use. Disadvantages include the necessity of editing software and equipment in some cases, as well as the need for support from other print materials. There is also danger of overuse, if other media or methods are more appropriate, and higher up-front costs. Producers of instructional videos must account for the costs of script development and hiring local performers as needed.

DVDs and CDs

Interactive DVDs and CDs, such as games, give viewers the opportunity to actively participate as they learn information. Additionally, videos are considered to be a professional method of sharing information. Compared to many other media formats, discs are comparatively inexpensive to make and are easy to transport due to their small size and weight. They are more resistant to damage and aging than older videotape technology, making them more durable. Some disadvantages include needing access to technology to play what is stored on the disc and access to certain software programs to add new content to a disc, especially if the producer wants to include video animation or audio commentary. Producers must also consider expenses concerning paid staff and production and labeling expenses. Content that would appear on DVDs and CDs can alternatively be shared through streaming services or digital files stored on a computer or other compatible device.

Television and Radio

Two media types are television and radio. Both are forms of mass media that reach many people. TV has the broadest reach and can market to the general public or be customized for target audiences, while radio only tends to reach specific target audiences. TV has the advantage of video plus audio, while radio broadcasts only feature audio. However, access to television programs is more expensive than access to radio broadcasts. A shared disadvantage is that TV and radio audiences can only interact directly during call-in programs. Additionally, programming times may be inconvenient, but tape, digital sound, and digital video recording (DVR) can remedy this. Many streaming services also provide access to these programs. Both television and radio are useful for communicating simple slogans and messages, and both can generate awareness, interest, and excitement.

Newspapers

Except for the occasional community columns, news releases, and letters to the editor, newspaper pages and features afford little opportunity for audience input or participation. However, they do reach and appeal to the general public. Cost is an advantage: hiring a PR writer and paying for a news advertisement costs much less than a radio or TV spot. Additionally, newspaper features are high-status, and audiences can reread and review them as often as they like. However, newspaper ads may have difficulty affecting the reader as deeply without audio or video, and they require a literate audience. Their publication is also subject to editors' whims and biases. Newspaper pieces combining advertising and editorial content—"advertorials"—provide inclusion of paid material, but are viewed as medium-status and cost more.

Websites, Blogs, Mobile Phones, and Text Messaging

Computer literacy is required for online material, but participation potential is high via websites, e-networking, and blogging. Mobile phones and text messaging are used for enormous direct, public, two-way and one-on-one communication, with timely information and reminders. Web media need a literate public and can be tailored for specific audiences. They afford global information, are accessible by increasingly technology-literate populations, and are high-status. Web media disadvantages include the necessity of computers and people to design, manage, and supply content, as well as to provide technical support. Mobile and text media are globally popular, but appeal especially to certain demographics like teens and young adults. They are increasingly available, especially in rural regions, and are decreasing in cost. Mobile and text media disadvantages include required brevity in texts and provider messaging charges. Links to related websites and pages within existing sites are also advantages of digital media.

Public Presentations and Slideshows

Public presentations have great potential for audience participation and can directly target various audiences. They can encourage the establishment of partnerships and groups, stimulate local ownership of issues and projects, and make information public. A drawback to public presentations is that they are limited to nights, weekends, or whenever audiences are available and do not always attract the intended audience.

Another method of presentation is to use **slideshows**. These presentations are best for sophisticated audiences like professionals, civil servants, and service organizations. Well-designed slideshows are good for stimulating audience interest, selling ideas, and marketing products. Also, they are accessible online as well as in-person so they can reach a broader audience. Slideshow disadvantages include the necessity of projectors and other equipment. Also, they are limited to communicating more general points, outlines, and summaries rather than conveying a multitude of information in more detail.

Posters and Brochures

Both **posters** and **brochures** can target audiences of the general public and more specific public sectors. Posters are better for communicating simple slogans and messages, while brochures can include more detail and are better for printing instructional information. Both can be inexpensive to produce, especially if printed only as needed and in-house. Posters can often be printed in-house without using outside printing companies. However, it is difficult to get feedback on both posters and brochures—unless they have been broadly tested, or if their publication is accompanied by workshops and other participatory events. A disadvantage of using posters is that they are designed to draw attention and communicate quickly, as they are mostly viewed in passing. This means that their messages must be simple and communicate efficiently. A disadvantage of using brochures is that they can only be distributed to a specific, limited group or area. Posters and brochures are also only understood when audiences are literate in both written language and visual elements.

Flyers and Fact Sheets

Flyers and fact sheets have one-way communication potential because readers cannot give feedback. Their target audiences are general. Some advantages of using this form of media include flexibility: people can distribute them at meetings or events, put them on car windshields in parking lots, leave them in stores or on bulletin boards at community agencies and schools, hand them out from booths and other displays, or mail them. When printed in black and white, they can be very inexpensive. They afford recipients the convenience of being able to review them at their leisure. Organizations and individuals can produce flyers and fact sheets in-house, or even at home with desktop publishing software. Disadvantages include their limitation to single facts or tips and specific information on specified topics.

Evaluating Media Information Sources

With the wealth of media in different formats available today, users are more likely to take media at face value. However, to understand the content of media, consumers must **critically evaluate each source**.

Users should ask themselves the following questions about media sources:

- Who is delivering this message, and why?
- What methods do a media source's publishers employ to gain and maintain users' attention?
- Which points of view is the media source representing?
- What are the various ways a message could be interpreted?
- What information is missing from the message?
- Is the source scholarly, i.e., peer-reviewed?
- Does it include author names and their credentials as they relate to the topic?
- Who publishes it, and why?
- Who is the target audience?
- Is the language technically specific or non-technical?
- Are sources cited, research claims documented, conclusions based on furnished evidence, and references provided?
- Is the publication current?

Other Considerations for the Validity of Sources

For books, consider whether information is **up-to-date** and whether **historical perspectives** apply. Content is more likely to be **scholarly** if publishers are universities, government, or professional organizations. Book reviews can also provide useful information. For articles, identify the author, publisher, frequency of the periodical's publication, and what kind of advertising, if any, is included. Looking for book reviews also informs users. For articles, look for biographical author information, publisher name, frequency of the periodical's publication, and whether advertising is included and, if so, whether it is for certain occupations or disciplines. For web pages, check their domain names, identify publishers or sponsors, look for the author or publisher's contact information, check dates of most recent page updates, be alert to biases, and verify the validity of the information on the webpage. The quality and accuracy of web pages located through search engines rather than library databases varies widely and requires careful user inspection. Web page recommendations from reliable sources like university faculties can help indicate quality and accuracy. Citations of websites by credible or scholarly sources also show reliability. Authors' names, relevant credentials, affiliations, and contact information support their authority. Site functionality, such as ease of navigation, ability to search, site maps, and indexes, is also a criterion to consider.

Persuasive Media

Advertising, public relations, and advocacy media all use **persuasion**. Advertisers use persuasion to sell goods and services. The public relations field uses persuasion to give good impressions of companies, governments, or organizations. Advocacy groups use persuasion to garner support or votes. Persuasion can come through commercials, public service announcements, speeches, websites, and newsletters, among others. Activists, lobbyists, government officials, and politicians use political rhetoric involving persuasive techniques. Basic techniques include using celebrity spokespersons, whom consumers admire or aspire to resemble; or, conversely, "everyday people" (albeit often portrayed by actors) with whom consumers identify. Using expert testimonials lends credibility. Explicit claims of content, effectiveness, quality, and reliability—which often cannot be proven or disproven—are used to persuade. While news and advocacy messages mostly eschew humor for credibility's sake (except in political satire), advertising often persuades via humor, which gets consumer attention and associates its pleasure with advertised products and services. Qualifiers and other misleading terms, sometimes called "Weasel words," are often combined with exaggerated claims. Intensifiers, such as hyperboles, superlatives, and repetitions, and sentimental appeals are also persuasive.

Intermediate Techniques

Dangerous propagandist Adolf Hitler said people suspect little lies more than big ones; hence the "Big Lie" is a persuasion method that cannot be identified without consumers' keen critical thinking. A related method is charisma, which can induce people to believe messages they would otherwise reject. Euphemisms substitute abstract, vague, or bland terms in place of more graphic, clear, and unpleasant ones. For example, the terms "layoffs" and "firing" are replaced by "downsizing," and "torture" is replaced with "intensive interrogation techniques." Extrapolation bases sweeping conclusions on small amounts of minor information to appeal to what consumers wish or hope. Flattery appeals to consumer self-esteem needs, such as L'Oreal's "You're worth it." Flattery is sometimes accomplished through contrast, like ads showing others' mistakes to make consumers feel superior and smarter. "Glittering generalities" refer to claims based on concepts such as beauty, love, health, democracy, freedom, and science. Persuaders use this tactic to gain consumer acceptance without consumers questioning what they mean. The opposite is name-calling to persuade consumers to reject someone or something.

American citizens love new ideas and technology. Persuaders exploit this by emphasizing the **newness** of products, services, and candidates. Conversely, they also use **nostalgia** to evoke consumers' happy memories, which they often remember more than unhappy ones. Citing "scientific evidence" is an intermediate version of the basic technique of expert testimonials. Consumers may accept this as proof, but some advertisers, politicians, and other persuaders may present inaccurate or misleading "evidence." Another intermediate technique is the "simple solution." Although the natures of people and life are complex, when consumers feel overwhelmed by complexity, persuaders exploit this by offering policies, products, or services they claim will solve complicated problems by simple means. Persuaders also use symbols, or images, words, and names we associate with more general, emotional concepts like lifestyle, country, family, religion, and gender. While symbols have power, their significance also varies across individuals. For example, some consumers regard the Hummer SUV as a prestigious status symbol, while others regard it as environmentally harmful and irresponsible.

Advanced Techniques

Ad hominem, Latin for "against the man"—also called "shoot the messenger"—attacks the person delivering a message, not the message itself. It operates by association; problems with the message must indicate problems with the messenger. **"Stacking the deck"** misleads by presenting only selected information that supports one position. **Apophasis**, or a false denial, allows the speaker or writer to indirectly bring attention to a flaw in an opponent's credibility. For example, a politician saying, "I won't mention my opponent's tax evasion issues" manages to mention them while seeming less accusatory. Persuaders may also use **majority belief**, making statements such as "Four out of five dentists recommend this brand" or "[insert number] people can't be wrong." In an intensified version, persuaders exploit group dynamics at rallies, speeches, and other live-audience events where people are vulnerable to surrounding crowd influences. **Scapegoating**, blaming one person or group for complex problems, is a form of the intermediate "simple solution" technique, a practice common in politics. **Timing** also persuades, like advertising flowers and candy in the weeks preceding Valentine's Day, ad campaigns preceding new technology rollouts, and politician speeches following big news events.

Visual Media

Some images have the power to communicate more information than an entire paragraph. Images can contain several elements and be interpreted different ways, making them an effective vessel for abstract and emotionally appealing ideas. Humans are also able to understand images before they fully acquire language, meaning that images can reach more people than language can at any time. Images are also more quickly comprehended than text, making them a highly efficient method of communication. People can remember or memorize images more easily than text, also. Historically, images have been used for propaganda and subliminal messaging. Images are also used by different companies as an effective technique to entice customers to buy their products. Though images do not always contain text, they can still convey explicit and implicit meanings. An image's explicit meaning would be the most recognizable shape or concept in the image. The implicit meaning may be obscured within the image through the use of negative space, background images, or out-of-focus shapes.

Interpreting and Evaluating Persuasive Media

Most messages can be interpreted in different ways. They can be interpreted explicitly, where the literal meaning of the words in the message creates the meaning of the message, and no context is considered. Alternatively, other contexts can be considered alongside the explicit meaning of the message. These create alternative, not clearly stated meanings called implicit meanings. Politics, current events, regional norms, and even emotions are examples of contexts that can add implicit meanings to a message. These implicit meanings can change the effect a message has on its recipient. Many products have slogans with both implicit and explicit meanings. These implicit meanings must be considered to fully interpret a message.

Messages come in different forms, and each form has a unique way of communicating both explicit and implicit meanings. Images can come with captions that communicate a message, but some images carry subliminal messages. This means that their implicit meaning is received by the viewer, but the viewer is not aware of it. The term propaganda describes messages that advocate for a specific opinion or way of thinking. Most propaganda is politically driven and has been used during historical periods, most notably World War II. Unlike messages with hidden or veiled implicit meanings, most propaganda aggressively communicates its entire meaning and is difficult to misinterpret. Documentaries are another prominent form of communication. Documentaries are informational videos that focus on a specific figure, subject, phenomenon, or time period. While documentaries are primarily fact based and contain excerpts from interviews and testimonials, documentaries feature a limited view of their subject and sometimes attempt to persuade viewers to take action or embrace their central message. While some documentaries communicate this clearly, some hide an implicit meaning through the way they present each piece of information.

English Conventions

Foundations of Grammar

The Eight Parts of Speech

Nouns

When you talk about a person, place, thing, or idea, you are talking about a **noun**. The two main types of nouns are **common** and **proper** nouns. Also, nouns can be abstract (i.e., general) or concrete (i.e., specific).

Common Nouns

Common nouns are generic names for people, places, and thing. Common nouns are not usually capitalized. Examples of common nouns:

> *People*: boy, girl, worker, manager
>
> *Places*: school, bank, library, home
>
> *Things*: dog, cat, truck, car

Proper Nouns

Proper nouns name specific people, places, or things. All proper nouns are capitalized. Examples of proper nouns:

> *People*: Abraham Lincoln; George Washington; Martin Luther King, Jr.
>
> *Places*: Los Angeles, California; New York; Asia
>
> *Things*: Statue of Liberty, Earth*, Lincoln Memorial
>
> Note: When referring to the planet that we live on, capitalize *Earth*. When referring to the dirt, rocks, or land, lowercase *earth*.

General and Specific Nouns

General nouns are the names of conditions or ideas. **Specific nouns** name people, places, and things that are understood by using your senses.

General nouns:

> *Condition*: beauty, strength
>
> *Idea*: truth, peace

Specific nouns:

> *People*: baby, friend, father
>
> *Places*: town, park, city hall
>
> *Things*: rainbow, cough, apple, silk, gasoline

Collective Nouns

Collective nouns are the names for a group of people, places, or things that may act as a whole. The following are examples of collective nouns: *class, company, dozen, group, herd, team,* and *public.* Collective nouns usually require an article, which denotes the noun as being a single unit. For instance, a choir is a group of singers. Even though there are many singers in a choir, the word choir is grammatically treated as a single unit. If we refer to the members of the group, and not the group itself, it is no longer a collective noun.

Incorrect: The **choir are** going to compete nationally this year.

Correct: The **choir is** going to compete nationally this year.

Incorrect: The **members** of the choir **is** competing nationally this year.

Correct: The **members** of the choir **are** competing nationally this year.

Pronouns

Pronouns are words that are used to stand in for nouns. A pronoun may be classified as personal, intensive, relative, interrogative, demonstrative, indefinite, and reciprocal.

Personal: *Nominative* is the case for nouns and pronouns that are the subject of a sentence. *Objective* is the case for nouns and pronouns that are an object in a sentence. *Possessive* is the case for nouns and pronouns that show possession or ownership.

Singular

	Nominative	Objective	Possessive
First Person	I	me	my, mine
Second Person	you	you	your, yours
Third Person	he, she, it	him, her, it	his, her, hers, its

Plural

	Nominative	Objective	Possessive
First Person	we	us	our, ours
Second Person	you	you	your, yours
Third Person	they	them	their, theirs

Intensive: I myself, you yourself, he himself, she herself, the (thing) itself, we ourselves, you yourselves, they themselves

Relative: which, who, whom, whose

Interrogative: what, which, who, whom, whose

Demonstrative: this, that, these, those

Indefinite: all, any, each, everyone, either/neither, one, some, several

Reciprocal: each other, one another

Review Video: Nouns and Pronouns
Visit mometrix.com/academy and enter code: 312073

VERBS

If you want to write a sentence, then you need a verb. Without a verb, you have no sentence. The verb of a sentence indicates action or being. In other words, the verb shows something's action or state of being or the action that has been done to something.

TRANSITIVE AND INTRANSITIVE VERBS

A **transitive verb** is a verb whose action (e.g., drive, run, jump) indicates a receiver (e.g., car, dog, kangaroo). **Intransitive verbs** do not indicate a receiver of an action. In other words, the action of the verb does not point to a subject or object.

> **Transitive**: He plays the piano. | The piano was played by him.
>
> **Intransitive**: He plays. | John plays well.

A dictionary will tell you whether a verb is transitive or intransitive. Some verbs can be transitive and intransitive.

ACTION VERBS AND LINKING VERBS

Action verbs show what the subject is doing. In other words, an action verb shows action. Unlike most types of words, a single action verb, in the right context, can be an entire sentence. **Linking verbs** link the subject of a sentence to a noun or pronoun, or they link a subject with an adjective. You always need a verb if you want a complete sentence. However, linking verbs on their own cannot be a complete sentence.

Common linking verbs include *appear, be, become, feel, grow, look, seem, smell, sound,* and *taste.* However, any verb that shows a condition and connects to a noun, pronoun, or adjective that describes the subject of a sentence is a linking verb.

Action: He sings. | Run! | Go! | I talk with him every day. | She reads.

Linking:

> Incorrect: I am.
>
> Correct: I am John. | I smell roses. | I feel tired.

Note: Some verbs are followed by words that look like prepositions, but they are a part of the verb and a part of the verb's meaning. These are known as phrasal verbs, and examples include *call off, look up*, and *drop off.*

Review Video: Action Verbs and Linking Verbs
Visit mometrix.com/academy and enter code: 743142

VOICE

Transitive verbs come in active or passive **voice**. If something does an action or is acted upon, then you will know whether a verb is active or passive. When the subject of the sentence is doing the action, the verb is in **active voice**. When the subject is acted upon, the verb is in **passive voice**.

> **Active**: Jon drew the picture. (The subject *Jon* is doing the action of *drawing a picture*.)
>
> **Passive**: The picture is drawn by Jon. (The subject *picture* is receiving the action from Jon.)

Verb Tenses

A verb **tense** shows the different form of a verb to point to the time of an action. The present and past tense are indicated the verb's form. An action in the present, *I talk,* can change form for the past: *I talked*. However, for the other tenses, an auxiliary (i.e., helping) verb is needed to show the change in form. These helping verbs include *am, are, is* | *have, has, had* | *was, were, will* (or *shall*).

Present: I talk	Present perfect: I have talked
Past: I talked	Past perfect: I had talked
Future: I will talk	Future perfect: I will have talked

Present: The action happens at the current time.

Example: He *walks* to the store every morning.

To show that something is happening right now, use the progressive present tense: I *am walking*.

Past: The action happened in the past.

Example: He *walked* to the store an hour ago.

Future: The action is going to happen later.

Example: I *will walk* to the store tomorrow.

Present perfect: The action started in the past and continues into the present or took place previously at an unspecified time

Example: I *have walked* to the store three times today.

Past perfect: The second action happened in the past. The first action came before the second.

Example: Before I walked to the store (Action 2), I *had walked* to the library (Action 1).

Future perfect: An action that uses the past and the future. In other words, the action is complete before a future moment.

Example: When she comes for the supplies (future moment), I *will have walked* to the store (action completed before the future moment).

Conjugating Verbs

When you need to change the form of a verb, you are **conjugating** a verb. The key forms of a verb are singular, present tense (dream); singular, past tense (dreamed); and the past participle (have dreamed). Note: the past participle needs a helping verb to make a verb tense. For example, I *have dreamed* of this day. The following tables demonstrate some of the different ways to conjugate a verb:

Singular

Tense	First Person	Second Person	Third Person
Present	I dream	You dream	He, she, it dreams
Past	I dreamed	You dreamed	He, she, it dreamed
Past Participle	I have dreamed	You have dreamed	He, she, it has dreamed

Plural

Tense	First Person	Second Person	Third Person
Present	We dream	You dream	They dream
Past	We dreamed	You dreamed	They dreamed
Past Participle	We have dreamed	You have dreamed	They have dreamed

Mood

There are three **moods** in English: the indicative, the imperative, and the subjunctive.

The **indicative mood** is used for facts, opinions, and questions.

Fact: You can do this.

Opinion: I think that you can do this.

Question: Do you know that you can do this?

The **imperative** is used for orders or requests.

Order: You are going to do this!

Request: Will you do this for me?

The **subjunctive mood** is for wishes and statements that go against fact.

Wish: I wish that I were famous.

Statement against fact: If I were you, I would do this. (This goes against fact because I am not you. You have the chance to do this, and I do not have the chance.)

Review Video: Verb Tenses
Visit mometrix.com/academy and enter code: 269472

Adjectives

An **adjective** is a word that is used to modify a noun or pronoun. An adjective answers a question: *Which one? What kind?* or *How many?* Usually, adjectives come before the words that they modify, but they may also come after a linking verb.

Which one? The *third* suit is my favorite.

What kind? This suit is *navy blue.*

How many? I am going to buy *four* pairs of socks to match the suit?

Articles

Articles are adjectives that are used to distinguish nouns as definite or indefinite. **Definite** nouns are preceded by the article *the* and indicate a specific person, place, thing, or idea. **Indefinite** nouns are preceded by *a* or *an* and do not indicate a specific person, place, thing, or idea. A, an, and the are the only articles. Note: *An* comes before words that start with a vowel sound. For example, "Are you going to get an **u**mbrella?".

Definite: I lost *the* bottle that belongs to me.

Indefinite: Does anyone have *a* bottle to share?

COMPARISON WITH ADJECTIVES

Some adjectives are relative and other adjectives are absolute. Adjectives that are **relative** can show the comparison between things. **Absolute** adjectives can show comparison. However, they show comparison in a different way. Let's say that you are reading two books. You think that one book is perfect, and the other book is not exactly perfect. It is not possible for one book to be more perfect than the other. Either you think that the book is perfect, or you think that the book is imperfect. In this case, perfect and imperfect are absolute adjectives.

Relative adjectives will show the different **degrees** of something or someone to something else or someone else. The three degrees of adjectives include positive, comparative, and superlative.

The **positive** degree is the normal form of an adjective.

Example: This work is *difficult.* | She is *smart.*

The **comparative** degree compares one person or thing to another person or thing.

Example: This work is *more difficult* than your work. | She is *smarter* than me.

The **superlative** degree compares more than two people or things.

Example: This is the *most difficult* work of my life. | She is the *smartest* lady in school.

Review Video: Adjectives
Visit mometrix.com/academy and enter code: 470154

ADVERBS

An **adverb** is a word that is used to **modify** a verb, adjective, or another adverb. Usually, adverbs answer one of these questions: *When?*, *Where?*, *How?*, and *Why?*. The negatives *not* and *never* are considered adverbs. Adverbs that modify adjectives or other adverbs **strengthen** or **weaken** the words that they modify.

Examples:

He walks *quickly* through the crowd.

The water flows *smoothly* on the rocks.

Note: Adverbs are usually indicated by the morpheme -ly, which has been added to the root word. For instance, *quick* can be made into an adverb by adding *-ly* to construct *quickly*. Some words that end in *-ly* do not follow this rule and can behave as other parts of speech. Examples of adjectives ending in *-ly* include: *early, friendly, holy, lonely, silly*, and *ugly*. To know if a word that ends in *-ly* is an adjective or adverb, check your dictionary. Also, while many adverbs end in *-ly*, you need to remember that not all adverbs end in *-ly*.

Examples:

He is *never* angry.

You walked *across* the bridge.

Comparison with Adverbs

The rules for comparing adverbs are the same as the rules for adjectives.

The **positive** degree is the standard form of an adverb.

Example: He arrives *soon*. | She speaks *softly* to her friends.

The **comparative** degree compares one person or thing to another person or thing.

Example: He arrives *sooner* than Sarah. | She speaks *more softly* than him.

The **superlative** degree compares more than two people or things.

Example: He arrives *soonest* of the group. | She speaks the *most softly* of any of her friends.

Review Video: Adverbs
Visit mometrix.com/academy and enter code: 713951

Prepositions

A **preposition** is a word placed before a noun or pronoun that shows the relationship between an object and another word in the sentence.

Common prepositions:

about	before	during	on	under
after	beneath	for	over	until
against	between	from	past	up
among	beyond	in	through	with
around	by	of	to	within
at	down	off	toward	without

Examples:

The napkin is *in* the drawer.

The Earth rotates *around* the Sun.

The needle is *beneath* the haystack.

Can you find "me" *among* the words?

Review Video: What is a Preposition?
Visit mometrix.com/academy and enter code: 946763

Conjunctions

Conjunctions join words, phrases, or clauses and they show the connection between the joined pieces. **Coordinating conjunctions** connect equal parts of sentences. **Correlative conjunctions**

show the connection between pairs. **Subordinating conjunctions** join subordinate (i.e., dependent) clauses with independent clauses.

Coordinating Conjunctions

The **coordinating conjunctions** include: *and, but, yet, or, nor, for,* and *so*

Examples:

The rock was small, *but* it was heavy.

She drove in the night, *and* he drove in the day.

Correlative Conjunctions

The **correlative conjunctions** are: *either...or* | *neither...nor* | *not only...but also*

Examples:

Either you are coming *or* you are staying.

He *not only* ran three miles *but also* swam 200 yards.

Review Video: Coordinating and Correlative Conjunctions
Visit mometrix.com/academy and enter code: 390329

Subordinating Conjunctions

Common **subordinating conjunctions** include:

after	since	whenever
although	so that	where
because	unless	wherever
before	until	whether
in order that	when	while

Examples:

I am hungry *because* I did not eat breakfast.

He went home *when* everyone left.

Review Video: Subordinating Conjunctions
Visit mometrix.com/academy and enter code: 958913

Interjections

Interjections are words of exclamation (i.e., audible expression of great feeling) that are used alone or as a part of a sentence. Often, they are used at the beginning of a sentence for an introduction. Sometimes, they can be used in the middle of a sentence to show a change in thought or attitude.

Common Interjections: Hey! | Oh, | Ouch! | Please! | Wow!

Agreement and Sentence Structure

Subjects and Predicates

Subjects

The **subject** of a sentence names who or what the sentence is about. The subject may be directly stated in a sentence, or the subject may be the implied *you*. The **complete subject** includes the simple subject and all of its modifiers. To find the complete subject, ask *Who* or *What* and insert the verb to complete the question. The answer, including any modifiers (adjectives, prepositional phrases, etc.), is the complete subject. To find the **simple subject**, remove all of the modifiers in the complete subject. Being able to locate the subject of a sentence helps with many problems, such as those involving sentence fragments and subject-verb agreement.

Examples:

The small, red car is the one that he wants for Christmas.

(The simple subject is the *car*, and the complete subject is *the small, red car.*)

The young artist is coming over for dinner.

(The simple subject is the *artist*, and the complete subject is *the young artist.*)

Review Video: Subjects
Visit mometrix.com/academy and enter code: 444771

In **imperative** sentences, the verb's subject is understood (e.g., [You] Run to the store), but is not actually present in the sentence. Normally, the subject comes before the verb. However, the subject comes after the verb in sentences that begin with *There are* or *There was.*

Direct:

John knows the way to the park.

(Who knows the way to the park? Answer: *John*)

The cookies need ten more minutes.

(What needs ten minutes? Answer: *The cookies*)

By five o'clock, Bill will need to leave.

(Who needs to leave? Answer: *Bill*)

Remember: The subject can come after the verb.

There are five letters on the table for him.

(What is on the table? Answer: *Five letters*)

There were coffee and doughnuts in the house.

(What was in the house? Answer: *Coffee and doughnuts*)

Implied:

Go to the post office for me.

(Who is going to the post office? Answer: *You.*)

Come and sit with me, please?

(Who needs to come and sit? Answer: *You.*)

Predicates

In a sentence, you always have a predicate and a subject. The subject tells what the sentence is about, and the **predicate** explains or describes the subject.

Think about the sentence *He sings.* In this sentence, we have a subject (He) and a predicate (sings). This is all that is needed for a sentence to be complete. Most sentences contain more information, but if this is all the information that you are given, then you have a complete sentence.

Now, let's look at another sentence:

John and Jane sing on Tuesday nights at the dance hall.

What is the subject of this sentence?

Answer: John and Jane.

What is the predicate of this sentence?

Answer: sing on Tuesday nights at the dance hall (everything else in the sentence).

Subject-Verb Agreement

Verbs **agree** with their subjects in number. In other words, *singular* subjects need *singular* verbs. *Plural* subjects need *plural* verbs. **Singular** is for **one** person, place, or thing. **Plural** is for **more than one** person, place, or thing. Subjects and verbs must also share the same point of view, as in first, second, or third person. The present tense ending *-s* is used on a verb if its subject is third person singular; otherwise, the verb' sending is not modified.

Review Video: Subject-Verb Agreement
Visit mometrix.com/academy and enter code: 479190

Number Agreement Examples:

Single Subject and Verb: *Dan calls home.*

(Dan is one person. So, the singular verb *calls* is needed.)

Plural Subject and Verb: *Dan and Bob call home.*

(More than one person needs the plural verb *call.*)

Person Agreement Examples:

First Person: I *am* walking.

Second Person: You *are* walking.

Third Person: He *is* walking.

Complications with Subject-Verb Agreement

Words Between Subject and Verb

Words that come between the simple subject and the verb have no bearing on subject-verb agreement.

Examples:

The joy of my life returns home tonight.

(**Singular Subject**: joy **Singular Verb**: returns)

The phrase *of my life* does not influence the verb *returns.*

The question that still remains unanswered is "Who are you?"

(**Singular Subject**: question **Singular Verb**: is)

Don't let the phrase "*that still remains...*" trouble you. The subject *question* goes with *is.*

Compound Subjects

A compound subject is formed when two or more nouns joined by *and*, *or*, or *nor* jointly act as the subject of the sentence.

Joined by And

When a compound subject is joined by *and*, it is treated as a plural subject and requires a plural verb.

Examples:

You and Jon are invited to come to my house.

(**Plural Subject**: You and Jon. **Plural Verb**: are)

The pencil and paper belong to me.

(**Plural Subject**: pencil and paper. **Plural Verb**: belong)

Joined by Or/Nor

For a compound subject joined by *or* or *nor*, the verb must agree in number with the part of the subject that is closest to the verb (italicized in the examples below).

Examples:

Today or *tomorrow is* the day.

(**Subject**: Today / tomorrow **Verb**: is)

Stan or *Phil wants* to read the book.

(**Subject**: Stan / Phil **Verb**: wants)

Neither the books nor the *pen is* on the desk.

(**Subject**: books / pen **Verb**: is)

Either the blanket or *pillows arrive* this afternoon.

(**Subject**: blanket / pillows **Verb**: arrive)

Indefinite Pronouns as Subject

An indefinite pronoun is a pronoun that does not refer to a specific noun. Different indefinite pronouns may only function as a singular noun, only function as a plural noun, or change depending on how they are used.

Always Singular

Pronouns such as *each*, *either*, *everybody*, *anybody*, *somebody*, and *nobody* are always singular.

Examples:

Each of the runners *has* a different bib number.

(**Singular Subject**: Each **Singular Verb**: has)

Is either of you ready for the game?

(**Singular Subject**: either **Singular Verb**: Is)

Note: The words *each* and *either* can also be used as adjectives (e.g., *each* person is unique). When one of these adjectives modifies the subject of a sentence, it is always a singular subject.

Everybody grows a day older every day.

(**Singular Subject**: Everybody **Singular Verb**: grows)

Anybody is welcome to bring a tent.

(**Singular Subject**: Anybody **Singular Verb**: is)

Always Plural

Pronouns such as *both*, *several*, and *many* are always plural.

Examples:

Both of the siblings *were* too tired to argue.

(**Plural Subject**: Both **Plural Verb**: were)

Many have tried, but none have succeeded.

(**Plural Subject**: Many **Plural Verb**: have tried)

Depend on Context

Pronouns such as *some*, *any*, *all*, *none*, *more*, and *most* can be either singular or plural depending on what they are representing in the context of the sentence.

Examples:

> *All* of my dog's food *was* still there in his bowl
>
> (**Singular Subject**: All **Singular Verb**: was)
>
> By the end of the night, *all* of my guests *were* already excited about coming to my next party.
>
> (**Plural Subject**: all **Plural Verb**: were)

Other Cases Involving Plural or Irregular Form

Some nouns are **singular in meaning but plural in form**: news, mathematics, physics, and economics.

> The *news is* coming on now.
>
> *Mathematics is* my favorite class.

Some nouns are plural in form and meaning, and have **no singular equivalent**: scissors and pants.

> Do these *pants come* with a shirt?
>
> The *scissors are* for my project.

Mathematical operations are **irregular** in their construction, but are normally considered to be **singular in meaning**.

> *One plus one is* two.
>
> *Three times three is* nine.

Note: Look to your **dictionary** for help when you aren't sure whether a noun with a plural form has a singular or plural meaning.

Complements

A complement is a noun, pronoun, or adjective that is used to give more information about the subject or verb in the sentence.

Direct Objects

A direct object is a noun or pronoun that takes or receives the **action** of a verb. (Remember: a complete sentence does not need a direct object, so not all sentences will have them. A sentence needs only a subject and a verb.) When you are looking for a direct object, find the verb and ask *who* or *what.*

Examples:

I took the blanket. (Who or what did I take? *The blanket*)

Jane read books. (Who or what does Jane read? *Books*)

Indirect Objects

An indirect object is a word or group of words that show how an action had an **influence** on someone or something. If there is an indirect object in a sentence, then you always have a direct object in the sentence. When you are looking for the indirect object, find the verb and ask *to/for whom or what.*

Examples:

We taught the old dog a new trick.

(To/For whom or what was taught? *The old dog*)

I gave them a math lesson.

(To/For whom or what was given? *Them*)

Review Video: Direct and Indirect Objects
Visit mometrix.com/academy and enter code: 817385

Predicate Nominatives and Predicate Adjectives

As we looked at previously, verbs may be classified as either action verbs or linking verbs. A linking verb is so named because it links the subject to words in the predicate that describe or define the subject. These words are called predicate nominatives (if nouns or pronouns) or predicate adjectives (if adjectives).

Examples:

My father is a *lawyer.*

(Father is the **subject**. Lawyer is the **predicate nominative.**)

Your mother is *patient.*

(Mother is the **subject**. Patient is the **predicate adjective.**)

Pronoun Usage

The **antecedent** is the noun that has been replaced by a pronoun. A pronoun and its antecedent **agree** when they have the same number (singular or plural) and gender (male, female, or neutral).

Examples:

Singular agreement: *John* came into town, and *he* played for us.

(The word *he* replaces *John.*)

Plural agreement: *John and Rick* came into town, and *they* played for us.

(The word *they* replaces *John and Rick.*)

To determine which is the correct pronoun to use in a compound subject or object, try each pronoun **alone** in place of the compound in the sentence. Your knowledge of pronouns will tell you which one is correct.

Example:

Bob and (I, me) will be going.

Test: (1) *I will be going* or (2) *Me will be going*. The second choice cannot be correct because *me* cannot be used as the subject of a sentence. Instead, *me* is used as an object.

Answer: Bob and I will be going.

When a pronoun is used with a noun immediately following (as in "we boys"), try the sentence **without the added noun**.

Example:

(We/Us) boys played football last year.

Test: (1) *We played football last ye*ar or (2) *Us played football last year*. Again, the second choice cannot be correct because *us* cannot be used as a subject of a sentence. Instead, *us* is used as an object.

Answer: We boys played football last year.

Review Video: Pronoun Usage
Visit mometrix.com/academy and enter code: 666500

A pronoun should point clearly to the **antecedent**. Here is how a pronoun reference can be unhelpful if it is puzzling or not directly stated.

Unhelpful: Ron and Jim went to the store, and *he* bought soda.

(Who bought soda? Ron or Jim?)

Helpful: Jim went to the store, and *he* bought soda.

(The sentence is clear. Jim bought the soda.)

Some pronouns change their form by their placement in a sentence. A pronoun that is a **subject** in a sentence comes in the **subjective case**. Pronouns that serve as **objects** appear in the **objective case**. Finally, the pronouns that are used as **possessives** appear in the **possessive case**.

Examples:

Subjective case: *He* is coming to the show.

(The pronoun *He* is the subject of the sentence.)

Objective case: Josh drove *him* to the airport.

(The pronoun *him* is the object of the sentence.)

Possessive case: The flowers are *mine*.

(The pronoun *mine* shows ownership of the flowers.)

The word *who* is a subjective-case pronoun that can be used as a **subject**. The word *whom* is an objective-case pronoun that can be used as an **object**. The words *who* and *whom* are common in subordinate clauses or in questions.

Examples:

Subject: He knows who wants to come.

(*Who* is the subject of the verb *wants*.)

Object: He knows the man whom we want at the party.

(*Whom* is the object of *we want*.)

CLAUSES

A clause is a group of words that contains both a subject and a predicate (verb). There are two types of clauses: independent and dependent. An **independent clause** contains a complete thought, while a **dependent (or subordinate) clause** does not. A dependent clause includes a subject and a verb, and may also contain objects or complements, but it cannot stand as a complete thought without being joined to an independent clause. Dependent clauses function within sentences as adjectives, adverbs, or nouns.

Example:

Independent Clause: I am running

Dependent Clause: because I want to stay in shape

The clause *I am running* is an independent clause: it has a subject and a verb, and it gives a complete thought. The clause *because I want to stay in shape* is a dependent clause: it has a subject and a verb, but it does not express a complete thought. It adds detail to the independent clause to which it is attached.

Combined: I am running because I want to stay in shape.

Review Video: Independent and Dependent Clauses
Visit mometrix.com/academy and enter code: 556903

TYPES OF DEPENDENT CLAUSES

ADJECTIVE CLAUSES

An **adjective clause** is a dependent clause that modifies a noun or a pronoun. Adjective clauses begin with a relative pronoun (*who, whose, whom, which,* and *that*) or a relative adverb (*where, when,* and *why*).

Also, adjective clauses come after the noun that the clause needs to explain or rename. This is done to have a clear connection to the independent clause.

Examples:

I learned the reason *why I won the award.*

This is the place *where I started my first job.*

An adjective clause can be an essential or nonessential clause. An essential clause is very important to the sentence. **Essential clauses** explain or define a person or thing. **Nonessential clauses** give more information about a person or thing but are not necessary to define them. Nonessential clauses are set off with commas while essential clauses are not.

Examples:

Essential: A person *who works hard at first* can often rest later in life.

Nonessential: Neil Armstrong, *who walked on the moon*, is my hero.

Review Video: Adjective Clauses and Phrases
Visit mometrix.com/academy and enter code: 520888

Adverb Clauses

An **adverb clause** is a dependent clause that modifies a verb, adjective, or adverb. In sentences with multiple dependent clauses, adverb clauses are usually placed immediately before or after the independent clause. An adverb clause is introduced with words such as *after, although, as, before, because, if, since, so, unless, when, where,* and *while.*

Examples:

When you walked outside, I called the manager.

I will go with you *unless you want to stay.*

Noun Clauses

A **noun clause** is a dependent clause that can be used as a subject, object, or complement. Noun clauses begin with words such as *how, that, what, whether, which, who,* and *why*. These words can also come with an adjective clause. Unless the noun clause is being used as the subject of the sentence, it should come after the verb of the independent clause.

Examples:

The real mystery is *how you avoided serious injury.*

What you learn from each other depends on your honesty with others.

Subordination

When two related ideas are not of equal importance, the ideal way to combine them is to make the more important idea an independent clause and the less important idea a dependent or subordinate clause. This is called **subordination**.

Example:

Separate ideas: The team had a perfect regular season. The team lost the championship.

Subordinated: Despite having a perfect regular season, *the team lost the championship.*

PHRASES

A phrase is a group of words that functions as a single part of speech, usually a noun, adjective, or adverb. A phrase is not a complete thought, but it adds **detail** or **explanation** to a sentence, or **renames** something within the sentence.

PREPOSITIONAL PHRASES

One of the most common types of phrases is the prepositional phrase. A **prepositional phrase** begins with a preposition and ends with a noun or pronoun that is the object of the preposition. Normally, the prepositional phrase functions as an **adjective** or an **adverb** within the sentence.

Examples:

The picnic is *on the blanket.*

I am sick *with a fever* today.

Among the many flowers, John found a four-leaf clover.

VERBAL PHRASES

A **verbal** is a word or phrase that is formed from a verb but does not function as a verb. Depending on its particular form, it may be used as a noun, adjective, or adverb. A verbal does **not** replace a verb in a sentence.

Examples:

Correct: *Walk* a mile daily.

(*Walk* is the verb of this sentence. The subject is the implied *you*.)

Incorrect: *To walk* a mile.

(*To walk* is a type of verbal. This is not a sentence since there is no functional verb)

There are three types of verbal: **participles**, **gerunds**, and **infinitives**. Each type of verbal has a corresponding **phrase** that consists of the verbal itself along with any complements or modifiers.

PARTICIPLES

A **participle** is a type of verbal that always functions as an adjective. The present participle always ends with *-ing*. Past participles end with *-d, -ed, -n,* or *-t*.

Examples: Verb: *dance* | Present Participle: *dancing* | Past Participle: *danced*

Participial phrases most often come right before or right after the noun or pronoun that they modify.

Examples:

Shipwrecked on an island, the boys started to fish for food.

Having been seated for five hours, we got out of the car to stretch our legs.

Praised for their work, the group accepted the first-place trophy.

GERUNDS

A **gerund** is a type of verbal that always functions as a **noun**. Like present participles, gerunds always end with *-ing*, but they can be easily distinguished from one another by the part of speech they represent (participles always function as adjectives). Since a gerund or gerund phrase always functions as a noun, it can be used as the subject of a sentence, the predicate nominative, or the object of a verb or preposition.

Examples:

We want to be known for *teaching the poor.* (Object of preposition)

Coaching this team is the best job of my life. (Subject)

We like *practicing our songs* in the basement. (Object of verb)

INFINITIVES

An **infinitive** is a type of verbal that can function as a noun, an adjective, or an adverb. An infinitive is made of the word *to* and the basic form of the verb. As with all other types of verbal phrases, an infinitive phrase includes the verbal itself and all of its complements or modifiers.

Examples:

To join the team is my goal in life. (Noun)

The animals have enough food *to eat for the night.* (Adjective)

People lift weights *to exercise their muscles.* (Adverb)

Review Video: Gerunds, Infinitives, and Participles
Visit mometrix.com/academy and enter code: 634263

APPOSITIVE PHRASES

An **appositive** is a word or phrase that is used to explain or rename nouns or pronouns. Noun phrases, gerund phrases, and infinitive phrases can all be used as appositives.

Examples:

Terriers, *hunters at heart,* have been dressed up to look like lap dogs.

(The noun phrase *hunters at heart* renames the noun *terriers.*)

His plan, *to save and invest his money,* was proven as a safe approach.

(The infinitive phrase explains what the plan is.)

Appositive phrases can be **essential** or **nonessential**. An appositive phrase is essential if the person, place, or thing being described or renamed is too general for its meaning to be understood without the appositive.

Examples:

Essential: Two of America's Founding Fathers, George Washington and Thomas Jefferson, served as presidents.

Nonessential: George Washington and Thomas Jefferson, two Founding Fathers, served as presidents.

ABSOLUTE PHRASES

An absolute phrase is a phrase that consists of **a noun followed by a participle**. An absolute phrase provides **context** to what is being described in the sentence, but it does not modify or explain any particular word; it is essentially independent.

Examples:

The alarm ringing, he pushed the snooze button.

The music paused, she continued to dance through the crowd.

PARALLELISM

When multiple items or ideas are presented in a sentence in series, such as in a list, the items or ideas must be stated in grammatically equivalent ways. In other words, if one idea is stated in gerund form, the second cannot be stated in infinitive form. For example, to write, *I enjoy reading and to study* would be incorrect. An infinitive and a gerund are not equivalent. Instead, you should write *I enjoy reading and studying*. In lists of more than two, all items must be parallel.

Example:

Incorrect: He stopped at the office, grocery store, and the pharmacy before heading home.

The first and third items in the list of places include the article *the*, so the second item needs it as well.

Correct: He stopped at the office, *the* grocery store, and the pharmacy before heading home.

Example:

Incorrect: While vacationing in Europe, she went biking, skiing, and climbed mountains.

The first and second items in the list are gerunds, so the third item must be as well.

Correct: While vacationing in Europe, she went biking, skiing, and *mountain climbing*.

Review Video: Parallel Construction
Visit mometrix.com/academy and enter code: 831988

Sentence Purpose

There are four types of sentences: declarative, imperative, interrogative, and exclamatory.

A **declarative** sentence states a fact and ends with a period.

Example: *The football game starts at seven o'clock.*

An **imperative** sentence tells someone to do something and generally ends with a period. (An urgent command might end with an exclamation point instead.)

Example: *Don't forget to buy your ticket.*

An **interrogative** sentence asks a question and ends with a question mark.

Example: *Are you going to the game on Friday?*

An **exclamatory** sentence shows strong emotion and ends with an exclamation point.

Example: *I can't believe we won the game!*

Review Video: Functions of a Sentence
Visit mometrix.com/academy and enter code: 475974

Sentence Structure

Sentences are classified by structure based on the type and number of clauses present. The four classifications of sentence structure are the following:

Simple: A simple sentence has one independent clause with no dependent clauses. A simple sentence may have **compound elements** (i.e., compound subject or verb).

Examples:

Judy *watered* the lawn. (single subject, single *verb*)

Judy and Alan *watered* the lawn. (compound subject, single *verb*)

Judy *watered* the lawn and *pulled* weeds. (single subject, compound *verb*)

Judy and Alan *watered* the lawn and *pulled* weeds. (compound subject, compound *verb*)

Compound: A compound sentence has two or more independent clauses with no dependent clauses. Usually, the independent clauses are joined with a comma and a coordinating conjunction or with a semicolon.

Examples:

The time has come, and we are ready.

I woke up at dawn; the sun was just coming up.

Complex: A complex sentence has one independent clause and at least one *dependent clause.*

Examples:

Although he had the flu, Harry went to work.

Marcia got married *after she finished college*.

Compound-Complex: A compound-complex sentence has at least two independent clauses and at least one *dependent clause*.

Examples:

John is my friend *who went to India*, and he brought back souvenirs.

You may not realize this, but we heard the music *that you played last night*.

Review Video: Sentence Structure
Visit mometrix.com/academy and enter code: 700478

Sentence variety is important to consider when writing an essay or speech. A variety of sentence lengths and types creates rhythm, makes a passage more engaging, and gives writers an opportunity to demonstrate their writing style. Writing that uses the same length or type of sentence without variation can be boring or difficult to read. To evaluate a passage for effective sentence variety, it is helpful to note whether the passage contains diverse sentence structures and lengths. It is also important to pay attention to the way each sentence starts and avoid beginning with the same words or phrases.

SENTENCE FRAGMENTS

Recall that a group of words must contain at least one **independent clause** in order to be considered a sentence. If it doesn't contain even one independent clause, it would be called a **sentence fragment**.

The appropriate process for **repairing** a sentence fragment depends on what type of fragment it is. If the fragment is a dependent clause, it can sometimes be as simple as removing a subordinating word (e.g., when, because, if) from the beginning of the fragment. Alternatively, a dependent clause can be incorporated into a closely related neighboring sentence. If the fragment is missing some required part, like a subject or a verb, the fix might be as simple as adding the missing part.

Examples:

Fragment: Because he wanted to sail the Mediterranean.

Removed subordinating word: He wanted to sail the Mediterranean.

Combined with another sentence: Because he wanted to sail the Mediterranean, he booked a Greek island cruise.

RUN-ON SENTENCES

Run-on sentences consist of multiple independent clauses that have not been joined together properly. Run-on sentences can be corrected in several different ways:

Join clauses properly: This can be done with a comma and coordinating conjunction, with a semicolon, or with a colon or dash if the second clause is explaining something in the first.

Example:

Incorrect: I went on the trip, we visited lots of castles.

Corrected: I went on the trip, and we visited lots of castles.

Split into separate sentences: This correction is most effective when the independent clauses are very long or when they are not closely related.

Example:

Incorrect: The drive to New York takes ten hours, my uncle lives in Boston.

Corrected: The drive to New York takes ten hours. My uncle lives in Boston.

Make one clause dependent: This is the easiest way to make the sentence correct and more interesting at the same time. It's often as simple as adding a subordinating word between the two clauses or before the first clause.

Example:

Incorrect: I finally made it to the store and I bought some eggs.

Corrected: When I finally made it to the store, I bought some eggs.

Reduce to one clause with a compound verb: If both clauses have the same subject, remove the subject from the second clause, and you now have just one clause with a compound verb.

Example:

Incorrect: The drive to New York takes ten hours, it makes me very tired.

Corrected: The drive to New York takes ten hours and makes me very tired.

Note: While these are the simplest ways to correct a run-on sentence, often the best way is to completely reorganize the thoughts in the sentence and rewrite it.

Review Video: Fragments and Run-on Sentences
Visit mometrix.com/academy and enter code: 541989

Dangling and Misplaced Modifiers

Dangling Modifiers

A dangling modifier is a dependent clause or verbal phrase that does not have a **clear logical connection** to a word in the sentence.

Example:

Dangling: *Reading each magazine article*, the stories caught my attention.

The word *stories* cannot be modified by *Reading each magazine article*. People can read, but stories cannot read. Therefore, the subject of the sentence must be a person.

Corrected: Reading each magazine article, *I* was entertained by the stories.

Example:

> **Dangling**: Ever since childhood, my grandparents have visited me for Christmas.
>
> The speaker in this sentence can't have been visited by her grandparents when *they* were children, since she wouldn't have been born yet. Either the modifier should be **clarified** or the sentence should be **rearranged** to specify whose childhood is being referenced.
>
> **Clarified**: Ever since I was a child, my grandparents have visited for Christmas.
>
> **Rearranged**: I have enjoyed my grandparents visiting for Christmas, ever since childhood.

Misplaced Modifiers

Because modifiers are grammatically versatile, they can be put in many different places within the structure of a sentence. The danger of this versatility is that a modifier can accidentally be placed where it is modifying the wrong word or where it is not clear which word it is modifying.

Example:

> **Misplaced**: She read the book to a crowd *that was filled with beautiful pictures.*
>
> The book was filled with beautiful pictures, not the crowd.
>
> **Corrected**: She read the book *that was filled with beautiful pictures* to a crowd.

Example:

> **Ambiguous**: Derek saw a bus nearly hit a man *on his way to work.*
>
> Was Derek on his way to work? Or was the other man?
>
> **Derek**: *On his way to work*, Derek saw a bus nearly hit a man.
>
> **The other man**: Derek saw a bus nearly hit a man *who was on his way to work.*

Split Infinitives

A split infinitive occurs when a modifying word comes between the word *to* and the verb that pairs with *to.*

> Example: To *clearly* explain vs. *To explain* clearly | To *softly* sing vs. *To sing* softly

Though considered improper by some, split infinitives may provide better clarity and simplicity in some cases than the alternatives. As such, avoiding them should not be considered a universal rule.

Double Negatives

Standard English allows **two negatives** only when a **positive** meaning is intended. For example, *The team was not displeased with their performance.* Double negatives to emphasize negation are not used in standard English.

Negative modifiers (e.g., never, no, and not) should not be paired with other negative modifiers or negative words (e.g., none, nobody, nothing, or neither). The modifiers *hardly, barely*, and *scarcely* are also considered negatives in standard English, so they should not be used with other negatives.

Punctuation

End Punctuation

Periods

Use a period to end **all** sentences **except** direct questions and exclamations. Periods are also used for abbreviations.

Examples: 3 p.m. | 2 a.m. | Mr. Jones | Mrs. Stevens | Dr. Smith | Bill, Jr. | Pennsylvania Ave.

Note: An abbreviation is a shortened form of a word or phrase.

Question Marks

Question marks should be used following a **direct question**. A polite request can be followed by a period instead of a question mark.

Direct Question: What is for lunch today? | How are you? | Why is that the answer?

Polite Requests: Can you please send me the item tomorrow. | Will you please walk with me on the track.

Review Video: Question Marks
Visit mometrix.com/academy and enter code: 118471

Exclamation Marks

Exclamation marks are used after a word group or sentence that shows much feeling or has special importance. Exclamation marks should not be overused. They are saved for proper **exclamatory interjections**.

Example: We're going to the finals! | You have a beautiful car! | "That's crazy!" she yelled.

Review Video: Exclamation Points
Visit mometrix.com/academy and enter code: 199367

Commas

The comma is a punctuation mark that can help you understand connections in a sentence. Not every sentence needs a comma. However, if a sentence needs a comma, you need to put it in the right place. A comma in the wrong place (or an absent comma) will make a sentence's meaning unclear. These are some of the rules for commas:

1. Use a comma **before a coordinating conjunction** joining independent clauses.
   Example: Bob caught three fish, and I caught two fish.

2. Use a comma after an introductory phrase or an adverbial clause.
   Examples:
   After the final out, we went to a restaurant to celebrate.
   Studying the stars, I was surprised at the beauty of the sky.

3. Use a comma between items in a series.

Example: I will bring the turkey, the pie, and the coffee.

4. Use a comma **between coordinate adjectives** not joined with *and.*

   Incorrect: The kind, brown dog followed me home.
   Correct: The *kind, loyal* dog followed me home.
   Not all adjectives are **coordinate** (i.e., equal or parallel). There are two simple ways to know if your adjectives are coordinate. One, you can join the adjectives with *and*: *The kind and loyal dog*. Two, you can change the order of the adjectives: *The loyal, kind dog*.

5. Use commas for **interjections** and **after *yes* and *no*** responses.

   Examples:

   Interjection: Oh, I had no idea. | Wow, you know how to play this game.
   Yes and No: *Yes,* I heard you. | *No,* I cannot come tomorrow.

6. Use commas to separate nonessential modifiers and nonessential appositives.

   Examples:

   Nonessential Modifier: John Frank, who is coaching the team, was promoted today.
   Nonessential Appositive: Thomas Edison, an American inventor, was born in Ohio.

7. Use commas to separate nouns of direct address, interrogative tags, and contrast.

   Examples:

   Direct Address: You, *John,* are my only hope in this moment.
   Interrogative Tag: This is the last time, *correct*?
   Contrast: You are my friend, *not my enemy.*

8. Use commas when writing dates, addresses, geographical names, and titles.

   Examples:

   Date: *July 4, 1776,* is an important date to remember.
   Address: He is meeting me at *456 Delaware Avenue, Washington, D.C.,* tomorrow morning.
   Geographical Name: *Paris, France,* is my favorite city.
   Title: John Smith, *PhD,* will be visiting your class today.

9. Use commas to **separate expressions like *he said* and *she said*** if they appear between two parts of a quote.

   Examples:

   "I want you to know," he began, "that I always wanted the best for you."
   "You can start," Jane said, "with an apology."

Review Video: Commas
Visit mometrix.com/academy and enter code: 786797

SEMICOLONS

The semicolon is used to connect major sentence pieces of equal value. Some rules for semicolons include:

1. Use a semicolon **between closely connected independent clauses** that are not connected with a coordinating conjunction.

Examples:

She is outside; we are inside.
You are right; we should go with your plan.

2. Use a semicolon between independent clauses linked with a transitional word.

   Examples:

   I think that we can agree on this; *however,* I am not sure about my friends.
   You are looking in the wrong places; *therefore,* you will not find what you need.

3. Use a semicolon between items in a series that has internal punctuation.

   Example:

   I have visited New York, New York; Augusta, Maine; and Baltimore, Maryland.

Review Video: Semicolon Usage
Visit mometrix.com/academy and enter code: 370605

Colons

The colon is used to call attention to the words that follow it. A colon must come after a **complete independent clause**. The rules for colons are as follows:

1. Use a colon after an independent clause to **make a list.**

   Example:

   I want to learn many languages: Spanish, German, and Italian.

2. Use a colon for explanations or to give a quote.

   Examples:

   Quote: He started with an idea: "We are able to do more than we imagine."
   Explanation: There is one thing that stands out on your resume: responsibility.

3. Use a colon after the greeting in a formal letter, to show hours and minutes, and to separate a title and subtitle.

   Examples:

   Greeting in a formal letter: Dear Sir: | To Whom It May Concern:
   Time: It is 3:14 p.m.
   Title: The essay is titled "America: A Short Introduction to a Modern Country."

Review Video: Colons
Visit mometrix.com/academy and enter code: 868673

Parentheses

Parentheses are used for additional information. Also, they can be used to put labels for letters or numbers in a series. Parentheses should be not be used very often. If they are overused, parentheses can be a distraction instead of a help.

Examples:

Extra Information: The rattlesnake (see Image 2) is a dangerous snake of North and South America.

Series: Include in the email (1) your name, (2) your address, and (3) your question for the author.

Review Video: Parentheses
Visit mometrix.com/academy and enter code: 947743

Quotation Marks

Use quotation marks to close off **direct quotations** of a person's spoken or written words. Do not use quotation marks around indirect quotations. An indirect quotation gives someone's message without using the person's exact words. Use **single quotation marks** to close off a quotation inside a quotation.

Direct Quote: Nancy said, "I am waiting for Henry to arrive."

Indirect Quote: Henry said that he is going to be late to the meeting.

Quote inside a Quote: The teacher asked, "Has everyone read 'The Gift of the Magi'?"

Quotation marks should be used around the titles of **short works**: newspaper and magazine articles, poems, short stories, songs, television episodes, radio programs, and subdivisions of books or websites.

Examples:

"Rip Van Winkle" (short story by Washington Irving)

"O Captain! My Captain!" (poem by Walt Whitman)

Although it is not standard usage, quotation marks are sometimes used to highlight **irony** or the use of words to mean something other than their dictionary definition. This type of usage should be employed sparingly, if at all.

Examples:

The boss warned Frank that he was walking on "thin ice."

(Frank is not walking on real ice. Instead, Frank is being warned to avoid mistakes.)

The teacher thanked the young man for his "honesty."

(In this example, the quotation marks around *honesty* show that the teacher does not believe the young man's explanation.)

Review Video: Quotation Marks
Visit mometrix.com/academy and enter code: 884918

Periods and commas are put **inside** quotation marks. Colons and semicolons are put **outside** the quotation marks. Question marks and exclamation points are placed inside quotation marks when they are part of a quote. When the question or exclamation mark goes with the whole sentence, the mark is left outside of the quotation marks.

Examples:

Period and comma: We read "The Gift of the Magi," "The Skylight Room," and "The Cactus."

Semicolon: They watched "The Nutcracker"; then, they went home.

Exclamation mark that is a part of a quote: The crowd cheered, "Victory!"

Question mark that goes with the whole sentence: Is your favorite short story "The Tell-Tale Heart"?

APOSTROPHES

An apostrophe is used to show **possession** or the **deletion of letters in contractions**. An apostrophe is not needed with the possessive pronouns *his, hers, its, ours, theirs, whose*, and *yours*.

Singular Nouns: David's car | a book's theme | my brother's board game

Plural Nouns that end with -*s*: the scissors' handle | boys' basketball

Plural Nouns that end without -*s*: Men's department | the people's adventure

Review Video: Apostrophes
Visit mometrix.com/academy and enter code: 213068

Review Video: Punctuation Errors in Possessive Pronouns
Visit mometrix.com/academy and enter code: 221438

HYPHENS

Hyphens are used to **separate compound words**. Use hyphens in the following cases:

1. **Compound numbers** from 21 to 99 when written out in words
   Example: This team needs *twenty-five* points to win the game.

2. Written-out fractions that are used as adjectives
   Incorrect: *One-fourth* of the road is under construction.
   Correct: The recipe says that we need a *three-fourths* cup of butter.

3. Compound adjectives that come before a noun
   Incorrect: The dog was *well-fed* for his nap.
   Correct: The *well-fed* dog took a nap.

4. Unusual compound words that would be hard to read or easily confused with other words
   Examples: Semi-irresponsible | Anti-itch | Re-sort

Note: This is not a complete set of the rules for hyphens. A dictionary is the best tool for knowing if a compound word needs a hyphen.

Review Video: Hyphens
Visit mometrix.com/academy and enter code: 981632

Dashes

Dashes are used to show a **break** or a **change in thought** in a sentence or to act as parentheses in a sentence. When typing, use two hyphens to make a dash. Do not put a space before or after the dash. The following are the functions of dashes:

1. To set off parenthetical statements or an appositive with internal punctuation

   Example:

   The three trees—oak, pine, and magnolia—are coming on a truck tomorrow.

2. To show a break or change in tone or thought

   Example:

   The first question—how silly of me—does not have a correct answer.

Ellipsis Marks

The ellipsis mark has **three** periods (...) to show when **words have been removed** from a quotation. If a **full sentence or more** is removed from a quoted passage, you need to use **four** periods to show the removed text and the end punctuation mark. The ellipsis mark should not be used at the beginning of a quotation. The ellipsis mark should also not be used at the end of a quotation unless some words have been deleted from the end of the final sentence.

Example:

"Then he picked up the groceries...paid for them...later he went home."

Brackets

There are two main reasons to use brackets:

1. When placing parentheses inside of parentheses

   Example:

   The hero of this story, Paul Revere (a silversmith and industrialist [see Ch. 4]), rode through towns of Massachusetts to warn of advancing British troops.

2. When adding clarification or detail to a quotation that is not part of the quotation

   Example:

   The father explained, "My children are planning to attend my alma mater [State University]."

Review Video: Brackets
Visit mometrix.com/academy and enter code: 727546

Common Usage Mistakes

WORD CONFUSION

WHICH, THAT, AND WHO

Which is used for things only.

Example: John's dog, *which is called Max,* is large and fierce.

That is used for people or things.

Example: Is this the only book *that Louis L'Amour wrote?*

Example: Is Louis L'Amour the author *that wrote Western novels?*

Who is used for people only.

Example: Mozart was the composer *who wrote those operas.*

HOMOPHONES

Homophones are words that sound alike (or similar) but have different **spellings** and **definitions**. A homophone is a type of **homonym**, which is a pair or group of words that are pronounced or spelled the same, but do not mean the same thing.

TO, TOO, AND TWO

To can be an adverb or a preposition for showing direction, purpose, and relationship. See your dictionary for the many other ways to use *to* in a sentence.

Examples: I went to the store. | I want to go with you.

Too is an adverb that means *also, as well, very,* or *in excess.*

Examples: I can walk a mile too. | You have eaten too much.

Two is the second number in the series of numbers (e.g., one (1), two, (2), three (3)...).

Example: You have two minutes left.

THERE, THEIR, AND THEY'RE

There can be an adjective, adverb, or pronoun. Often, *there* is used to show a place or to start a sentence.

Examples: I went there yesterday. | There is something in his pocket.

Their is a pronoun that is used to show ownership.

Examples: He is their father. | This is their fourth apology this week.

They're is a contraction of *they are.*

Example: Did you know that they're in town?

Knew and New

Knew is the past tense of *know*.

Example: I knew the answer.

New is an adjective that means something is current, has not been used, or is modern.

Example: This is my new phone.

Then and Than

Then is an adverb that indicates sequence or order:

Example: I'm going to run to the library and then come home.

Than is special-purpose word used only for comparisons:

Example: Susie likes chips more than candy.

Its and It's

Its is a pronoun that shows ownership.

Example: The guitar is in its case.

It's is a contraction of *it is*.

Example: It's an honor and a privilege to meet you.

Note: The *h* in honor is silent, so the sound of the vowel *o* must have the article *an*.

Your and You're

Your is a pronoun that shows ownership.

Example: This is your moment to shine.

You're is a contraction of *you are*.

Example: Yes, you're correct.

Saw and Seen

Saw is the past-tense form of *see*.

Example: I saw a turtle on my walk this morning.

Seen is the past participle of *see*.

Example: I have seen this movie before.

Affect and Effect

There are two main reasons that *affect* and *effect* are so often confused: 1) both words can be used as either a noun or a verb, and 2) unlike most homophones, their usage and meanings are closely related to each other. Here is a quick rundown of the four usage options:

Affect (n): feeling, emotion, or mood that is displayed

Example: The patient had a flat *affect*. (i.e., his face showed little or no emotion)

Affect (v): to alter, to change, to influence

Example: The sunshine *affects* the plant's growth.

Effect (n): a result, a consequence

Example: What *effect* will this weather have on our schedule?

Effect (v): to bring about, to cause to be

Example: These new rules will *effect* order in the office.

The noun form of *affect* is rarely used outside of technical medical descriptions, so if a noun form is needed on the test, you can safely select *effect*. The verb form of *effect* is not as rare as the noun form of *affect*, but it's still not all that likely to show up on your test. If you need a verb and you can't decide which to use based on the definitions, choosing *affect* is your best bet.

HOMOGRAPHS

Homographs are words that share the same spelling, but have different meanings and sometimes different pronunciations. To figure out which meaning is being used, you should be looking for context clues. The context clues give hints to the meaning of the word. For example, the word *spot* has many meanings. It can mean "a place" or "a stain or blot." In the sentence "After my lunch, I saw a spot on my shirt," the word *spot* means "a stain or blot." The context clues of "After my lunch" and "on my shirt" guide you to this decision. A homograph is another type of homonym.

BANK

(noun): an establishment where money is held for savings or lending

(verb): to collect or pile up

CONTENT

(noun): the topics that will be addressed within a book

(adjective): pleased or satisfied

(verb): to make someone pleased or satisfied

FINE

(noun): an amount of money that acts a penalty for an offense

(adjective): very small or thin

(adverb): in an acceptable way

(verb): to make someone pay money as a punishment

INCENSE

(noun): a material that is burned in religious settings and makes a pleasant aroma

(verb): to frustrate or anger

LEAD

(noun): the first or highest position

(noun): a heavy metallic element

(verb): to direct a person or group of followers

(adjective): containing lead

OBJECT

(noun): a lifeless item that can be held and observed

(verb): to disagree

PRODUCE

(noun): fruits and vegetables

(verb): to make or create something

REFUSE

(noun): garbage or debris that has been thrown away

(verb): to not allow

SUBJECT

(noun): an area of study

(verb): to force or subdue

TEAR

(noun): a fluid secreted by the eyes

(verb): to separate or pull apart

The Writing Process

BRAINSTORMING

Brainstorming is a technique that is used to find a creative approach to a subject. This can be accomplished by simple **free-association** with a topic. For example, with paper and pen, write every thought that you have about the topic in a word or phrase. This is done without critical thinking. You should put everything that comes to your mind about the topic on your scratch paper. Then, you need to read the list over a few times. Next, you look for patterns, repetitions, and clusters of ideas. This allows a variety of fresh ideas to come as you think about the topic.

FREE WRITING

Free writing is a more structured form of brainstorming. The method involves taking a limited amount of time (e.g., 2 to 3 minutes) to write everything that comes to mind about the topic in complete sentences. When time expires, review everything that has been written down. Many of your sentences may make little or no sense, but the insights and observations that can come from free writing make this method a valuable approach. Usually, free writing results in a fuller expression of ideas than brainstorming because thoughts and associations are written in complete sentences. However, both techniques can be used to complement each other.

Planning

Planning is the process of planning a piece of writing before composing a draft. Planning can include creating an outline or a graphic organizer, such as a Venn diagram, a spider-map, or a flowchart. These methods should help the writer identify their topic, main ideas, and the general organization of the composition. Preliminary research can also take place during this stage. Planning helps writers organize all of their ideas and decide if they have enough material to begin their first draft. However, writers should remember that the decisions they make during this step will likely change later in the process, so their plan does not have to be perfect.

Drafting

Writers may then use their plan, outline, or graphic organizer to compose their first draft. They may write subsequent drafts to improve their writing. Writing multiple drafts can help writers consider different ways to communicate their ideas and address errors that may be difficult to correct without rewriting a section or the whole composition. Most writers will vary in how many drafts they choose to write, as there is no "right" number of drafts. Writing drafts also takes away the pressure to write perfectly on the first try, as writers can improve with each draft they write.

Revising, Editing, and Proofreading

Once a writer completes a draft, they can move on to the revising, editing, and proofreading steps to improve their draft. These steps begin with making broad changes that may apply to large sections of a composition and then making small, specific corrections. **Revising** is the first and broadest of these steps. Revising involves ensuring that the composition addresses an appropriate audience, includes all necessary material, maintains focus throughout, and is organized logically. Revising may occur after the first draft to ensure that the following drafts improve upon errors from the first draft. Some revision should occur between each draft to avoid repeating these errors. The **editing** phase of writing is narrower than the revising phase. Editing a composition should include steps such as improving transitions between paragraphs, ensuring each paragraph is on topic, and improving the flow of the text. The editing phase may also include correcting grammatical errors that cannot be fixed without significantly altering the text. **Proofreading** involves fixing misspelled words, typos, other grammatical errors, and any remaining surface-level flaws in the composition.

Recursive Writing Process

However you approach writing, you may find comfort in knowing that the revision process can occur in any order. The **recursive writing process** is not as difficult as the phrase may make it seem. Simply put, the recursive writing process means that you may need to revisit steps after completing other steps. It also implies that the steps are not required to take place in any certain order. Indeed, you may find that planning, drafting, and revising can all take place at about the same time. The writing process involves moving back and forth between planning, drafting, and revising, followed by more planning, more drafting, and more revising until the writing is satisfactory.

Review Video: Recursive Writing Process
Visit mometrix.com/academy and enter code: 951611

Technology in the Writing Process

Modern technology has yielded several tools that can be used to make the writing process more convenient and organized. Word processors and online tools, such as databases and plagiarism detectors, allow much of the writing process to be completed in one place, using one device.

Technology for Planning and Drafting

For the planning and drafting stages of the writing process, word processors are a helpful tool. These programs also feature formatting tools, allowing users to create their own planning tools or create digital outlines that can be easily converted into sentences, paragraphs, or an entire essay draft. Online databases and references also complement the planning process by providing convenient access to information and sources for research. Word processors also allow users to keep up with their work and update it more easily than if they wrote their work by hand. Online word processors often allow users to collaborate, making group assignments more convenient. These programs also allow users to include illustrations or other supplemental media in their compositions.

Technology for Revising, Editing, and Proofreading

Word processors also benefit the revising, editing, and proofreading stages of the writing process. Most of these programs indicate errors in spelling and grammar, allowing users to catch minor errors and correct them quickly. There are also websites designed to help writers by analyzing text for deeper errors, such as poor sentence structure, inappropriate complexity, lack of sentence variety, and style issues. These websites can help users fix errors they may not know to look for or may have simply missed. As writers finish these steps, they may benefit from checking their work for any plagiarism. There are several websites and programs that compare text to other documents and publications across the internet and detect any similarities within the text. These websites show the source of the similar information, so users know whether or not they referenced the source and unintentionally plagiarized its contents.

Technology for Publishing

Technology also makes managing written work more convenient. Digitally storing documents keeps everything in one place and is easy to reference. Digital storage also makes sharing work easier, as documents can be attached to an email or stored online. This also allows writers to publish their work easily, as they can electronically submit it to other publications or freely post it to a personal blog, profile, or website.

Outlining and Organizing Ideas

Main Ideas, Supporting Details, and Outlining a Topic

A writer often begins the first paragraph of a paper by stating the **main idea** or point, also known as the **topic sentence**. The rest of the paragraph supplies particular details that develop and support the main point. One way to visualize the relationship between the main point and supporting information is by considering a table: the tabletop is the main point, and each of the table's legs is a supporting detail or group of details. Both professional authors and students can benefit from planning their writing by first making an outline of the topic. Outlines facilitate quick identification of the main point and supporting details without having to wade through the additional language that will exist in the fully developed essay, article, or paper. Outlining can also help readers to analyze a piece of existing writing for the same reason. The outline first summarizes the main idea in one sentence. Then, below that, it summarizes the supporting details in a numbered list. Writing the paper then consists of filling in the outline with detail, writing a paragraph for each supporting point, and adding an introduction and conclusion.

Introduction

The purpose of the introduction is to capture the reader's attention and announce the essay's main idea. Normally, the introduction contains 50-80 words, or 3-5 sentences. An introduction can begin with an interesting quote, a question, or a strong opinion—something that will **engage** the reader's interest and prompt them to keep reading. If you are writing your essay to a specific prompt, your introduction should include a **restatement or summarization** of the prompt so that the reader will have some context for your essay. Finally, your introduction should briefly state your **thesis or main idea**: the primary thing you hope to communicate to the reader through your essay. Don't try to include all of the details and nuances of your thesis, or all of your reasons for it, in the introduction. That's what the rest of the essay is for!

Review Video: Introduction
Visit mometrix.com/academy and enter code: 961328

Thesis Statement

The thesis is the main idea of the essay. A temporary thesis, or working thesis, should be established early in the writing process because it will serve to keep the writer focused as ideas develop. This temporary thesis is subject to change as you continue to write.

The temporary thesis has two parts: a topic (i.e., the focus of your essay based on the prompt) and a comment. The comment makes an important point about the topic. A temporary thesis should be interesting and specific. Also, you need to limit the topic to a manageable scope. These three questions are useful tools to measure the effectiveness of any temporary thesis:

- Does the focus of my essay have enough interest to hold an audience?
- Is the focus of my essay specific enough to generate interest?
- Is the focus of my essay manageable for the time limit? Too broad? Too narrow?

The thesis should be a generalization rather than a fact because the thesis prepares readers for facts and details that support the thesis. The process of bringing the thesis into sharp focus may help in outlining major sections of the work. Once the thesis and introduction are complete, you can address the body of the work.

Review Video: Thesis Statements
Visit mometrix.com/academy and enter code: 691033

Supporting the Thesis

Throughout your essay, the thesis should be **explained clearly and supported** adequately by additional arguments. The thesis sentence needs to contain a clear statement of the purpose of your essay and a comment about the thesis. With the thesis statement, you have an opportunity to state what is noteworthy of this particular treatment of the prompt. Each sentence and paragraph should build on and support the thesis.

When you respond to the prompt, use parts of the passage to support your argument or defend your position. With supporting evidence from the passage, you strengthen your argument because readers can see your attention to the entire passage and your response to the details and facts within the passage. You can use facts, details, statistics, and direct quotations from the passage to uphold your position. Be sure to point out which information comes from the original passage and base your argument around that evidence.

Body

In an essay's introduction, the writer establishes the thesis and may indicate how the rest of the piece will be structured. In the body of the piece, the writer **elaborates** upon, **illustrates**, and

explains the **thesis statement**. How writers arrange supporting details and their choices of paragraph types are development techniques. Writers may give examples of the concept introduced in the thesis statement. If the subject includes a cause-and-effect relationship, the author may explain its causality. A writer will explain or analyze the main idea of the piece throughout the body, often by presenting arguments for the veracity or credibility of the thesis statement. Writers may use development to define or clarify ambiguous terms. Paragraphs within the body may be organized using natural sequences, like space and time. Writers may employ **inductive reasoning**, using multiple details to establish a generalization or causal relationship, or **deductive reasoning**, proving a generalized hypothesis or proposition through a specific example or case.

Review Video: Drafting Body Paragraphs
Visit mometrix.com/academy and enter code: 724590

Paragraphs

After the introduction of a passage, a series of body paragraphs will carry a message through to the conclusion. Each paragraph should be **unified around a main point**. Normally, a good topic sentence summarizes the paragraph's main point. A topic sentence is a general sentence that gives an introduction to the paragraph.

The sentences that follow support the topic sentence. However, though it is usually the first sentence, the topic sentence can come as the final sentence to the paragraph if the earlier sentences give a clear explanation of the paragraph's topic. This allows the topic sentence to function as a concluding sentence. Overall, the paragraphs need to stay true to the main point. This means that any unnecessary sentences that do not advance the main point should be removed.

The main point of a paragraph requires adequate development (i.e., a substantial paragraph that covers the main point). A paragraph of two or three sentences does not cover a main point. This is especially true when the main point of the paragraph gives strong support to the argument of the thesis. An occasional short paragraph is fine as a transitional device. However, a well-developed argument will have paragraphs with more than a few sentences.

Methods of Developing Paragraphs

Common methods of adding substance to paragraphs include examples, illustrations, analogies, and cause and effect.

- **Examples** are the supporting details to the main idea of a paragraph or a passage. When authors write about something that their audience may not understand, they can provide an example to show their point. When authors write about something that is not easily accepted, they can give examples to prove their point.
- **Illustrations** are extended examples that require several sentences. Well-selected illustrations can be a great way for authors to develop a point that may not be familiar to their audience.
- **Analogies** make comparisons between items that appear to have nothing in common. Analogies are employed by writers to provoke fresh thoughts about a subject. These comparisons may be used to explain the unfamiliar, to clarify an abstract point, or to argue a point. Although analogies are effective literary devices, they should be used carefully in arguments. Two things may be alike in some respects but completely different in others.

- **Cause and effect** is an excellent device used when the cause and effect are accepted as true. One way that authors can use cause and effect is to state the effect in the topic sentence of a paragraph and add the causes in the body of the paragraph. With this method, an author's paragraphs can have structure which always strengthens writing.

Types of Paragraphs

A **paragraph of narration** tells a story or a part of a story. Normally, the sentences are arranged in chronological order (i.e., the order that the events happened). However, flashbacks (i.e., an anecdote from an earlier time) can be included.

A **descriptive paragraph** makes a verbal portrait of a person, place, or thing. When specific details are used that appeal to one or more of the senses (i.e., sight, sound, smell, taste, and touch), authors give readers a sense of being present in the moment.

A **process paragraph** is related to time order (i.e., First, you open the bottle. Second, you pour the liquid, etc.). Usually, this describes a process or teaches readers how to perform a process.

Comparing two things draws attention to their similarities and indicates a number of differences. When authors contrast, they focus only on differences. Both comparing and contrasting may be done point-by-point, noting both the similarities and differences of each point, or in sequential paragraphs, where you discuss the all the similarities and then all the differences, or vice versa.

Breaking Text into Paragraphs

For most forms of writing, you will need to use multiple paragraphs. As such, determining when to start a new paragraph is very important. Reasons for starting a new paragraph include:

- To mark off the introduction and concluding paragraphs
- To signal a shift to a new idea or topic
- To indicate an important shift in time or place
- To explain a point in additional detail
- To highlight a comparison, contrast, or cause and effect relationship

Paragraph Length

Most readers find that their comfort level for a paragraph is between 100 and 200 words. Shorter paragraphs cause too much starting and stopping, and give a choppy effect. Paragraphs that are too long often test the attention span of readers. Two notable exceptions to this rule exist. In scientific or scholarly papers, longer paragraphs suggest seriousness and depth. In journalistic writing, constraints are placed on paragraph size by the narrow columns in a newspaper format.

The first and last paragraphs of a text will usually be the introduction and conclusion. These special-purpose paragraphs are likely to be shorter than paragraphs in the body of the work. Paragraphs in the body of the essay follow the subject's outline (e.g., one paragraph per point in short essays and a group of paragraphs per point in longer works). Some ideas require more development than others, so it is good for a writer to remain flexible. A paragraph of excessive length may be divided, and shorter ones may be combined.

Coherent Paragraphs

A smooth flow of sentences and paragraphs without gaps, shifts, or bumps will lead to paragraph **coherence**. Ties between old and new information can be smoothed using several methods:

- **Linking ideas clearly**, from the topic sentence to the body of the paragraph, is essential for a smooth transition. The topic sentence states the main point, and this should be followed by specific details, examples, and illustrations that support the topic sentence. The support may be direct or indirect. In **indirect support**, the illustrations and examples may support a sentence that in turn supports the topic directly.
- The **repetition of key words** adds coherence to a paragraph. To avoid dull language, variations of the key words may be used.
- **Parallel structures** are often used within sentences to emphasize the similarity of ideas and connect sentences giving similar information.
- Maintaining a **consistent verb tense** throughout the paragraph helps. Shifting tenses affects the smooth flow of words and can disrupt the coherence of the paragraph.

Review Video: How to Write a Good Paragraph
Visit mometrix.com/academy and enter code: 682127

Sequence Words and Phrases

When a paragraph opens with the topic sentence, the second sentence may begin with a phrase like "First of all," introducing the first supporting detail or example. The writer may introduce the second supporting item with words or phrases like "Also," "In addition," and "Besides." The writer might introduce succeeding pieces of support with wording like, "Another thing," "Moreover" "Furthermore," or "Not only that, but." The writer may introduce the last piece of support with "Lastly," "Finally," or "Last but not least." Writers get off the point by presenting "off-target" items not supporting the main point. For example, a main point "My dog is not smart" is supported by the statement, "He's six years old and still doesn't answer to his name." But "He cries when I leave for school" is not supportive, as it does not indicate lack of intelligence. Writers stay on point by presenting only supportive statements that are directly relevant to and illustrative of their main point.

Transitions

Transitions between sentences and paragraphs guide readers from idea to idea. They also indicate relationships between sentences and paragraphs. Writers should be judicious in their use of transitions, inserting them sparingly. They should also be selected to fit the author's purpose—transitions can indicate time, comparison, and conclusion, among other purposes. Tone is also important to consider when using transitional phrases, varying the tone for different audiences. For example, in a scholarly essay, *in summary* would be preferable to the more informal *in short*.

When working with transitional words and phrases, writers usually find a natural flow that indicates when a transition is needed. In reading a draft of the text, it should become apparent where the flow is disrupted. At this point, the writer can add transitional elements during the revision process. Revising can also afford an opportunity to delete transitional devices that seem heavy handed or unnecessary.

Review Video: Transitions in Writing
Visit mometrix.com/academy and enter code: 233246

Types of Transitional Words

Time	Afterward, immediately, earlier, meanwhile, recently, lately, now, since, soon, when, then, until, before, etc.
Sequence	too, first, second, further, moreover, also, again, and, next, still, besides, and finally
Comparison	similarly, in the same way, likewise, also, again, and once more
Contrasting	but, although, despite, however, instead, nevertheless, on the one hand... on the other hand, regardless, yet, and in contrast.
Cause and Effect	because, consequently, thus, therefore, then, to this end, since, so, as a result, if... then, and accordingly
Examples	for example, for instance, such as, to illustrate, indeed, in fact, and specifically
Place	near, far, here, there, to the left/right, next to, above, below, beyond, opposite, and beside
Concession	granted that, naturally, of course, it may appear, and although it is true that
Repetition, Summary, or Conclusion	as mentioned earlier, as noted, in other words, in short, on the whole, to summarize, therefore, as a result, to conclude, and in conclusion
Addition	and, also, furthermore, moreover
Generalization	in broad terms, broadly speaking, in general

Review Video: Transitional Words and Phrases
Visit mometrix.com/academy and enter code: 197796

Review Video: Transitions
Visit mometrix.com/academy and enter code: 707563

Conclusion

Two important principles to consider when writing a conclusion are strength and closure. A strong conclusion gives the reader a sense that the author's main points are meaningful and important, and that the supporting facts and arguments are convincing, solid, and well developed. When a conclusion achieves closure, it gives the impression that the writer has stated all necessary information and points and completed the work, rather than simply stopping after a specified length. Some things to avoid when writing concluding paragraphs include:

- Introducing a completely new idea
- Beginning with obvious or unoriginal phrases like "In conclusion" or "To summarize"
- Apologizing for one's opinions or writing
- Repeating the thesis word for word rather than rephrasing it
- Believing that the conclusion must always summarize the piece

Review Video: Drafting Conclusions
Visit mometrix.com/academy and enter code: 209408

Organization within a Passage

Organization of the Text

The way a text is organized can help readers understand the author's intent and his or her conclusions. There are various ways to organize a text, and each one has a purpose and use. Usually, authors will organize information logically in a passage so the reader can follow and locate the information within the text. However, since not all passages are written with the same logical structure, you need to be familiar with several different types of passage structure.

Review Video: Organizational Methods to Structure Text
Visit mometrix.com/academy and enter code: 606263

Chronological

When using **chronological** order, the author presents information in the order that it happened. For example, biographies are typically written in chronological order. The subject's birth and childhood are presented first, followed by their adult life, and lastly the events leading up to the person's death.

Cause and Effect

One of the most common text structures is **cause and effect**. A **cause** is an act or event that makes something happen, and an **effect** is the thing that happens as a result of the cause. A cause-and-effect relationship is not always explicit, but there are some terms in English that signal causes, such as *since*, *because*, and *due to*. Furthermore, terms that signal effects include *consequently, therefore, this leads to*. As an example, consider the sentence *Because the sky was clear, Ron did not bring an umbrella*. The cause is the clear sky, and the effect is that Ron did not bring an umbrella. However, readers may find that sometimes the cause-and-effect relationship will not be clearly noted. For instance, the sentence *He was late and missed the meeting* does not contain any signaling words, but the sentence still contains a cause (he was late) and an effect (he missed the meeting).

Review Video: Cause and Effect
Visit mometrix.com/academy and enter code: 868099

Multiple Effects

Be aware of the possibility for a single cause to have **multiple effects.** (e.g., *Single cause*: Because you left your homework on the table, your dog engulfed the assignment. *Multiple effects*: As a result, you receive a failing grade, your parents do not allow you to go out with your friends, you miss out on the new movie, and one of your classmates spoils it for you before you have another chance to watch it).

Multiple Causes

Also, there is the possibility for a single effect to have **multiple causes.** (e.g., *Single effect*: Alan has a fever. *Multiple causes*: An unexpected cold front came through the area, and Alan forgot to take his multi-vitamin to avoid getting sick.) Additionally, an effect can in turn be the cause of another effect, in what is known as a cause-and-effect chain. (e.g., As a result of her disdain for procrastination, Lynn prepared for her exam. This led to her passing her test with high marks. Consequently, her resume was accepted and her application was approved.)

Cause and Effect in Persuasive Essays

Persuasive essays, in which an author tries to make a convincing argument and change the minds of readers, usually include cause-and-effect relationships. However, these relationships should not always be taken at face value. Frequently, an author will assume a cause or take an effect for granted. To read a persuasive essay effectively, readers need to judge the cause-and-effect relationships that the author is presenting. For instance, imagine an author wrote the following: *The parking deck has been unprofitable because people would prefer to ride their bikes.* The relationship is clear: the cause is that people prefer to ride their bikes, and the effect is that the parking deck has been unprofitable. However, readers should consider whether this argument is conclusive. Perhaps there are other reasons for the failure of the parking deck: a down economy, excessive fees, etc. Too often, authors present causal relationships as if they are fact rather than opinion. Readers should be on the alert for these dubious claims.

Problem-Solution

Some nonfiction texts are organized to **present a problem** followed by a solution. For this type of text, the problem is often explained before the solution is offered. In some cases, as when the problem is well known, the solution may be introduced briefly at the beginning. Other passages may focus on the solution, and the problem will be referenced only occasionally. Some texts will outline multiple solutions to a problem, leaving readers to choose among them. If the author has an interest or an allegiance to one solution, he or she may fail to mention or describe accurately some of the other solutions. Readers should be careful of the author's agenda when reading a problem-solution text. Only by understanding the author's perspective and interests can one develop a proper judgment of the proposed solution.

Compare and Contrast

Many texts follow the **compare-and-contrast** model in which the similarities and differences between two ideas or things are explored. Analysis of the similarities between ideas is called **comparison**. In an ideal comparison, the author places ideas or things in an equivalent structure, i.e., the author presents the ideas in the same way. If an author wants to show the similarities between cricket and baseball, then he or she may do so by summarizing the equipment and rules for each game. Be mindful of the similarities as they appear in the passage and take note of any differences that are mentioned. Often, these small differences will only reinforce the more general similarity.

Review Video: Compare and Contrast Essays
Visit mometrix.com/academy and enter code: 798319

Thinking critically about ideas and conclusions can seem like a daunting task. One way to ease this task is to understand the basic elements of ideas and writing techniques. Looking at the way different ideas relate to each other can be a good way for readers to begin their analysis. For instance, sometimes authors will write about two ideas that are in opposition to each other. Or, one author will provide his or her ideas on a topic, and another author may respond in opposition. The analysis of these opposing ideas is known as **contrast**. Contrast is often marred by the author's obvious partiality to one of the ideas. A discerning reader will be put off by an author who does not engage in a fair fight. In an analysis of opposing ideas, both ideas should be presented in clear and reasonable terms. If the author does prefer a side, you need to read carefully to determine the areas where the author shows or avoids this preference. In an analysis of opposing ideas, you should proceed through the passage by marking the major differences point by point with an eye that is looking for an explanation of each side's view. For instance, in an analysis of capitalism and communism, there is an importance in outlining each side's view on labor, markets, prices, personal responsibility, etc. Additionally, as you read through the passages, you should note whether the opposing views present each side in a similar manner.

Sequence

Readers must be able to identify a text's **sequence**, or the order in which things happen. Often, when the sequence is very important to the author, the text is indicated with signal words like *first, then, next,* and *last*. However, a sequence can be merely implied and must be noted by the reader. Consider the sentence *He walked through the garden and gave water and fertilizer to the plants.* Clearly, the man did not walk through the garden before he collected water and fertilizer for the plants. So, the implied sequence is that he first collected water, then he collected fertilizer, next he walked through the garden, and last he gave water or fertilizer as necessary to the plants. Texts do not always proceed in an orderly sequence from first to last. Sometimes they begin at the end and start over at the beginning. As a reader, you can enhance your understanding of the passage by taking brief notes to clarify the sequence.

Style and Form

Writing Style and Linguistic Form

Linguistic form encodes the literal meanings of words and sentences. It comes from the phonological, morphological, syntactic, and semantic parts of a language. **Writing style** consists of different ways of encoding the meaning and indicating figurative and stylistic meanings. An author's writing style can also be referred to as his or her **voice**.

Writers' stylistic choices accomplish three basic effects on their audiences:

- They **communicate meanings** beyond linguistically dictated meanings,
- They communicate the **author's attitude**, such as persuasive or argumentative effects accomplished through style, and
- They communicate or **express feelings**.

Within style, component areas include: narrative structure; viewpoint; focus; sound patterns; meter and rhythm; lexical and syntactic repetition and parallelism; writing genre; representational, realistic, and mimetic effects; representation of thought and speech; meta-representation (representing representation); irony; metaphor and other indirect meanings; representation and use of historical and dialectal variations; gender-specific and other group-specific speech styles, both real and fictitious; and analysis of the processes for inferring meaning from writing.

Level of Formality

The relationship between writer and reader is important in choosing a **level of formality** as most writing requires some degree of formality. **Formal writing** is for addressing a superior in a school or work environment. Business letters, textbooks, and newspapers use a moderate to high level of formality. **Informal writing** is appropriate for private letters, personal emails, and business correspondence between close associates.

For your exam, you will want to be aware of informal and formal writing. One way that this can be accomplished is to watch for shifts in point of view in the essay. For example, unless writers are using a personal example, they will rarely refer to themselves (e.g., "*I* think that *my* point is very clear.") to avoid being informal when they need to be formal.

Also, be mindful of an author who addresses his or her audience **directly** in their writing (e.g., "Readers, *like you*, will understand this argument.") as this can be a sign of informal writing. Good writers understand the need to be consistent with their level of formality. Shifts in levels of formality or point of view can confuse readers and cause them to discount the message.

Clichés

Clichés are phrases that have been **overused** to the point that the phrase has no importance or has lost the original meaning. These phrases have no originality and add very little to a passage. Therefore, most writers will avoid the use of clichés. Another option is to make changes to a cliché so that it is not predictable and empty of meaning.

Examples:

> When life gives you lemons, make lemonade.
>
> Every cloud has a silver lining.

Jargon

Jargon is a **specialized vocabulary** that is used among members of a trade or profession. Since jargon is understood by only a small audience, writers will use jargon in passages that will only be read by a specialized audience. For example, medical jargon should be used in a medical journal but not in a New York Times article. Jargon includes exaggerated language that tries to impress rather than inform. Sentences filled with jargon are not precise and are difficult to understand.

Examples:

> "He is going to *toenail* these frames for us." (Toenail is construction jargon for nailing at an angle.)
>
> "They brought in a *kip* of material today." (Kip refers to 1000 pounds in architecture and engineering.)

Slang

Slang is an **informal** and sometimes private language that is understood by some individuals. Slang terms have some usefulness, but they can have a small audience. So, most formal writing will not include this kind of language.

Examples:

> "Yes, the event was a blast!" (In this sentence, *blast* means that the event was a great experience.)
>
> "That attempt was an epic fail." (By *epic fail*, the speaker means that his or her attempt was not a success.)

Colloquialism

A colloquialism is a word or phrase that is found in informal writing. Unlike slang, **colloquial language** will be familiar to a greater range of people. However, colloquialisms are still considered inappropriate for formal writing. Colloquial language can include some slang, but these are limited to contractions for the most part.

Examples:

> "Can *y'all* come back another time?" (Y'all is a contraction of "you all.")
>
> "Will you stop him from building this *castle in the air*?" (A "castle in the air" is an improbable or unlikely event.)

Academic Language

In educational settings, students are often expected to use academic language in their schoolwork. Academic language is also commonly found in dissertations and theses, texts published by academic journals, and other forms of academic research. Academic language conventions may vary between fields, but general academic language is free of slang, regional terminology, and noticeable grammatical errors. Specific terms may also be used in academic language, and it is important to understand their proper usage. A writer's command of academic language impacts their ability to communicate in an academic or professional context. While it is acceptable to use colloquialisms, slang, improper grammar, or other forms of informal speech in social settings or at home, it is inappropriate to practice academic language in academic contexts.

Tone

Tone may be defined as the writer's **attitude** toward the topic, and to the audience. This attitude is reflected in the language used in the writing. The tone of a work should be **appropriate to the topic** and to the intended audience. Some texts should not contain slang or jargon, while it may be fine to use such terms in a different piece. Tone can range from humorous to serious and any level in between. It may be more or less formal, depending on the purpose of the writing and its intended audience. All these nuances in tone can flavor the entire writing and should be kept in mind as the work evolves.

Word Selection

A writer's choice of words is a signature of their style. Careful thought about the use of words can improve a piece of writing. A passage can be an exciting piece to read when attention is given to the use of vivid or specific nouns rather than general ones.

Example:

> General: His kindness will never be forgotten.
>
> Specific: His thoughtful gifts and bear hugs will never be forgotten.

Attention should also be given to the kind of verbs that are used in sentences. Active verbs (e.g., run, swim) should be about an action. Whenever possible, an **active verb should replace a linking verb** to provide clear examples for arguments and to strengthen a passage overall. When using an active verb, one should be sure that the verb is used in the active voice instead of the passive voice. Verbs are in the active voice when the subject is the one doing the action. A verb is in the passive voice when the subject is the recipient of an action.

Example:

> Passive: The winners were called to the stage by the judges.
>
> Active: The judges called the winners to the stage.

Review Video: Word Usage
Visit mometrix.com/academy and enter code: 197863

Conciseness

Conciseness is writing that communicates a message in the fewest words possible. Writing concisely is valuable because short, uncluttered messages allow the reader to understand the author's message more easily and efficiently. Planning is important in writing concise messages. If you have in mind what you need to write beforehand, it will be easier to make a message short and to the point. Do not state the obvious.

Revising is also important. After the message is written, make sure you have effective, pithy sentences that efficiently get your point across. When reviewing the information, imagine a conversation taking place, and concise writing will likely result.

Appropriate Kinds of Writing for Different Tasks, Purposes, and Audiences

When preparing to write a composition, consider the audience and purpose to choose the best type of writing. Three common types of writing are persuasive, expository, and narrative. **Persuasive**, or argumentative writing, is used to convince the audience to take action or agree with the author's claims. **Expository** writing is meant to inform the audience of the author's observations or research on a topic. **Narrative** writing is used to tell the audience a story and often allows more room for creativity. While task, purpose, and audience inform a writer's mode of writing, these factors also impact elements such as tone, vocabulary, and formality.

For example, students who are writing to persuade their parents to grant them some additional privilege, such as permission for a more independent activity, should use more sophisticated vocabulary and diction that sounds more mature and serious to appeal to the parental audience. However, students who are writing for younger children should use simpler vocabulary and sentence structure, as well as choose words that are more vivid and entertaining. They should treat their topics more lightly, and include humor when appropriate. Students who are writing for their classmates may use language that is more informal, as well as age-appropriate.

Review Video: Writing Purpose and Audience
Visit mometrix.com/academy and enter code: 146627

Modes of Writing

Essays

Essays usually focus on one topic, subject, or goal. There are several types of essays, including informative, persuasive, and narrative. An essay's structure and level of formality depend on the type of essay and its goal. While narrative essays typically do not include outside sources, other types of essays often require some research and the integration of primary and secondary sources.

The basic format of an essay typically has three major parts: the introduction, the body, and the conclusion. The body is further divided into the writer's main points. Short and simple essays may have three main points, while essays covering broader ranges and going into more depth can have almost any number of main points, depending on length.

An essay's introduction should answer three questions:

1. What is the **subject** of the essay?

   If a student writes an essay about a book, the answer would include the title and author of the book and any additional information needed—such as the subject or argument of the book.

2. How does the essay **address** the subject?

   To answer this, the writer identifies the essay's organization by briefly summarizing main points and the evidence supporting them.

3. What will the essay **prove**?

   This is the thesis statement, usually the opening paragraph's last sentence, clearly stating the writer's message.

The body elaborates on all the main points related to the thesis, introducing one main point at a time, and includes supporting evidence with each main point. Each body paragraph should state the point in a topic sentence, which is usually the first sentence in the paragraph. The paragraph should then explain the point's meaning, support it with quotations or other evidence, and then explain how this point and the evidence are related to the thesis. The writer should then repeat this procedure in a new paragraph for each additional main point.

The conclusion reiterates the content of the introduction, including the thesis, to remind the reader of the essay's main argument or subject. The essay writer may also summarize the highlights of the argument or description contained in the body of the essay, following the same sequence originally used in the body. For example, a conclusion might look like: Point 1 + Point 2 + Point 3 = Thesis, or Point 1 → Point 2 → Point 3 → Thesis Proof. Good organization makes essays easier for writers to compose and provides a guide for readers to follow. Well-organized essays hold attention better and are more likely to get readers to accept their theses as valid.

Informative vs. Persuasive Writing

Informative writing, also called explanatory or expository writing, begins with the basis that something is true or factual, while **persuasive** writing strives to prove something that may or may not be true or factual. Whereas argumentative text is written to **persuade** readers to agree with the author's position, informative text merely **provides information and insight** to readers. Informative writing concentrates on **informing** readers about why or how something is as it is. This can include offering new information, explaining how a process works, and developing a concept for readers. To accomplish these objectives, the essay may name and distinguish various things within a category; provide definitions; provide details about the parts of something; explain a particular function or behavior; and give readers explanations for why a fact, object, event, or process exists or occurs.

Review Video: Informative Text
Visit mometrix.com/academy and enter code: 924964

Review Video: Argumentative Writing
Visit mometrix.com/academy and enter code: 561544

Narrative Writing

Put simply, **narrative** writing tells a story. The most common examples of literary narratives are novels. Non-fictional biographies, autobiographies, memoirs, and histories are also narratives. Narratives should tell stories in such a way that the readers learn something or gain insight or understanding. Students can write more interesting narratives by describing events or experiences that were meaningful to them. Narratives should start with the story's actions or events, rather than begin with long descriptions or introductions. Students should ensure that there is a point to each story by describing what they learned from the experience they narrate. To write an effective description, students should include sensory details, asking themselves what they saw, heard, felt or touched, smelled, and tasted during the experiences they describe. In narrative writing, the details should be **concrete** rather than **abstract**. Using concrete details enables readers to imagine everything that the writer describes.

Review Video: Narratives
Visit mometrix.com/academy and enter code: 280100

Sensory Details

Students need to use vivid descriptions when writing descriptive essays. Narratives should also include descriptions of characters, things, and events. Students should remember to describe not only the visual detail of what someone or something looks like, but details from other senses, as well. For example, they can contrast the feeling of a sea breeze to that of a mountain breeze, describe how they think something inedible would taste, and compare sounds they hear in the same location at different times of day and night. Readers have trouble visualizing images or imagining sensory impressions and feelings from abstract descriptions, so concrete descriptions make these more real.

Concrete vs. Abstract Descriptions in Narrative

Concrete language provides information that readers can grasp and may empathize with, while **abstract language**, which is more general, can leave readers feeling disconnected, empty, or even confused. "It was a lovely day" is abstract, but "The sun shone brightly, the sky was blue, the air felt warm, and a gentle breeze wafted across my skin" is concrete. "Ms. Couch was a good teacher" uses abstract language, giving only a general idea of the writer's opinion. But "Ms. Couch is excellent at helping us take our ideas and turn them into good essays and stories" uses concrete language, giving more specific examples of what makes Ms. Couch a good teacher. "I like writing poems but not essays" gives readers a general idea that the student prefers one genre over another, but not why. But by reading, "I like writing short poems with rhythm and rhyme, but I hate writing five-page essays that go on and on about the same ideas," readers understand that the student prefers the brevity, rhyme, and meter of short poetry over the length and redundancy of longer prose.

Autobiographical Narratives

Autobiographical narratives are narratives written by an author about an event or period in their life. Autobiographical narratives are written from one person's perspective, in first person, and often include the author's thoughts and feelings alongside their description of the event or period. Structure, style, or theme varies between different autobiographical narratives, since each narrative is personal and specific to its author and their experience.

Reflective Essay

A less common type of essay is the reflective essay. **Reflective essays** allow the author to reflect, or think back on, an experience and analyze what they recall. They should consider what they learned from the experience, what they could have done differently, what would have helped them during the experience, or anything else that they have realized from looking back on the experience. Reflection essays incorporate both objective reflection on one's own actions and subjective explanation of thoughts and feelings. These essays can be written for a number of experiences in a formal or informal context.

JOURNALS AND DIARIES

A **journal** is a personal account of events, experiences, feelings, and thoughts. Many people write journals to express their feelings and thoughts or to help them process experiences they have had. Since journals are **private documents** not meant to be shared with others, writers may not be concerned with grammar, spelling, or other mechanics. However, authors may write journals that they expect or hope to publish someday; in this case, they not only express their thoughts and feelings and process their experiences, but they also attend to their craft in writing them. Some authors compose journals to record a particular time period or a series of related events, such as a cancer diagnosis, treatment, surviving the disease, and how these experiences have changed or affected them. Other experiences someone might include in a journal are recovering from addiction, journeys of spiritual exploration and discovery, time spent in another country, or anything else someone wants to personally document. Journaling can also be therapeutic, as some people use journals to work through feelings of grief over loss or to wrestle with big decisions.

EXAMPLES OF DIARIES IN LITERATURE

The Diary of a Young Girl by Dutch Jew Anne Frank (1947) contains her life-affirming, nonfictional diary entries from 1942-1944 while her family hid in an attic from World War II's genocidal Nazis. *Go Ask Alice* (1971) by Beatrice Sparks is a cautionary, fictional novel in the form of diary entries by Alice, an unhappy, rebellious teen who takes LSD, runs away from home and lives with hippies, and eventually returns home. Frank's writing reveals an intelligent, sensitive, insightful girl, raised by intellectual European parents—a girl who believes in the goodness of human nature despite surrounding atrocities. Alice, influenced by early 1970s counterculture, becomes less optimistic. However, similarities can be found between them: Frank dies in a Nazi concentration camp while the fictitious Alice dies from a drug overdose. Both young women are also unable to escape their surroundings. Additionally, adolescent searches for personal identity are evident in both books.

Review Video: Journals, Diaries, Letters, and Blogs
Visit mometrix.com/academy and enter code: 432845

LETTERS

Letters are messages written to other people. In addition to letters written between individuals, some writers compose letters to the editors of newspapers, magazines, and other publications, while some write "Open Letters" to be published and read by the general public. Open letters, while intended for everyone to read, may also identify a group of people or a single person whom the letter directly addresses. In everyday use, the most-used forms are business letters and personal or friendly letters. Both kinds share common elements: business or personal letterhead stationery; the writer's return address at the top; the addressee's address next; a salutation, such as "Dear [name]" or some similar opening greeting, followed by a colon in business letters or a comma in personal letters; the body of the letter, with paragraphs as indicated; and a closing, like "Sincerely/Cordially/Best regards/etc." or "Love," in intimate personal letters.

EARLY LETTERS

The Greek word for "letter" is *epistolē*, which became the English word "epistle." The earliest letters were called epistles, including the New Testament's epistles from the apostles to the Christians. In ancient Egypt, the writing curriculum in scribal schools included the epistolary genre. Epistolary novels frame a story in the form of letters. Examples of noteworthy epistolary novels include:

- *Pamela* (1740), by 18th-century English novelist Samuel Richardson
- *Shamela* (1741), Henry Fielding's satire of *Pamela* that mocked epistolary writing.
- *Lettres persanes* (1721) by French author Montesquieu
- *The Sorrows of Young Werther* (1774) by German author Johann Wolfgang von Goethe
- *The History of Emily Montague* (1769), the first Canadian novel, by Frances Brooke
- *Dracula* (1897) by Bram Stoker
- *Frankenstein* (1818) by Mary Shelley
- *The Color Purple* (1982) by Alice Walker

Blogs

The word "blog" is derived from "weblog" and refers to writing done exclusively on the internet. Readers of reputable newspapers expect quality content and layouts that enable easy reading. These expectations also apply to blogs. For example, readers can easily move visually from line to line when columns are narrow, while overly wide columns cause readers to lose their places. Blogs must also be posted with layouts enabling online readers to follow them easily. However, because the way people read on computer, tablet, and smartphone screens differs from how they read print on paper, formatting and writing blog content is more complex than writing newspaper articles. Two major principles are the bases for blog-writing rules: The first is while readers of print articles skim to estimate their length, online they must scroll down to scan; therefore, blog layouts need more subheadings, graphics, and other indications of what information follows. The second is onscreen reading can be harder on the eyes than reading printed paper, so legibility is crucial in blogs.

Rules and Rationales for Writing Blogs

1. Format all posts for smooth page layout and easy scanning.
2. Column width should not be too wide, as larger lines of text can be difficult to read
3. Headings and subheadings separate text visually, enable scanning or skimming, and encourage continued reading.
4. Bullet-pointed or numbered lists enable quick information location and scanning.
5. Punctuation is critical, so beginners should use shorter sentences until confident.
6. Blog paragraphs should be far shorter—two to six sentences each—than paragraphs written on paper to enable "chunking" because reading onscreen is more difficult.
7. Sans-serif fonts are usually clearer than serif fonts, and larger font sizes are better.
8. Highlight important material and draw attention with **boldface**, but avoid overuse. Avoid hard-to-read *italics* and ALL CAPITALS.
9. Include enough blank spaces: overly busy blogs tire eyes and brains. Images not only break up text but also emphasize and enhance text and can attract initial reader attention.
10. Use background colors judiciously to avoid distracting the eye or making it difficult to read.
11. Be consistent throughout posts, since people read them in different orders.
12. Tell a story with a beginning, middle, and end.

Specialized Modes of Writing

Editorials

Editorials are articles in newspapers, magazines, and other serial publications. Editorials express an opinion or belief belonging to the majority of the publication's leadership. This opinion or belief generally refers to a specific issue, topic, or event. These articles are authored by a member, or a small number of members, of the publication's leadership and are often written to affect their readers, such as persuading them to adopt a stance or take a particular action.

Resumes

Resumes are brief, but formal, documents that outline an individual's experience in a certain area. Resumes are most often used for job applications. Such resumes will list the applicant's work experience, certification, and achievements or qualifications related to the position. Resumes should only include the most pertinent information. They should also use strategic formatting to highlight the applicant's most impressive experiences and achievements, ensure the document can be read quickly and easily, and to eliminate both visual clutter and excessive negative space.

Reports

Reports summarize the results of research, new methodology, or other developments in an academic or professional context. Reports often include details about methodology and outside influences and factors. However, a report should focus primarily on the results of the research or development. Reports are objective and deliver information efficiently, sacrificing style for clear and effective communication.

Memoranda

A memorandum, also called a memo, is a formal method of communication used in professional settings. Memoranda are printed documents that include a heading listing the sender and their job title, the recipient and their job title, the date, and a specific subject line. Memoranda often include an introductory section explaining the reason and context for the memorandum. Next, a memorandum includes a section with details relevant to the topic. Finally, the memorandum will conclude with a paragraph that politely and clearly defines the sender's expectations of the recipient.

Research

Research Writing

Writing for research is essentially writing to answer a question or a problem about a particular **research topic**. A **problem statement** is written to clearly define what a problem with the topic is before asking about how to solve the problem. A **research question** serves to ask what can be done to address the problem. Before a researcher should try to solve a problem, the researcher should spend significant time performing a **literature review** to find out what has already been learned about the topic and if there are already solutions in place. The literature review can help to re-evaluate the research question as well. If the question has not been thoroughly answered, then it is proper to do more broad research to learn about the topic and build up the body of literature. If the literature review provides plenty of background, but no practical solutions to the problem, then the research question should be targeted at solving a problem more directly. After the research has been performed, a **thesis** can act as a proposal for a solution or as a recommendation to future researchers to continue to learn more about the topic. The thesis should then be supported by significant contributing evidence to help support the proposed solution.

Example of Research Writing Elements

Topic	The general idea the research is about. This is usually broader than the problem itself. Example: Clean Water
Problem Statement	A problem statement is a brief, clear description of a problem with the topic. Example: Not all villages in third-world countries have ready access to clean water.
Research Question	A research question asks a specific question about what needs to be learned or done about the problem statement. Example: What can local governments do to improve access to clean water?
Literature Review	A review of the body of literature by the researcher to show what is already known about the topic and the problem. If the literature review shows that the research question has already been thoroughly answered, the researcher should consider changing problem statements to something that has not been solved.
Thesis	A brief proposal of a solution to a problem. Theses do not include their own support, but are supported by later evidence. Example: Local governments can improve access to clean water by installing sealed rain-water collection units.
Body Paragraphs	Paragraphs focused on the primary supporting evidence for the main idea of the thesis. There are usually three body paragraphs, but there can be more if needed.
Conclusion	A final wrap-up of the research research project. The conclusion should reiterate the problem, question, thesis, and briefly mention how the main evidences support the thesis.

The Research Process

Researchers should prepare some information before gathering sources. Researchers who have chosen a **research question** should choose key words or names that pertain to their question. They should also identify what type of information and sources they are looking for. Researchers should consider whether secondary or primary sources will be most appropriate for their research project. As researchers find credible and appropriate sources, they should be prepared to adjust the scope of their research question or topic in response to the information and insights they gather.

Using Sources and Synthesizing Information

As researchers find potential sources for their research project, it is important to keep a **record** of the material they find and note how each source may impact their work. When taking these notes, researchers should keep their research question or outline in mind and consider how their chosen references would complement their discussion. **Literature reviews** and **annotated bibliographies** are helpful tools for evaluating sources, as they require the researcher to consider the qualities and offerings of the sources they choose to use. These tools also help researchers synthesize the information they find.

Synthesizing Information

Synthesizing information requires the researcher to integrate sources and their own thoughts by quoting, paraphrasing, or summarizing outside information in their research project. Synthesizing information indicates that the research complements the writer's claims, ensures that the ideas in the composition flow logically, and makes including small details and quotes easier. Paraphrasing is one of the simplest ways to integrate a source. **Paraphrasing** allows the writer to support their ideas with research while presenting the information in their own words, rather than using the source's original wording. Paraphrasing also allows the writer to reference the source's main ideas instead of specific details. While paraphrasing does not require the writer to quote the source, it still entails a direct reference to the source, meaning that any paraphrased material still requires a citation.

Citing Sources

While researchers should combine research with their own ideas, the information and ideas that come from outside sources should be attributed to the author of the source. When conducting research, it is helpful to record the publication information for each source so that **citations** can be easily added within the composition. Keeping a close record of the source of each idea in a composition or project is helpful for avoiding plagiarism, as both direct and indirect references require documentation.

Plagiarism

Understanding what is considered to be plagiarism is important to preventing unintentional plagiarism. Using another person's work in any way without proper attribution is **plagiarism**. However, it is easy to mistakenly commit plagiarism by improperly citing a source or creating a citation that is not intended for the way the source was used. Even when an honest attempt to attribute information is made, small errors can still result in plagiarized content. For this reason, it is important to create citations carefully and review citations before submitting or publishing research. It is also possible to plagiarize one's own work. This occurs when a writer has published work with one title and purpose and then attempts to publish it again as new material under a new title or purpose.

Literature Review

One of the two main parts of a literature review is searching through existing literature. The other is actually writing the review. Researchers must take care not to get lost in the information and inhibit progress toward their research goal. A good precaution is to write out the research question and keep it nearby. It is also wise to make a search plan and establish a time limit in advance. Finding a seemingly endless number of references indicates a need to revisit the research question because the topic is too broad. Finding too little material means that the research topic is too narrow. With new or cutting-edge research, one may find that nobody has investigated this particular question. This requires systematic searching, using abstracts in periodicals for an overview of available literature, research papers or other specific sources to explore its reference, and references in books and other sources.

When searching published literature on a research topic, one must take thorough notes. It is common to find a reference that could be useful later in the research project, but is not needed yet. In situations like this, it is helpful to make a note of the reference so it will be easy to find later. These notes can be grouped in a word processing document, which also allows for easy compiling of links and quotes from internet research. Researchers should explore the internet regularly, view resources for their research often, learn how to use resources correctly and efficiently, experiment with resources available within the disciplines, open and examine databases, become familiar with reference desk materials, find publications with abstracts of articles and books on one's topic, use papers' references to locate the most utile journals and important authors, identify keywords for refining and narrowing database searches, and peruse library catalogues online for available sources—all while taking notes.

As one searches for references, one will gradually develop an overview of the body of literature available for his or her subject. This signals the time to prepare for writing the literature review. The researcher should assemble his or her notes along with copies of all the journal articles and all the books he or she has acquired. Then one should write the research question again at the top of a page and list below it all of the author names and keywords discovered while searching. It is also helpful to observe whether any groups or pairs of these stand out. These activities are parts of structuring one's literature review—the first step for writing a thesis, dissertation, or research paper. Writers should rewrite their work as necessary rather than expecting to write only one draft. However, stopping to edit along the way can distract from the momentum of writing the first draft. If the writer is dissatisfied with a certain part of the draft, it may be better to skip to a later portion of the paper and revisit the problem section at another time.

Body and Conclusion in Literature Review

The first step of a literature review paper is to create a rough draft. The next step is to edit: rewrite for clarity, eliminate unnecessary verbiage, and change terminology that could confuse readers. After editing, a writer should ask others to read and give feedback. Additionally, the writer should read the paper aloud to hear how it sounds, editing as needed. Throughout a literature review, the writer should not only summarize and comment on each source reviewed, but should also relate these findings to the original research question. The writer should explicitly state in the conclusion how the research question and pertinent literature interaction is developed throughout the body, reflecting on insights gained through the process.

Review Video: Drafting Conclusions
Visit mometrix.com/academy and enter code: 209408

Summaries and Abstracts

When preparing to submit or otherwise publish research, it may be necessary to compose a summary or abstract to accompany the research composition.

A summary is a brief description of the contents of a longer work that provides an overview of the work and may include its most important details. One common type of summary is an abstract. Abstracts are specialized summaries that are most commonly used in the context of research. Abstracts may include details such as the purpose for the research, the researcher's methodology, and the most significant results of the research. Abstracts sometimes include sections and headings, where most summaries are limited to one or a few paragraphs with no special groupings.

Editing and Revising

After composing a rough draft of a research paper, the writer should **edit** it. The purpose of the paper is to communicate the answer to one's research question in an efficient and effective manner. The writing should be as **concise** and **clear** as possible, and the style should also be consistent. Editing is often easier to do after writing the first draft rather than during it, as taking time between writing and editing allows writers to be more objective. If the paper includes an abstract and an introduction, the writer should compose these after writing the rest, when he or she will have a better grasp of the theme and arguments. Not all readers understand technical terminology or long words, so writers should use these sparingly. Finally, writers should consult a writing and style guide address any industry- or institution-specific issues that may arise as they edit.

Review Video: Revising and Editing
Visit mometrix.com/academy and enter code: 674181

Sources for Research

Primary Sources

In literature review, one may examine both primary and secondary sources. Primary sources contain original information that was witnessed, gathered, or otherwise produced by the source's author. Primary sources can include firsthand accounts, found in sources such as books, autobiographies, transcripts, speeches, videos, photos, and personal journals or diaries. Primary sources may also include records of information, such as government documents, or personally-conducted research in sources like reports and essays. They may be found in academic books, journals and other periodicals, and authoritative databases. Using primary sources allows researchers to develop their own conclusions about the subject. Primary sources are also reliable for finding information about a person or their personal accounts and experiences. Primary sources such as photos, videos, audio recordings, transcripts, and government documents are often reliable, as they are usually objective and can be used to confirm information from other sources.

Secondary Sources

Secondary sources are sources that reference information originally provided by another source. The original source may be cited, quoted, paraphrased, or described in a secondary source. Secondary sources may be articles, essays, videos, or books found in periodicals, magazines, newspapers, films, databases, or websites. A secondary source can be used to reference another researcher's analysis or conclusion from a primary source. This information can inform the researcher of the existing discussions regarding their subject. These types of sources may also support the researcher's claims by providing a credible argument that contributes to the researcher's argument. Secondary sources may also highlight connections between primary sources or criticize both primary and other secondary sources. These types of secondary sources are valuable because they provide information and conclusions the researcher may not have considered or found, otherwise.

Review Video: Primary and Secondary Sources
Visit mometrix.com/academy and enter code: 383328

Types of Sources

- **Textbooks** are specialized materials that are designed to thoroughly instruct readers on a particular topic. Textbooks often include features such as a table of contents, visuals, an index, a glossary, headings, and practice questions and exercises.
- **Newspapers** are collections of several written pieces and are primarily used to distribute news stories to their audience. In addition to news articles, newspapers may also include advertisements or pieces meant to entertain their audience, such as comic strips, columns, and letters from readers. Newspapers are written for a variety of audiences, as they are published on both the local and national levels.

- **Manuals** are instructional documents that accompany a product or explain an important procedure. Manuals include a table of contents, guidelines, and instructional content. Instructional manuals often include information about safe practices, risks, and product warranty. The instructions in manuals are often presented as step-by-step instructions, as they are meant to help users properly use a product or complete a task.
- **Electronic texts** are written documents that are read digitally and are primarily accessed online or through a network. Many electronic texts have characteristics similar to printed texts, such as a table of contents, publication information, a main text, and supplemental materials. However, electronic texts are more interactive and can be navigated more quickly. Electronic texts can also provide more accessibility, as they can be easily resized or narrated by text-to-speech software.

Finding Sources

Finding sources for a research project may be intimidating or difficult. There are numerous sources available, and several research tools to help researchers find them. Starting with one of these tools can help narrow down the number of sources a researcher is working with at one time.

- **Libraries** house independent, printed publications that are organized by subject. This makes finding sources easy, since researchers can visit sections with sources relevant to their topic and immediately see what sources are available. Many libraries also offer printed journals and collections that include sources related to a common subject or written by the same author.
- **Databases** offer digital access to sources from a wide variety of libraries and online containers. To use a database, users search for keywords related to their topic or the type of source they want to use. The database then lists results related to or featuring those key words. Users can narrow their results using filters that will limit their results based on factors such as publication year, source type, or whether the sources are peer-reviewed. Database search results also list individual articles and methods of accessing the article directly. While databases help users find sources, they do not guarantee users access to each source.
- **Academic Journals** are collections of articles that cover a particular topic or fit within a certain category. These journals are often offered both online and in print. Academic journals typically contain peer-reviewed works or works that have undergone another type of reviewing process.

Credibility

There are innumerable primary and secondary sources available in print and online. However, not every published or posted source is appropriate for a research project. When finding sources, the researcher must know how to evaluate each source for credibility and relevance. Not only must the sources be reliable and relevant to the research subject, but they must also be appropriate and help form an answer to the research question. As researchers progress in their research and composition, the relevance of each source will become clear. Appropriate sources will contribute valuable information and arguments to the researcher's own thoughts and conclusions, providing useful evidence to bolster the researcher's claims. The researcher has the freedom to choose which sources they reference or even change their research topic and question in response to the sources they find. However, the researcher should not use unreliable sources, and determining a source's credibility is not always easy.

Considerations for Evaluating the Credibility of a Source

- The author and their purpose for writing the source

- The author's qualifications to write on the topic
- Whether the source is peer-reviewed or included in a scholarly publication
- The publisher
- The target audience
- The jargon or dialect the source is written in (e.g., academic, technical)
- The presence of bias or manipulation of information
- The date of publication
- The author's use of other sources to support their claims
- Whether any outside sources are cited appropriately in the source
- The accuracy of information presented

Author's Purpose and Credibility

Knowing who wrote a source and why they wrote it is important to determining whether a source is appropriate for a research project. The author should be qualified to write on the subject of the material. Their purpose may be to inform their audience of information, to present and defend an analysis, or even to criticize a work or other argument. The researcher must decide whether the author's purpose makes the source appropriate to use. The source's container and publisher are important to note because they indicate the source's reputability and whether other qualified individuals have reviewed the information in the source. Credible secondary sources should also reference other sources, primary or secondary, that support or inform the source's content. Evaluating the accuracy of the information or the presence of bias in a source will require careful reading and critical thinking on the part of the researcher. However, a source with excellent credentials may still contain pieces of inaccurate information or bias, so it is the researcher's responsibility to be careful in their use of each source.

Integrating References and Quotations

In research papers, one can include studies whose conclusions agree with one's position (Reed 284; Becker and Fagen 93), as well as studies that disagree (Limbaugh 442, Beck 69) by including parenthetical citations as demonstrated in this sentence. Quotations should be selective: writers should compose an original sentence and incorporate only a few words from a research source. If students cannot use more original words than quotation, they are likely padding their compositions. However, including quotations appropriately increases the credibility of the writer and their argument.

Properly Integrating Quotations

When using sources in a research paper, it is important to integrate information so that the flow of the composition is not interrupted as the two compositions are combined. When quoting outside sources, it is necessary to lead into the quote and ensure that the whole sentence is logical, is grammatically correct, and flows well. Below is an example of an incorrectly integrated quote.

> During the Industrial Revolution, many unions organized labor strikes "child labor, unregulated working conditions, and excessive working hours" in America.

Below is the same sentence with a properly integrated quote.

> During the Industrial Revolution, many unions organized labor strikes to protest the presence of "child labor, unregulated working conditions, and excessive working hours" in America.

In the first example, the connection between "strikes" and the quoted list is unclear. In the second example, the phrase "to protest the presence of" link the ideas together and successfully creates a suitable place for the quotation.

When quoting sources, writers should work quotations and references seamlessly into their sentences instead of interrupting the flow of their own argument to summarize a source. Summarizing others' content is often a ploy to bolster word counts. Writing that analyzes the content, evaluates it, and synthesizes material from various sources demonstrates critical thinking skills and is thus more valuable.

Properly Incorporating Outside Sources

Writers do better to include short quotations rather than long. For example, quoting six to eight long passages in a 10-page paper is excessive. It is also better to avoid wording like "This quotation shows," "As you can see from this quotation," or "It talks about." These are amateur, feeble efforts to interact with other authors' ideas. Also, writing about sources and quotations wastes words that should be used to develop one's own ideas. Quotations should be used to stimulate discussion rather than taking its place. Ending a paragraph, section, or paper with a quotation is not incorrect per se, but using it to prove a point, without including anything more in one's own words regarding the point or subject, suggests a lack of critical thinking about the topic and consideration of multiple alternatives. It can also be a tactic to dissuade readers from challenging one's propositions. Writers should include references and quotations that challenge as well as support their thesis statements. Presenting evidence on both sides of an issue makes it easier for reasonably skeptical readers to agree with a writer's viewpoint.

Citing Sources

Formal research writers must **cite all sources** used—books, articles, interviews, conversations, and anything else that contributed to the research. One reason is to **avoid plagiarism** and give others credit for their ideas. Another reason is to help readers find the sources consulted in the research and access more information about the subject for further reading and research. Additionally, citing sources helps to make a paper academically authoritative. To prepare, research writers should keep a running list of sources consulted, in an electronic file or on file cards. For every source used, the writer needs specific information. For books, a writer needs to record the author's and editor's name, book title, publication date, city, and publisher name. For articles, one needs the author name, article title, journal (or magazine or newspaper) name, volume and issue number, publication date, and page numbers. For electronic resources, a writer will need the author's name, article information plus the URL, database name, name of the database's publisher, and the date of access.

Common Reference Styles

Three common reference styles are **MLA** (Modern Language Association), **APA** (American Psychological Association), and **Turabian** (created by author Kate Turabian, also known as the Chicago Manual of Style). Each style formats citation information differently. Professors and instructors often specify that students use one of these. Generally, APA style is used in psychology and sociology papers, and MLA style is used in English literature papers and similar scholarly projects. To understand how these styles differ, consider an imaginary article cited in each of these styles. This article is titled "Ten Things You Won't Believe Dragons Do," written by author Andra Gaines, included in the journal *Studies in Fantasy Fiction*, and published by Quest for Knowledge Publishing.

MLA:

Gaines, Andra. "Ten Things You Won't Believe Dragons Do". *Studies in Fantasy Fiction*, vol. 3, no. 8, Quest for Knowledge Publishing, 21 Aug. 2019.

APA:

Gaines, A. (2019). Ten Things You Won't Believe Dragons Do. *Studies in Fantasy Fiction, 3(8)*, 42-65.

Chicago:

Gaines, Andra. "Ten Things You Won't Believe Dragons Do," *Studies in Fantasy Fiction* 3, no. 8 (2019): 42-65.

Within each of these styles, citations, though they vary according to the type of source and how its used, generally follow a structure and format similar to those above. For example, citations for whole books will probably not include a container title or a volume number, but will otherwise look very similar.

Review Video: Citing Sources
Visit mometrix.com/academy and enter code: 993637

Vocabulary and Word Relationships

Synonyms and Antonyms

When you understand how words relate to each other, you will discover more in a passage. This is explained by understanding **synonyms** (e.g., words that mean the same thing) and **antonyms** (e.g., words that mean the opposite of one another). As an example, *dry* and *arid* are synonyms, and *dry* and *wet* are antonyms.

There are many pairs of words in English that can be considered synonyms, despite having slightly different definitions. For instance, the words *friendly* and *collegial* can both be used to describe a warm interpersonal relationship, and one would be correct to call them synonyms. However, *collegial* (kin to *colleague*) is often used in reference to professional or academic relationships, and *friendly* has no such connotation.

If the difference between the two words is too great, then they should not be called synonyms. *Hot* and *warm* are not synonyms because their meanings are too distinct. A good way to determine whether two words are synonyms is to substitute one word for the other word and verify that the meaning of the sentence has not changed. Substituting *warm* for *hot* in a sentence would convey a different meaning. Although warm and hot may seem close in meaning, warm generally means that the temperature is moderate, and hot generally means that the temperature is excessively high.

Antonyms are words with opposite meanings. *Light* and *dark*, *up* and *down*, *right* and *left*, *good* and *bad*: these are all sets of antonyms. Be careful to distinguish between antonyms and pairs of words that are simply different. *Black* and *gray*, for instance, are not antonyms because gray is not the opposite of black. *Black* and *white*, on the other hand, are antonyms.

Not every word has an antonym. For instance, many nouns do not. What would be the antonym of *chair*? During your exam, the questions related to antonyms are more likely to concern adjectives. You will recall that adjectives are words that describe a noun. Some common adjectives include *purple*, *fast*, *skinny*, and *sweet*. From those four adjectives, *purple* is the item that lacks a group of obvious antonyms.

Review Video: Synonyms and Antonyms
Visit mometrix.com/academy and enter code: 105612

AFFIXES

Affixes in the English language are morphemes that are added to words to create related but different words. Derivational affixes form new words based on and related to the original words. For example, the affix *–ness* added to the end of the adjective *happy* forms the noun *happiness.* Inflectional affixes form different grammatical versions of words. For example, the plural affix *–s* changes the singular noun *book* to the plural noun *books*, and the past tense affix *–ed* changes the present tense verb *look* to the past tense *looked.* Prefixes are affixes placed in front of words. For example, *heat* means to make hot; *preheat* means to heat in advance. Suffixes are affixes placed at the ends of words. The *happiness* example above contains the suffix *–ness.* Circumfixes add parts both before and after words, such as how *light* becomes *enlighten* with the prefix *en-* and the suffix *–en.* Interfixes create compound words via central affixes: *speed* and *meter* become *speedometer* via the interfix *–o–*.

Review Video: Affixes
Visit mometrix.com/academy and enter code: 782422

WORD ROOTS, PREFIXES, AND SUFFIXES TO HELP DETERMINE MEANINGS OF WORDS

Many English words were formed from combining multiple sources. For example, the Latin *habēre* means "to have," and the prefixes *in-* and *im-* mean a lack or prevention of something, as in *insufficient* and *imperfect.* Latin combined *in-* with *habēre* to form *inhibēre,* whose past participle was *inhibitus*. This is the origin of the English word *inhibit,* meaning to prevent from having. Hence by knowing the meanings of both the prefix and the root, one can decipher the word meaning. In Greek, the root *enkephalo-* refers to the brain. Many medical terms are based on this root, such as encephalitis and hydrocephalus. Understanding the prefix and suffix meanings (*-itis* means inflammation; *hydro-* means water) allows a person to deduce that encephalitis refers to brain inflammation and hydrocephalus refers to water (or other fluid) on the brain.

Review Video: Determining Word Meanings
Visit mometrix.com/academy and enter code: 894894

PREFIXES

While knowing prefix meanings helps ESL and beginning readers learn new words, other readers take for granted the meanings of known words. However, prefix knowledge will also benefit them for determining meanings or definitions of unfamiliar words. For example, native English speakers and readers familiar with recipes know what *preheat* means. Knowing that *pre-* means in advance can also inform them that *presume* means to assume in advance, that *prejudice* means advance judgment, and that this understanding can be applied to many other words beginning with *pre-*. Knowing that the prefix *dis-* indicates opposition informs the meanings of words like *disbar, disagree, disestablish,* and many more. Knowing *dys-* means bad, impaired, abnormal, or difficult informs *dyslogistic, dysfunctional, dysphagia,* and *dysplasia.*

SUFFIXES

In English, certain suffixes generally indicate both that a word is a noun, and that the noun represents a state of being or quality. For example, *-ness* is commonly used to change an adjective into its noun form, as with *happy* and *happiness, nice* and *niceness,* and so on. The suffix *–tion* is commonly used to transform a verb into its noun form, as with *converse* and *conversation or move* and *motion*. Thus, if readers are unfamiliar with the second form of a word, knowing the meaning of the transforming suffix can help them determine meaning.

DENOTATIVE VS. CONNOTATIVE MEANING

The **denotative** meaning of a word is the literal meaning. The **connotative** meaning goes beyond the denotative meaning to include the emotional reaction that a word may invoke. The connotative meaning often takes the denotative meaning a step further due to associations the reader makes with the denotative meaning. Readers can differentiate between the denotative and connotative meanings by first recognizing how authors use each meaning. Most non-fiction, for example, is fact-based and authors do not use flowery, figurative language. The reader can assume that the writer is using the denotative meaning of words. In fiction, the author may use the connotative meaning. Readers can determine whether the author is using the denotative or connotative meaning of a word by implementing context clues.

Review Video: Denotation and Connotation
Visit mometrix.com/academy and enter code: 310092

NUANCES OF WORD MEANING RELATIVE TO CONNOTATION, DENOTATION, DICTION, AND USAGE

A word's denotation is simply its objective dictionary definition. However, its connotation refers to the subjective associations, often emotional, that specific words evoke in listeners and readers. Two or more words can have the same dictionary meaning, but very different connotations. Writers use diction (word choice) to convey various nuances of thought and emotion by selecting synonyms for other words that best communicate the associations they want to trigger for readers. For example, a car engine is naturally greasy; in this sense, "greasy" is a neutral term. But when a person's smile, appearance, or clothing is described as "greasy," it has a negative connotation. Some words have even gained additional or different meanings over time. For example, *awful* used to be used to describe things that evoked a sense of awe. When *awful* is separated into its root word, awe, and suffix, -ful, it can be understood to mean "full of awe." However, the word is now commonly used to describe things that evoke repulsion, terror, or another intense, negative reaction.

Review Video: Word Usage
Visit mometrix.com/academy and enter code: 197863

CONTEXT CLUES

Readers of all levels will encounter words that they have either never seen or have encountered only on a limited basis. The best way to define a word in **context** is to look for nearby words that can assist in revealing the meaning of the word. For instance, unfamiliar nouns are often accompanied by examples that provide a definition. Consider the following sentence: *Dave arrived at the party in hilarious garb: a leopard-print shirt, buckskin trousers, and bright green sneakers.* If a reader was unfamiliar with the meaning of garb, he or she could read the examples (i.e., a leopard-print shirt, buckskin trousers, and high heels) and quickly determine that the word means *clothing*. Examples will not always be this obvious. Consider this sentence: *Parsley, lemon, and flowers were just a few of the items he used as garnishes.* Here, the word *garnishes* is exemplified by parsley, lemon, and flowers. Readers who have eaten in a variety of restaurants will probably be able to identify a garnish as something used to decorate a plate.

Review Video: Context
Visit mometrix.com/academy and enter code: 613660

Using Contrast in Context Clues

In addition to looking at the context of a passage, readers can use contrast to define an unfamiliar word in context. In many sentences, the author will not describe the unfamiliar word directly; instead, he or she will describe the opposite of the unfamiliar word. Thus, you are provided with some information that will bring you closer to defining the word. Consider the following example: *Despite his intelligence, Hector's low brow and bad posture made him look obtuse.* The author writes that Hector's appearance does not convey intelligence. Therefore, *obtuse* must mean unintelligent. Here is another example: *Despite the horrible weather, we were beatific about our trip to Alaska*. The word *despite* indicates that the speaker's feelings were at odds with the weather. Since the weather is described as *horrible*, then *beatific* must mean something positive.

Substitution to Find Meaning

In some cases, there will be very few contextual clues to help a reader define the meaning of an unfamiliar word. When this happens, one strategy that readers may employ is **substitution**. A good reader will brainstorm some possible synonyms for the given word, and he or she will substitute these words into the sentence. If the sentence and the surrounding passage continue to make sense, then the substitution has revealed at least some information about the unfamiliar word. Consider the sentence: *Frank's admonition rang in her ears as she climbed the mountain.* A reader unfamiliar with *admonition* might come up with some substitutions like *vow, promise, advice, complaint*, or *compliment*. All of these words make general sense of the sentence though their meanings are diverse. However, this process has suggested that an admonition is some sort of message. The substitution strategy is rarely able to pinpoint a precise definition, but this process can be effective as a last resort.

Occasionally, you will be able to define an unfamiliar word by looking at the descriptive words in the context. Consider the following sentence: *Fred dragged the recalcitrant boy kicking and screaming up the stairs.* The words *dragged, kicking*, and *screaming* all suggest that the boy does not want to go up the stairs. The reader may assume that *recalcitrant* means something like unwilling or protesting. In this example, an unfamiliar adjective was identified.

Additionally, using description to define an unfamiliar noun is a common practice compared to unfamiliar adjectives, as in this sentence: *Don's wrinkled frown and constantly shaking fist identified him as a curmudgeon of the first order*. Don is described as having a *wrinkled frown and constantly shaking fist*, suggesting that a *curmudgeon* must be a grumpy person. Contrasts do not always provide detailed information about the unfamiliar word, but they at least give the reader some clues.

Words with Multiple Meanings

When a word has more than one meaning, readers can have difficulty determining how the word is being used in a given sentence. For instance, the verb *cleave*, can mean either *join* or *separate*. When readers come upon this word, they will have to select the definition that makes the most sense. Consider the following sentence: *Hermione's knife cleaved the bread cleanly.* Since a knife cannot join bread together, the word must indicate separation. A slightly more difficult example would be the sentence: *The birds cleaved to one another as they flew from the oak tree.* Immediately, the presence of the words *to one another* should suggest that in this sentence *cleave* is being used to mean *join*. Discovering the intent of a word with multiple meanings requires the same tricks as defining an unknown word: look for contextual clues and evaluate the substituted words.

Context Clues to Help Determine Meanings of Words

If readers simply bypass unknown words, they can reach unclear conclusions about what they read. However, looking for the definition of every unfamiliar word in the dictionary can slow their reading progress. Moreover, the dictionary may list multiple definitions for a word, so readers must search the word's context for meaning. Hence context is important to new vocabulary regardless of reader methods. Four types of context clues are examples, definitions, descriptive words, and opposites. Authors may use a certain word, and then follow it with several different examples of what it describes. Sometimes authors actually supply a definition of a word they use, which is especially true in informational and technical texts. Authors may use descriptive words that elaborate upon a vocabulary word they just used. Authors may also use opposites with negation that help define meaning.

Examples and Definitions

An author may use a word and then give examples that illustrate its meaning. Consider this text: "Teachers who do not know how to use sign language can help students who are deaf or hard of hearing understand certain instructions by using gestures instead, like pointing their fingers to indicate which direction to look or go; holding up a hand, palm outward, to indicate stopping; holding the hands flat, palms up, curling a finger toward oneself in a beckoning motion to indicate 'come here'; or curling all fingers toward oneself repeatedly to indicate 'come on', 'more', or 'continue.'" The author of this text has used the word "gestures" and then followed it with examples, so a reader unfamiliar with the word could deduce from the examples that "gestures" means "hand motions." Readers can find examples by looking for signal words "for example," "for instance," "like," "such as," and "e.g.."

While readers sometimes have to look for definitions of unfamiliar words in a dictionary or do some work to determine a word's meaning from its surrounding context, at other times an author may make it easier for readers by defining certain words. For example, an author may write, "The company did not have sufficient capital, that is, available money, to continue operations." The author defined "capital" as "available money," and heralded the definition with the phrase "that is." Another way that authors supply word definitions is with appositives. Rather than being introduced by a signal phrase like "that is," "namely," or "meaning," an appositive comes after the vocabulary word it defines and is enclosed within two commas. For example, an author may write, "The Indians introduced the Pilgrims to pemmican, cakes they made of lean meat dried and mixed with fat, which proved greatly beneficial to keep settlers from starving while trapping." In this example, the appositive phrase following "pemmican" and preceding "which" defines the word "pemmican."

Descriptions

When readers encounter a word they do not recognize in a text, the author may expand on that word to illustrate it better. While the author may do this to make the prose more picturesque and vivid, the reader can also take advantage of this description to provide context clues to the meaning of the unfamiliar word. For example, an author may write, "The man sitting next to me on the airplane was obese. His shirt stretched across his vast expanse of flesh, strained almost to bursting."

The descriptive second sentence elaborates on and helps to define the previous sentence's word "obese" to mean extremely fat. A reader unfamiliar with the word "repugnant" can decipher its meaning through an author's accompanying description: "The way the child grimaced and shuddered as he swallowed the medicine showed that its taste was particularly repugnant."

Opposites

Text authors sometimes introduce a contrasting or opposing idea before or after a concept they present. They may do this to emphasize or heighten the idea they present by contrasting it with something that is the reverse. However, readers can also use these context clues to understand familiar words. For example, an author may write, "Our conversation was not cheery. We sat and talked very solemnly about his experience and a number of similar events." The reader who is not familiar with the word "solemnly" can deduce by the author's preceding use of "not cheery" that "solemn" means the opposite of cheery or happy, so it must mean serious or sad. Or if someone writes, "Don't condemn his entire project because you couldn't find anything good to say about it," readers unfamiliar with "condemn" can understand from the sentence structure that it means the opposite of saying anything good, so it must mean reject, dismiss, or disapprove. "Entire" adds another context clue, meaning total or complete rejection.

Syntax to Determine Part of Speech and Meanings of Words

Syntax refers to sentence structure and word order. Suppose that a reader encounters an unfamiliar word when reading a text. To illustrate, consider an invented word like "splunch." If this word is used in a sentence like "Please splunch that ball to me," the reader can assume from syntactic context that "splunch" is a verb. We would not use a noun, adjective, adverb, or preposition with the object "that ball," and the prepositional phrase "to me" further indicates "splunch" represents an action. However, in the sentence, "Please hand that splunch to me," the reader can assume that "splunch" is a noun. Demonstrative adjectives like "that" modify nouns. Also, we hand someone some*thing*—a thing being a noun; we do not hand someone a verb, adjective, or adverb. Some sentences contain further clues. For example, from the sentence, "The princess wore the glittering splunch on her head," the reader can deduce that it is a crown, tiara, or something similar from the syntactic context, without knowing the word.

Syntax to Indicate Different Meanings of Similar Sentences

The syntax, or structure, of a sentence affords grammatical cues that aid readers in comprehending the meanings of words, phrases, and sentences in the texts that they read. Seemingly minor differences in how the words or phrases in a sentence are ordered can make major differences in meaning. For example, two sentences can use exactly the same words but have different meanings based on the word order:

- "The man with a broken arm sat in a chair.
- "The man sat in a chair with a broken arm."

While both sentences indicate that a man sat in a chair, differing syntax indicates whether the man's or chair's arm was broken.

Determining Meaning of Phrases and Paragraphs

Like unknown words, the meanings of phrases, paragraphs, and entire works can also be difficult to discern. Each of these can be better understood with added context. However, for larger groups of words, more context is needed. Unclear phrases are similar to unclear words, and the same methods can be used to understand their meaning. However, it is also important to consider how the individual words in the phrase work together. Paragraphs are a bit more complicated. Just as words must be compared to other words in a sentence, paragraphs must be compared to other paragraphs in a composition or a section.

Determining Meaning in Various Types of Compositions

To understand the meaning of an entire composition, the type of composition must be considered. Expository writing is generally organized so that each paragraph focuses on explaining one idea, or part of an idea, and its relevance. Persuasive writing uses paragraphs for different purposes to organize the parts of the argument. Unclear paragraphs must be read in the context of the paragraphs around them for their meaning to be fully understood. The meaning of full texts can also be unclear at times. The purpose of composition is also important for understanding the meaning of a text. To quickly understand the broad meaning of a text, look to the introductory and concluding paragraphs. Fictional texts are different. Some fictional works have implicit meanings, but some do not. The target audience must be considered for understanding texts that do have an implicit meaning, as most children's fiction will clearly state any lessons or morals. For other fiction, the application of literary theories and criticism may be helpful for understanding the text.

Additional Resources for Determining Word Meaning and Usage

While these strategies are useful for determining the meaning of unknown words and phrases, sometimes additional resources are needed to properly use the terms in different contexts. Some words have multiple definitions, and some words are inappropriate in particular contexts or modes of writing. The following tools are helpful for understanding all meanings and proper uses for words and phrases.

- **Dictionaries** provide the meaning of a multitude of words in a language. Many dictionaries include additional information about each word, such as its etymology, its synonyms, or variations of the word.
- **Glossaries** are similar to dictionaries, as they provide the meanings of a variety of terms. However, while dictionaries typically feature an extensive list of words and comprise an entire publication, glossaries are often included at the end of a text and only include terms and definitions that are relevant to the text they follow.
- **Spell Checkers** are used to detect spelling errors in typed text. Some spell checkers may also detect the misuse of plural or singular nouns, verb tenses, or capitalization. While spell checkers are a helpful tool, they are not always reliable or attuned to the author's intent, so it is important to review the spell checker's suggestions before accepting them.
- **Style Manuals** are guidelines on the preferred punctuation, format, and grammar usage according to different fields or organizations. For example, the Associated Press Stylebook is a style guide often used for media writing. The guidelines within a style guide are not always applicable across different contexts and usages, as the guidelines often cover grammatical or formatting situations that are not objectively correct or incorrect.

STAAR Practice Test #1

Questions 1 – 12 pertain to the following passage:

Mammie

(1) Characters:

ANTHONY – The young husband

MANDIE – The young wife

MAMMIE – Anthony's mother

(2) Setting:

Mammie's kitchen; the appliances are old, and a farmhouse table dominates the small room.

(3) The scene opens with Mandie clinging to Anthony. They are alone in the kitchen.

(4) MANDIE: Please don't leave me here with... her. She doesn't like me.

(5) ANTHONY: Of course she likes you. Don't be silly. Why wouldn't she like you?

(6) MANDIE: Oh, I don't know. She just doesn't. You don't know how she can be.

(7) ANTHONY: Don't I? I only lived with her for the first twenty years of my life.

(8) MANDIE: (pleading) Anthony, you can't go. Just take me with you. We can come back for dinner, just like you promised Mammie.

(9) ANTHONY: (taking Mandie firmly by the shoulders) No, Mandie. You're here, and you're staying. I'll only be gone for an hour or two. I promise to be back for dinner.

(10) MANDIE: But, Anthony—

(11) ANTHONY: Shush! She'll hear you—Mammie!

(12) Mammie enters, straightening her apron. She looks Mandie up and down. Anthony moves to kiss Mammie's cheek and Mandie reluctantly does the same.

(13) MAMMIE: Hello, Anthony. Hello, Amanda.

(14) ANTHONY: Well, Mammie, I'm afraid it's hello and goodbye for me. I'm off to my meeting. (He kisses Mandie.) You two girls have fun. I'll be back for dinner.

(15) Anthony exits. Mandie and Mammie look at each other for several seconds. The silence becomes uncomfortable. Finally, Mammie turns her back on Mandie and begins preparing dinner. She takes pots, pans, and ingredients out of the cupboards.

(16) MANDIE: (clearing her throat) So, um, what are you making for dinner?

(17) MAMMIE: (without turning around) Baked chicken. Rice. Asparagus.

(18) MANDIE: Oh. (Pauses) Could I help with something?

(19) Mammie wordlessly takes out a large pot and a bag of rice. She hands the items to Mandie and turns back to her work.

(20) MAMMIE: You can make the rice.

(21) Mandie stands very still, holding the rice and the pot. She bites her lip. She looks very frightened. Finally, Mammie turns around to face Mandie.

(22) MAMMIE: Well, child? What is it?

(23) MANDIE: (looking at the floor) I-I don't know how to make rice.

(24) MAMMIE: Don't know how to make rice? Don't be silly. Everyone knows how to make rice.

(25) MANDIE: (starting to cry) Everyone... except... me!

(26) Mammie sighs and wipes her hands on her apron. She comes over and takes the pot and the rice away from Mandie. She sets them on the table and gently chucks Mandie under the chin.

(27) MAMMIE: Come, child. It's nothing to cry over. Hush now. What can you cook?

(28) MANDIE: (sniffling) I can make brownies, I guess.

(29) MAMMIE: Good. (Patting Mandie awkwardly on the shoulder) Get to work, then.

(30) Mandie starts opening cupboard doors and pulling out ingredients. Mammie hands her a mixing bowl and measuring cups.

(31) MANDIE: Thank you.

(32) They work in silence for a while. After Mammie puts the chicken in the oven and puts the rice on to cook, she turns and watches Mandie work. Her face softens.

(33) MAMMIE: I suppose it's just as well, you know. Anthony always did like brownies better than rice. (She smiles and sits at the table.) I remember that when he was little, he always used to stick his finger into the middle brownie as soon as I took the pan from the oven. He always burned himself something terrible, but he couldn't let anyone else have that soft, gooey center brownie.

(34) MANDIE: (giggling) He still does that.

(35) MAMMIE: (shocked) No! A big, grown man like Anthony?

(36) MANDIE: Every time I make a batch of brownies.

(37) Mandie pours the batter into a brownie pan. Mammie watches her intently.

(38) MAMMIE: (motioning to the chair beside her) Come, child. Have a seat. Tell me more about my Anthony.

(39) Mandie sits and they chat for a while. Anthony reenters and looks surprised to see them sitting together.

(40) ANTHONY: (kissing Mandie) Hello, ladies. Something smells good. (He looks around.) And is that a pan of brownies waiting to go into the oven?

(41) MANDIE: Yes, Anthony. Now, go make yourself comfortable in the living room. We'll call you for dinner.

(42) ANTHONY: (bewildered) Well, okay… I guess. Are you sure you don't want me to stay in here?

(43) MANDIE: I'm sure. We have work to do. Now, go on.

(44) Anthony leaves, shaking his head and muttering to himself.

(45) MAMMIE: Besides, we can't talk about him when he's here!

(46) They both laugh and move to finish the dinner preparations, chatting amiably.

1. Which of the following is the best definition of the word "dominates" as it is used in paragraph 2?

a. Diminishes
b. Takes over
c. Destroys
d. Bosses around

2. How would you describe Mandie's feelings at the beginning of the play in relation to being left alone with Mammie?

a. Desperate
b. Excited
c. Depressed
d. Contented

3. Which paragraph best depicts Anthony's dismissive attitude toward Mandie's concerns?

a. Paragraph 2
b. Paragraph 3
c. Paragraph 5
d. Paragraph 7

4. Based on the information presented in the play, who is Mammie to Anthony?

a. His aunt
b. His grandmother
c. His cousin
d. His mother

5. How does the use of action and silence in this play contribute to the development of Mammie's character?

a. It does not contribute to the development of Mammie's character
b. It shows she is a poor communicator
c. It demonstrates the awkwardness of her relationship with Mandie
d. It shows her love for Anthony

6. Which paragraph best demonstrates Mammie's critical tendencies?

a. Paragraph 17
b. Paragraph 20
c. Paragraph 22
d. Paragraph 24

7. Which paragraph best indicates Mandie's feelings about Mammie?

a. Paragraph 3
b. Paragraph 4
c. Paragraph 8
d. Paragraph 10

8. What experience do Mandie and Mammie have in common that opens the door for them to bond with each other?

a. Anthony hates both of their cooking
b. Their rice always ends up overdone
c. Anthony sticks his finger into both their brownie batches
d. They both know how to bake brownies

9. What is the author's main purpose in writing this play?

a. To show that shared experiences provide relational connections
b. To emphasize the importance of getting along as a family
c. To highlight the detriments of familial disharmony
d. To exhibit a "slice of life" view of everyday Americana

10. Which of the following is a minor detail in this play?

a. Mammie is Mandie's mother-in-law
b. Mandie is afraid of Mammie
c. Anthony is leaving Mandie alone with Mammie for a while
d. The kitchen is small and cramped

11. Which of the following is an opinion, rather than a summary of this play?

a. This play examines the dynamics between a young wife and her mother-in-law
b. This play is a powerful, poignant look at the importance of communication
c. This play shows how common experiences can help build relationships
d. This play offers a look at the relationships of a man, his mother, and his wife

12. Which word in paragraph 43 best illustrates the newfound camaraderie between Mandie and Mammie?

a. We
b. Sure
c. Go
d. Work

SHORT ANSWER QUESTION #1:

How does the relationship between Mandie and Mammie change over the course of this encounter? Support your answer with evidence from the text.

Questions 13 – 24 pertain to the following passage:

Vegetarian Victory

(1) I remember the day I came home and told my mom I was planning on becoming a vegetarian. It was the summer before my junior year of high school, and Mom just nodded and smiled knowingly. She assumed it was another phase, like my short-lived hot pink mohawk, or the now-passé pegged jeans. But it wasn't a phase. For the past decade, I have lived a vegetarian lifestyle because it is healthy, wallet-friendly, and environmentally wise.

(2) Most people are familiar with at least some of the health benefits of a vegetarian lifestyle. But many people also believe that sacrificing meat means sacrificing taste. Not true. I can easily get my required 50 grams of protein each day through beans, nuts, and seeds in dishes that are bursting with beautiful tastes. I use herbs and spices to make my food fun and flavorful. Best of all, by using plants to provide protein and punch in my diet I forego much of the fat and cholesterol that is so prevalent in animal products.

(3) By foregoing that fat and cholesterol, I also protect myself from a variety of common diseases and health conditions. Studies have shown, for example, that a vegetarian lifestyle reduces the risk of a variety of cancers and can even lower the incidence of Alzheimer's disease. In addition, a vegetarian lifestyle has been shown to improve digestion, lower blood pressure and cholesterol levels, and protect against type II diabetes. In essence, I consider vegetables my super-weapon in the war against weariness!

(4) While the vegetarian lifestyle is clearly beneficial to my health, it also boosts my finances. Many people believe vegetarian foods—including fresh fruits and vegetables and alternative protein sources like soy—are just too expensive. To a certain extent, that may be true. But while the foods I eat may cost more than processed, packaged junk, my reward is fewer trips to the doctor and dentist. With the reduced incidence of disease comes a reduced need for treatments and medications. In the long run, the savings on medical costs more than makes up for the price of healthy food.

(5) The cost savings do not end with medical costs, however. I also save the money I used to spend on fast food and vending machines. My first two years of high school, I was a junk-food junkie. If you could get it at the drive-through or from a machine, I ate it. But after a while, all that junk made a sizeable dent in my wallet. When I became

a vegetarian, I noticed that my cravings began to change. It didn't happen overnight, but over time I no longer craved the oily, greasy, and fatty food that drained my energy and my savings account. In fact, those types of foods actually started to make me sick. Now, I walk with a granola bar or tin of almonds in my pocket for convenient snacking. I'm saving my money and my health, all at once.

(6) Not only does my vegetarian lifestyle save my money and my health, it also helps save the environment. By choosing plant proteins over animal products, I am saving the lives of countless animals in my lifetime. I don't have to lie awake at night wondering about slaughterhouse horrors or inhumane living conditions. Whether or not all the stories of such things are true, I don't obsess about contributing to that industry anymore. More animals, raised more naturally, create a better prospect and future for our world.

(7) Many people do not realize that the livestock industry—run primarily for food consumption—is one of the largest contributors of greenhouse gases in our environment. Thousands of cattle milling about in dusty feed lots, long treks from farm to marketplace in large trucks, and other factors add up to a huge environmental impact. By choosing a vegetarian lifestyle, I reduce the demand for this industry, thereby reducing their level of production and both their carbon footprint and mine. My personal choice might not change the world, but I can do my best to change my corner of the community.

(8) Becoming a vegetarian is a very personal choice. I chose this lifestyle because it benefits my overall health and protects me from certain disease processes. I also chose this lifestyle because it benefits my finances by reducing my expenditures for health care and junk food. Finally, I chose this lifestyle because it benefits the environment, reducing the demands on the livestock industry and shrinking my carbon footprint. I know this choice works for me, but I never pressure my friends to become vegetarians. I tell them my story with pride, but I understand they must make the choice for themselves, and vegetarianism is not for everyone. Still, I never know when I might inspire someone else to have a vegetarian victory—just like mine!

13. Which of the following words is the best synonym for "passé" as it is used in paragraph 1?

a. Outdated
b. Fashionable
c. Foolish
d. Memorable

14. What are the three key benefits of a vegetarian lifestyle listed in this article?

a. Health benefits, social benefits, environmental benefits
b. Social benefits, financial benefits, environmental benefits
c. Health benefits, financial benefits, social benefits
d. Health benefits, financial benefits, environmental benefits

15. How long does the article say the author has been living a vegetarian lifestyle?

a. 5 years
b. 10 years
c. 15 years
d. The article does not give this information

16. What does the author compare the vegetarian lifestyle to in paragraph 3?

a. A cancer
b. A war
c. A disease
d. A weapon

17. What point of view was used to write this article?

a. First person
b. Second person
c. Third person
d. All of the above

18. Which of the following best describes the author's perspective in this article?

a. The vegetarian lifestyle is the only way to go
b. The vegetarian lifestyle doesn't work for most people
c. The vegetarian lifestyle offers many benefits
d. The vegetarian lifestyle is best lived short-term

19. According to the article, how many grams of protein does the author need each day?

a. 35
b. 45
c. 50
d. 10

20. What does paragraph 1 mean when it says, "Mom just nodded and smiled knowingly"?

a. Mom was, by nature, a very wise, happy person
b. Mom thought vegetarianism was just another phase
c. Mom was a vegetarian and was happy her child was too
d. Mom wasn't really listening because she was distracted

21. Which of the following is a controlling idea in this article?

a. Beans, nuts, and seeds can provide protein
b. The vegetarian lifestyle can improve finances
c. The vegetarian lifestyle can reduce cholesterol
d. Some slaughterhouses have inhumane conditions

22. Which of the following is an opinion about this article, rather than a summary?

a. This article clearly outlines the benefits of a vegetarian lifestyle
b. This article contains a lot of information about vegetarianism
c. This article uses opinions to guilt people into vegetarianism
d. This article urges people to consider a vegetarian lifestyle

23. Which of the following represents the author's main objective in writing this article?

a. To open readers' eyes to the benefits of vegetarianism
b. To force people to adopt a vegetarian lifestyle
c. To clearly demonstrate the evils of eating animal products
d. To illustrate the environmental impact of the livestock industry

24. Which paragraph best encapsulates the main ideas and purpose of this entire article?

a. Paragraph 1
b. Paragraph 3
c. Paragraph 7
d. Paragraph 8

Questions 25 – 29 pertain to the following short story:

Puck

(1) It was the second week of an unseasonably cool July. The sun had finally made a rare weekend appearance, and the suburban neighborhood sizzled with possibility. As the day slipped lazily into evening, sun-baked residents trickled back to their homes from the lakeshore and the park and the community pool. The air smelled of sunscreen, charcoal smoke, sweat, overcooked meat.

(2) Will Jensen tossed a football across the yard to his best friend, Troy Coons. Dusk was settling around them, but the thought of retreating to the confines of the house seemed sacrilegious.

(3) "Can you believe we're going to college in a few weeks?" Troy asked, lobbing the ball back to Will.

(4) "What I can't believe is that you and I will be six hundred miles apart," Will said, catching the ball easily. "I don't think we've gone more than three days without seeing each other since kindergarten."

(5) "Except for when you had chicken pox," Troy said. "And the time I went to Hawaii with my grandparents. Remember how we begged them to let you come in my luggage?"

(6) Will laughed and tossed the ball back. "Those things don't count," he argued.

(7) The ball went sideways and Troy lunged for it, tripping over a ragged little terrier lounging lazily on the lawn. Troy collapsed in a tangled heap and the ball bounced down, just beyond his outstretched hand.

(8) "Puck!" Troy groaned. "No dogs on the field!"

(9) Will sauntered over and scooped up the little dog. He plopped down onto the crisp brown grass and laughed at Troy. Will reached over and rolled the ball toward Troy.

(10) "Don't blame Puck for your clumsiness," Will said, idly scratching the dog's fuzzy scalp. "How was he supposed to know you'd come stumbling through his daydreams?"

(11) Troy chuckled. Then they sat in silence as darkness swirled around them. Light glowed from windows thrown hopefully open to the faint breeze. Above them, the stars winked on in the charcoal sky. In the distance, leftover fireworks crackled and fizzed. The night was ripe with memories to be made.

(12) "Are you taking Puck with you?" Troy finally asked, breaking the silence.

(13) "Nah. No dogs in the dorm. Besides, Puck would hate being locked up in a room. He's spent the last sixteen years being king of the castle. He'll be happier here. That way he can greet me whenever I make it back home."

(14) Will lifted Puck and held him in mid-air. Puck wriggled playfully and licked Will's nose with his doughy pink tongue. Will laughed and set him down.

(15) "I sure will miss him, though," Will said, wiping Puck's saliva from his nose. "Puck's been a part of every memory I've had since I was really little."

(16) Troy faked a sniffle. "Stop, man. Just stop. I'm tearing up over here."

(17) Will punched Troy's arm good-naturedly. "Shut up!"

(18) A low, loud car careened around the corner, shattering the stupor of the summer night. Puck ran barking toward the car as it wove across the street like a wayward pinball.

(19) Seized with sudden panic, Will scrambled to his feet. "Puck, no! Come back!"

(20) As Will reached the sidewalk, Puck darted into the street. In a terrible, slow-motion montage, Will heard the tires squeal and Puck's bark turn to a startled yelp. Then the car sped away, and silence smothered the chaos.

(21) Will ran into the street. People peeked from doorways and windows, searching for the source of the commotion. Will fell beside Puck's limp body. Puck whimpered quietly and struggled to lick Will's hand. Then he was still.

(22) "No, Puck! No!" Will screamed. Shock rang in his ears and he was dizzy with emotion. Troy put a hand on Will's shoulder, but Will shook it off. He didn't want to be comforted. He wanted to wallow and writhe in the pool of pain that was slowly spreading through his soul.

(23) Every memory he had with Puck flooded his mind. This was not how it was supposed to be. Puck was supposed to be waiting for him when he came home from college. He was supposed to watch at the window as Will drove away and be there wagging with excitement whenever Will came home. He was supposed to be the constant in Will's changing life. This was not part of the plan.

(24) Will stayed in the road for a long time, crouched over Puck's familiar, lifeless body. He felt numb, empty, and emotionless. Finally, Will's mother led him gently from the street. Troy and Will's father gathered Puck's body carefully into a sheet. Neighbors watched in sympathy as the sorrowful party crossed the lawn.

(25) They walked in silence as darkness swirled around them. Lights still glowed from windows thrown hopefully open to the faint breeze. Above them, stars still winked on in the charcoal sky. In the distance, leftover fireworks still crackled and fizzed. Everything was the same, and nothing was the same. Puck was gone. And Will knew things would never really be the same again.

25. In paragraph 2, what does "sacrilegious" mean?

a. Absurdly inappropriate
b. Nasty and evil
c. A waste of time
d. Holy and good

26. Which of the following best describes Will's attitude in paragraph 15?

a. Angry
b. Cheerful
c. Sentimental
d. Annoyed

27. What type of figurative language is used to describe the stars in paragraph 11?

a. Simile
b. Personification
c. Metaphor
d. Paradox

28. How is Puck's death an example of irony?

a. Will was worried about missing Puck while Will was away at college, and now he will miss him forever
b. Will wanted Puck to die so Will didn't have to think about him while he was away at college
c. Puck was always quiet and docile, but he was strangely driven to run after that one car
d. Troy hated Puck, and he wanted Puck to be hit by the passing car

29. Which of the following is a main idea in this story?

a. The passing car is playing loud music
b. Troy misses the ball when he trips over Puck
c. Will and Troy like to play football
d. Will has had Puck for a very long time

Questions 30 – 34 pertain to the following short story:

What I Will Always Remember

(1) I will always remember my grandfather, wiry and strong, hoisting me onto his shoulders as he showed me around the rail yard where he worked. His shock of shiny black hair glistened in the sunlight, flanked by silvery sideburns. High atop his shoulder, I owned the world. Everyone looked up to me, but I looked up to him. We played together like wayward children. He was larger than life, and I was proud he was my grandfather.

(2) I will always remember my grandfather, tainted with the first pangs of age, standing and proudly applauding at my high school graduation. He was grayer and weaker, but still robust. We stood eye to eye, but I still looked up to him. I craved his wisdom, his patience, his guidance. We talked together like two best pals. He was still larger than life, and I was proud he was my grandfather.

(3) I will always remember my grandfather, wrapped in the first throes of Parkinson's disease, watching me receive my college degree. He was paler and thinner and too weak to stand, but he applauded boisterously when my name was called. I towered above his wheelchair, but I still looked up to him. I needed his support, his affirmation, his

companionship. We sat together like two old friends. He was still larger than life, and I was proud he was my grandfather.

(4) I will always remember my grandfather, lost in the last weeks of his life, sitting quietly with me on the front porch. His skin was translucent with the pallor of death, and his body was wracked by endless tremors. I fed him with a syringe, gently coaxing the food down his throat. He was shrunken and powerless, but I still looked up to him. We clung to our memories together like two sailors lost at sea. He was still larger than life, and I was proud he was my grandfather.

(5) Today I remembered my grandfather, cocooned in his flag-draped coffin as they lowered him into the ground. He was surrounded by those he had impacted in life. Today we honored a soldier, a worker, a teacher, a friend. We honored a husband, a father, a mentor, a guide. He was strong, even in weakness. He was wise, even in silence. He gave me everything, even when he had nothing to give, and I looked up to him. He will always be larger than life to me, and I will always be proud he was my grandfather.

30. In paragraph 4, what does "pallor" mean?

a. Brightness
b. Paleness
c. Jaundice
d. Darkness

31. How would you properly classify this piece of writing?

a. Informational essay
b. Fiction
c. Persuasive essay
d. Memoir

32. What is the author's main purpose in writing this piece?

a. To honor and say goodbye to Grandfather
b. To illustrate the ravages of age
c. To show the effects of Parkinson's disease
d. To chronicle Grandfather's life

33. What technique is used throughout this piece to increase its power and impact?

a. Plotting
b. Dialogue
c. Repetition
d. Citation

34. In paragraph 4, what image best illustrates Grandfather's powerlessness?

a. Sitting quietly on the porch
b. Being wracked with tremors
c. Being fed with a syringe
d. Having translucent skin

Questions 35 – 38 pertain to both short stories "Puck" and "What I Will Always Remember":

35. What theme do these two passages have most in common?

a. Loss of a loved one
b. The silence of summer
c. Companionship
d. Grandparents and friends

36. What is the difference in point of view between these two stories?

a. There is no difference in point of view between these two stories
b. One is written in third person and the other is written in first person
c. One is written in second person and the other is written in third person
d. One is written in first person and the other is written in second person

37. Why does the expression of grief seem more vivid in "Puck" than it does in "What I Will Always Remember"?

a. It does not seem more vivid in "Puck"
b. Will seems younger than the narrator in the other piece
c. The grief in "Puck" is more sudden and described in greater detail
d. Losing an animal is more painful than losing a grandparent

38. What is the primary similarity between paragraph 23 of "Puck" and paragraph 5 of "What I Will Always Remember"?

a. They both have seven sentences
b. They both express reminiscence in the face of loss
c. They are both centered on excessive emotion
d. They are both near the end of the piece

SHORT ANSWER QUESTION #2:

How are the feelings of grief and loss similar in these two stories? How are they different? Support you answer with examples from both texts.

Writing Test

Composition Prompt #1 – Literary Composition

Imagine you are stranded in an airport in an unfamiliar foreign country. What country are you in? What do you see? What do you hear? Who do you meet? Write a literary composition telling about your experience in detail.

Composition Prompt #2 – Expository Composition

Discuss the role of achievement in motivation for success. Do achievements motivate people to further success in the future? Or do achievements cause people to rest on their laurels? Explain your answer thoroughly.

Questions 39 – 48 pertain to the following short story:

The Saga of "Sparky"

(1) Sparky was a loser, but he didn't stay that way. (2) You probably know Sparky better by his given name: Charles Schulz. (3) Nicknamed Sparky when he was a child, Charles schulz endured years of struggle before he finally found success. (4) Eventually, the loser became a winner. (5) Thanks to the hard work and perseverance of Sparky, the world will always remember a boy named Charlie Brown and the rest of the Peanuts gang.

(6) Sparky was born Charles Monroe Schulz on November 26, 1922, and he grew up in Minneapolis, Minnesota, where he struggled to fit in socially. (7) He skipped two grades, and as a result he struggled with his studies. (8) He was also painfully shy, so he never dated. (9) In addition, Sparky was inert at most sports. (10) But he loved to draw, drawing was his dream.

(11) Sparky poured his heart and soul into his drawings during his high school years. (12) He had a particular love for cartooning, and he unsuccessfully submitted several cartoons to his yearbook. (13) In the late 1940s, when Sparky was in his mid-twenties, his dream began to come true. (14) Although he was devastated when the cartoons were rejected by the yearbook committee, he remained determined to make a living through his art someday. (15) He sold some cartoons to magazines and newspapers. (16) Someone finally appriciated his artistic ability.

(17) In 1950, Sparky created what would become his legacy; a comic called Peanuts. (18) The central character—Charlie Brown—was based on Sparky himself and his lifelong struggle to fit in with the world around him. (19) Peanuts became an instant hit. (20) Adults and children alike were drawn to it because they could relate to the struggles of the characters.

(21) From its humble beginnings in the 1950s, Peanuts went on to become one of the most successful comics of all time. (22) Sparky lovingly hand-drew each of the 18,000 Peanuts comic strips, and they eventually appointed in over 2000 newspapers in more than 75 countries. (23) The Peanuts characters have appeared in comic strips, television specials, coloring books, children's books, and a variety of other media. (24) Although Sparky died in 2000, his work lives on. (25) His comics are still seen in dozens of newspapers each week. (26) Through hard work, perseverance, and believing in himself, Sparky turned his loser's lot into a story of success.

39. Which of the following is the most appropriate correction for sentence 3?

a. Change Sparky to sparky
b. Change Nicknamed to Nick-named
c. Remove the comma after child
d. Change Charles schulz to Charles Schulz

40. Which sentence in paragraph 1 functions as the thesis statement for this composition?

a. Sentence 2
b. Sentence 5
c. Sentence 3
d. Sentence 1

41. In sentence 9, what change is necessary?

a. Change inert to inept
b. Remove the comma after addition
c. Change Sparky to sparky
d. Change most to many

42. What change, if any, should be made in sentence 10?

a. No change is necessary
b. Remove the comma
c. Replace the comma with a semicolon
d. Replace the comma with a colon

43. What change would most improve the organization of the third paragraph of this composition?

a. Swap sentences 13 and 14
b. Move sentence 13 to the beginning of the paragraph
c. Swap sentences 11 and 16
d. Move sentence 12 to the end of the paragraph

44. What change, if any, should be made in sentence 16?

a. No change is necessary
b. Change finally to finaly
c. Change appriciated to appreciated
d. Change artistic to autistic

45. What change, if any, is needed in sentence 17?

a. No change is necessary
b. Replace the semicolon with a colon
c. Replace the semicolon with a period
d. Remove the semicolon

46. What punctuation change, if any, should be made in sentence 18?

a. No change is necessary
b. Remove the dashes
c. Replace the second dash with a comma
d. Replace the first dash with a colon

47. How does sentence 21 function as a transition between paragraph 4 and paragraph 5?

a. Sentence 21 does not function as a transition
b. It talks about a topic previously mentioned
c. It demonstrates transition with the phrase "went on"
d. It connects the history of Peanuts with the success of Sparky

48. In sentence 22, what word would be most appropriate to replace the misused word "appointed"?

a. Approximated
b. Appeared
c. Appropriated
d. Appositioned

Questions 49 – 58 pertain to the following essay:

The Very Best Season

(1) Ice cream cones shrink and drip in the stiffling heat. (2) Cool pools shimmer like a welcoming oasis. (3) The blazing sun hangs lazily for hours in the breathtakingly blue sky. (4) It's summer, and the whole world seems more content. (5) Summer is the very best season for three main reasons.

(6) First, Summer is the best season because school is out and the days are long and lazy. (7) Without structure and schedule, the nights were late and the afternoons roll on forever. (8) There is no homework, no pressure, and no deadlines. (9) There is no blaring alarm clock, just the endless cadence of birds and sprinklers and kids playing in the streets. (10) Everything feels more simpler and more relaxed.

(11) That sense of relaxation brings the second reason summer is the best season: the pace of life is slower. (12) No one seems to be in a hurry. (13) It is the season of hamocks and vacations and sandy seashores. (14) It is a time when the whole hectic, hurried world seems to pause and take a deep, cleansing breath. (15) The endless days and hazy nights seem to add to the pleasant stupor. (16) All is calm, and all is bright.

(17) Despite the universal sense of relaxation summer is also the best season because there is so much to do. (18) Warm, dry weather lends itself perfectly to outdoor activities: camping in the cool, quiet woods; swimming in a crystal-clear stream; sunning on an emerald carpet of fragrant grass. (19) It is also the season of fairs, festivals, and farmers' markets. (20) There is never a shortage of fun.

(21) While every season of the year has its own unique charms, summer will always be the best season to me. (22) The long, lazy, school-free days are loved by me. (23) I love the slower, more relaxed pace of life. (24) Finally, I love the many fun activities that can fill the empty hours. (25) All of these things—and many more—make summer the very best season.

49. What change, if any, needs to be made in sentence 1?

a. No change is necessary
b. Change stiffling to stifling
c. Change cream to Cream
d. Insert a comma after shrink

50. Which sentence functions as the thesis statement for this essay?

a. Sentence 1
b. Sentence 4
c. Sentence 5
d. Sentence 10

51. In sentence 6, what correction, if any, is necessary?

a. No correction is necessary
b. Remove the comma after first
c. Insert a comma after season
d. Change Summer to summer

52. Which of the following is the best version of sentence 7?

a. Without structure and schedule, the nights are late and the afternoons roll on forever
b. Without structure and schedule, the nights are late and the afternoons rolled on forever
c. Without structure and schedule, the nights were late and the afternoons rolled on forever
d. The sentence is correct as it is written.

53. What correction, if any, is needed in sentence 10?

a. No correction is needed.
b. Change more simpler to simpler
c. Change feels to felt
d. Insert a comma after simpler

54. What change, if any, is needed in sentence 11?

a. No change is needed
b. Replace the colon with a semicolon
c. Replace the colon with a comma
d. Remove the colon

55. In sentence 13, what spelling error needs to be corrected?

a. Change season to session
b. Change hamocks to hammocks
c. Change seashores to seeshores
d. There is no spelling error in sentence 13

56. What change, if any, should be made in sentence 17?

a. No change is necessary.
b. Insert a comma after season
c. Insert a comma after Despite
d. Insert a comma after relaxation

57. What is the error in sentence 22?

a. It is a sentence fragment
b. It is a run-on sentence
c. It has passive construction
d. It has parallel structure

58. What correction, if any, needs to be made in sentence 25?

a. No correction is necessary
b. Remove the dashes
c. Replace the first dash with a colon
d. Replace the second dash with a comma

Questions 59 – 68 pertain to the following short story:

Volunteer Fisherman

(1) As a new volunteer at the youth center, I was expected to help out with activities, like the upcoming fishing field trip. (2) When the director asked me to come along, I excepted right away. (3) I had never been fishing, but it looked easy enough on TV. (4) You just tossed a line into the water and waited for a fish to bite. (5) How hard could that be? (6) It ended up being much harder than I expected.

(7) Upon arrival at the Turner Family Trout Farm, I was assigned three rambunctious Kindergartners as my charges for the day. (8) They were tense with excited energy and frequently ran off in various directions. (9) Keeping them together while herding them toward the equipment shed took every ounce of my focus and every shred of my patience. (10) Finally, we found ourselves in line for poles and bait.

(11) Once we had collected our poles and bait, we marched our way to an empty spot on the rocky banks of a green-black pond. (12) I ordered the boys to line up so that I could bait their hooks. (13) When the first one thrust his read plastic cup full of soil and writhing nightcrawlers into my face, I almost gagged. (14) I looked away and plunged my fingers into the dirt, closing them on the first worm I could find. (15) I pulled him from the dirt and held him up triumphantly. (16) The boys clapped and cheered. (17) Success!

(18) I soon learned pulling the worm from the plastic cup was among the easiest parts of fishing. (19) The hook would not penetrate his tough skin. (20) Baiting the hook posed a whole new set of challenges. (21) The worm curled its slimy ridges eagerly around my dirty fingers. (22) I poked through my finger three times before I finally got the worm onto the hook. (23) I breathed a sigh of relief before I realized, I had two more hooks to bait.

(24) Finally, with all the hooks baited, I tried casting the first rod. (25) The hook plopped into the water about two feet out—not the 30-foot cast I had envisioned—and to my horror, the worm floated away. (26) I baited the hook again in discouraged disgust and finally got all the lines cast about five feet out. (27) My fishing wouldn't win any awards, but my kindergarden protégés were happy, and that was good enough for me.

(28) After nearly an hour of our fishing adventure had passed, we had three trout awkwardly dangling from our stringer. (29) The boys were thrilled, and I was exhausted. (30) Between baiting hooks, reeling in catches, and keeping the boys from falling into the pond, my energy was spent. (31) But when the whistle blew to load the bus for the trip home, I felt strangely saddened. (32) Despite the headaches and harrowing challenges, I was proud of all I had accomplished that day. (33) And I knew the next time they needed a volunteer fisherman, myself would be the first to sign up!

59. Which of the following is the most appropriate correction for sentence 2?

a. No correction is needed
b. Change along to alone
c. Change excepted to accepted
d. Change right to write

60. Which sentence functions as the thesis statement for this piece?

a. Sentence 1
b. Sentence 6
c. Sentence 7
d. Sentence 10

61. What is the proper correction for the capitalization error in sentence 7?

a. Change Farm to farm
b. Change Trout to trout
c. Change Kindergartners to kindergartners
d. There is no capitalization error in sentence 7

62. What correction, if any, needs to be made in sentence 13?

a. No correction is needed
b. Change writhing to rising
c. Change thrust to thirst
d. Change read to red

63. Where should sentence 19 be placed to improve the organization of this essay?

a. Before sentence 18
b. Right where it is
c. After sentence 20
d. After sentence 21

64. What change, if any, is necessary in sentence 22?

a. No change is necessary
b. Change through to threw
c. Change three to 3
d. Change onto to into

65. How can sentence 23 be corrected?

a. Sentence 23 is correct as it is written.
b. Remove the comma
c. Replace the comma with a semicolon
d. Replace the comma with a dash

66. What spelling correction, if any, is appropriate in sentence 27?

a. No spelling correction is needed
b. Change kindergarden to kindergarten
c. Change protégés to protoges
d. Change enough to enuogh

67. What change, if any, needs to be made in sentence 28?

a. No change is needed.
b. Change had passed to have passed
c. Change had three to have three
d. Change dangling to dangled

68. What type of error is present in sentence 33?

a. There is no error in sentence 33.
b. There is a comma splice
c. There is a verb form error
d. There is a misused reflexive pronoun

Answer Key and Explanations

TEKS Standard §110.31(b)(1)(A)

1. B: In Paragraph 2, "dominates" means "takes over." The author is using the word to show how much of the small room is taken up by the large table.

TEKS Standard §110.31(b)(5) and (4) and Figure: 19 TAC §110.30(b)(110.31)

2. A: "Desperate" is the best choice because to describe Mandie's feelings in the beginning of the play about being left alone with Mammie. She is clinging to her husband and begging him not to leave her alone with his mother.

TEKS Standard §110.31(b)(5) and (4) and Figure: 19 TAC §110.30(b)(110.31)

3. C: Paragraph 5 clearly shows Anthony's dismissive attitude when he calls Mandie "silly."

TEKS Standard §110.31(b)(5) and (4) and Figure: 19 TAC §110.30(b)(110.31)

4. D: The "Characters" section of this play (Paragraph 1) describes Mammie as Anthony's mother.

TEKS Standard §110.31(b)(5) and (4) and Figure: 19 TAC §110.30(b)(110.31)

5. C: Silence and action contribute to the development of Mammie's character by showing how awkwardly she relates to Mandie.

TEKS Standard §110.31(b)(5) and (4) and Figure: 19 TAC §110.30(b)(110.31)

6. D: Paragraph 24 clearly shows Mammie's critical tendencies in the way she responds to Mandie's ignorance, when she tells her to stop being silly, because everyone knows how to cook rice.

TEKS Standard §110.31(b)(5) and (4) and Figure: 19 TAC §110.30(b)(110.31)

7. B: Paragraph 4 shows Mandie's feelings about Mammie when she says, "She doesn't like me."

TEKS Standard §110.31(b)(5) and (4) and Figure: 19 TAC §110.30(b)(110.31)

8. C: Mandie's relationship with Mammie begins to improve when Mammie tells Mandy that when Anthony was growing up, he loved to stick his finger into the middle brownie after she baked them, and Mandy replies by laughing about the fact that he still does it.

TEKS Standard §110.31(b)(5) and (4) and Figure: 19 TAC §110.30(b)(110.31)

9. A: is The most important lesson of this short play is that people can get along with each other better when they share common interests or experiences.

TEKS Standard §110.31(b)(5) and (4) and Figure: 19 TAC §110.30(b)(110.31)

10. D: The fact that the kitchen is small and cramped doesn't have much of a bearing on the story at all, but the other three answer choices represent important points in the play.

TEKS Standard §110.31(b)(5) and (4) and (9)(A)

11. B is the correct answer because it is an expression of a person's view of the play, using the words "powerful" and "poignant," making it an opinion. A summary gives a factual description of a play, while an opinion is one person's unique take on it.

TEKS Standard §110.31(b)(5) and (4) and Figure: 19 TAC §110.30(b)(110.31)

12. A: When Mandie says "*we* have work to do", it illustrates the newfound camaraderie between herself and Mammie.

Sample Short Answer #1:

In the beginning of this play, the relationship between Mammie and Mandie is clearly tense. This is best demonstrated in paragraph 4, when Mandie says, "She doesn't like me." It is also shown in the stage directions in paragraph 12, where the play states Mandie "reluctantly" kisses Mammie, and in paragraph 15, when Mammie "turns her back on Mandie."

In contrast, their relationship at the end of the play shows a sense of camaraderie. They have bonded over the common link of Anthony. This is best shown in paragraph 38 when Mammie invites Mandie to have a seat with her and talk about Anthony. It is also shown in paragraph 43, when Mandie shoos Anthony from the kitchen and refers to herself and Mammie as "we."

TEKS Standard §110.31(b)(1)(A)

13. A: The word "passé" means "outdated."

TEKS Standard §110.31(b)(10) and Figure: 19 TAC §110.30(b)(110.31)

14. D: The three key benefits discussed in this article are health benefits, financial benefits, and environmental benefits.

TEKS Standard §110.31(b)(10) and Figure: 19 TAC §110.30(b)(110.31)

15. B: Paragraph 1 indicates that the author has been a vegetarian for a decade, which is 10 years.

TEKS Standard §110.31(b)(10) and Figure: 19 TAC §110.30(b)(110.31)

16. D: In paragraph 3, the vegetarian lifestyle is compared to a weapon.

TEKS Standard §110.31(b)(10) and Figure: 19 TAC §110.30(b)(110.31)

17. A: This article is written in first-person point of view.

TEKS Standard §110.31(b)(10)

18. C: The author's perspective is that being a vegetarian offers many benefits, but we know she doesn't feel that "it's the only way to go", because she says that she never pressures her friends to become vegetarians.

TEKS Standard §110.31(b)(10) and Figure: 19 TAC §110.30(b)(110.31)(B)

19. C: Paragraph 2 indicates that the author needs 50 grams of protein each day.

TEKS Standard §110.31(b)(10) and Figure: 19 TAC §110.30(b)(110.31)(B)

20. B: In Paragraph 1, when the author says, "Mom just nodded and smiled knowingly" , she follows it up in the next sentence by stating that her mother was assuming that vegetarianism was just going to another of the author's many phases.

TEKS Standard §110.31(b)(10) and Figure: 19 TAC §110.30(b)(110.31)(B)

21. B: A controlling idea is an idea that represents one of the main points the author is making. One of her main points is that being a vegetarian improves one's finances. She makes the other points, too, but they are subordinate to her overall main points.

TEKS Standard §110.31(b)(10) and (9)(A)

22. C is the only answer choice that is a personal opinion of this article, rather than a fact-based description of it.

TEKS Standard §110.31(b)(10)

23. A best represents the author's main objective in this article, which is to show people the benefits of vegetarianism that they may not be aware of. She is certainly not trying to force anyone to become a vegetarian. She does discuss the ill effects of factory farms and eating meat on animals and the environment, but they are minor points, not her main one.

TEKS Standard §110.31(b)(10)

24. D: Paragraph 8 best encapsulates both the main ideas and purpose of the article. As it's the final paragraph in the piece, this should come as no surprise, because many authors of short articles such as this one will use their final paragraph to recap and summarize the whole.

TEKS Standard §110.31(b)(1)(A)

25. A: is the best choice because the best definition of "sacrilegious" as it appears in paragraph 2 is "absurdly inappropriate." This is not the literal meaning of "sacreligious", which means "not showing proper respect to something holy." The author is using the word figuratively, to say that going inside would be a complete waste of the nice weather, and completely out of place because of all the activity that had taken place outdoors that day.

TEKS Standard §110.31(b)(5) and Figure: 19 TAC §110.30(b)(110.31)

26. C: Will's attitude in Paragraph 15 is best described as sentimental, because he's expressing strong emotions.

TEKS Standard §110.31(b)(7)

27. B: Personification is used to describe the stars in Paragraph 11, when the author says the stars "winked." Winking is something that human beings do, and personification is attributing a human trait or actions to something that isn't human.

TEKS Standard §110.31(b)(7)(A)

28. A best illustrates how Puck's death is an example of irony, which is when something happens in a way that's the opposite of what one would expect.

TEKS Standard §110.31(b)(5) and Figure: 19 TAC §110.30(b)(110.31)

29. D is the only option that is a main idea in this story. The other three answer selections are all supporting ideas, not main ideas in the story.

TEKS Standard §110.31(b)(1)(A)

30. B: "Pallor" means "paleness."

TEKS Standard §110.31(b)(6)

31. D: This essay is best classified as a memoir, or a personal recollection by a writer.

TEKS Standard §110.31(b)(6) and Figure: 19 TAC §110.30(b)(110.31)

32. A: The main purpose of this piece is to honor and say goodbye to Grandfather. The other answer choices represent aspects of the piece, but none of them are the main reason the author had in mind for writing this.

TEKS Standard §110.31(b)(6) and Figure: 19 TAC §110.30(b)(110.31)

33. C: The author uses repetition in this piece to increase its power and impact. Every paragraph but the last begins with the phrase "I will always remember my grandfather", which is followed by a snapshot of what he was like at that point in his life.

TEKS Standard §110.31(b)(6) and Figure: 19 TAC §110.30(b)(110.31)

34. C: Being fed with a syringe is the image that most strongly illustrates Grandfather's powerlessness, because being unable to feed one's self is a state of extreme weakness. The other answer choices represent age-related problems, but not powerlessness.

TEKS Standard §110.31(b)(2)(A) and Figure: 19 TAC §110.30(b)(110.31)

35. A: The common theme that most unites these passages is loss of a loved one. This is not to imply that the loss of a dog is equivalent to the loss of a grandparent, but only that both pieces are about deeply felt personal loss.

TEKS Standard Figure: 19 TAC §110.30(b)(110.31)

36. B: The first piece is written in third-person point of view and the second is in first-person point of view.

TEKS Standard Figure: 19 TAC §110.30(b)(110.31)

37. C: The reason the grief in "Puck" seems more vivid is because it comes as a sudden shock, whereas in the other piece, the grandfather's decline takes place over years, and is the natural process most people will experience as they age.

TEKS Standard Figure: 19 TAC §110.30(b)(110.31)

38. B: Both paragraphs express reminiscence in the face of loss.

Sample Short Answer #2:

We see grief and loss in the emotional pain of both stories. This is especially evident in paragraph 24 of "Puck" when Will stays crouched over Puck's lifeless body. In "What I Will Always Remember," it is shown in paragraph 4 when the narrator says, "We clung to our memories together like two sailors lost at sea." Both instances demonstrate a desire to hold onto the past in the face of a grief-filled future.

On the other hand, the narrator of "What I Will Always Remember" seems more pragmatic, prepared for, and disconnected from Grandfather's death. In "Puck," Will's reaction to Puck's death is much more visceral, as evidenced by his screaming and the description of his physical grief reaction in paragraph 22.

Sample Composition #1 – Literary Composition:

Alone, But Not Lonely

My flight was delayed—again. The next plane wasn't scheduled to leave until morning. That meant I had to spend the night in the airport. Already the shopkeepers were dropping gates across their darkened shops. With every clanking gate, the airport emptied further. It was a far cry from the typical, 24-hour bustle of the busy airport at home.

Down some unseen hallway, a baby cried. A man's voice echoed sharply in a distant corridor. Subdued reggae music drifted faintly through the nearly-empty terminal from the only shop that remained open. It was a combination coffee shop and magazine stand, and a young man with thick dreadlocks lounged behind the counter, sipping a coffee and browsing through a magazine.

Across the terminal from where I sat, a scruffy-looking custodian pushed a wide broom over the waxy floor. He whistled a chaotic counterpoint to the reggae. Every so often, he burst into song for a few notes, and then returned to his whistling. I studied his tufted hair and grizzled beard. His clothes hung from his narrow body like a scarecrow, and he danced through his work with a smile.

As he neared the coffee shop/magazine stand, the custodian called out to the young man behind the counter. They chatted for a few moments and then motioned toward me, continuing to talk and laugh. I was suddenly vividly aware of the emptiness of the terminal. I was alone, a young girl far from home, and I was afraid. When the young man with dreadlocks started across the terminal toward me, I considered running, but I was frozen to my seat with fatigue and fear.

"You not from here, I see," he said, taking a seat beside me. His voice had the unmistakable island lilt, and his smile seemed warm. "Look here—you don' hafta sit here by youself. Come on in my shop."

"I don't have any money left," I admitted.

"No problem, mon," he said, standing and pulling me to my feet. He grabbed my carry-on and slung it over his shoulder. "I make you a coffee and we jus' talk. It will make di time go fasta."

It did make the time go faster. Damian—that was his name—and I talked for hours and became good friends. That night, in a strange, faraway place, Damian taught me about reaching out without fear. Most of all, he taught me that being alone didn't mean I had to be lonely. Friends are waiting for me wherever I choose to make them.

Sample Composition #2 – Expository Composition:

Achievements: Springboards to Success

I can still vividly remember the moment I won my first speech competition. With the announcement of my name and the thundering applause came a trickle of disbelief followed by a flood of personal pride. That achievement became the first of many, a springboard to a new hobby and a career path. Achievements are important motivators for future success because they build confidence, fuel desire, and encourage dreaming.

Achievements contribute to future success by building confidence. Before I won that speech competition, I thought I could never speak in front of people or present information in public. After the contest, I had a new belief in myself and my abilities. Life's constant barrage of small setbacks can sap our strength and our belief in ourselves. The simple knowledge that we can succeed at something fills us with an assurance that future success is possible. Each achievement serves as the foundation for the next, creating a positive pyramid of possibilities for the future.

In addition to building confidence, achievement fuels desire. After I won that speech competition, I wanted to win more. I wanted to succeed at the regional and national levels. I wanted to see how far I could go. When we achieve goals, we tend to desire bigger and better things. Each accomplishment in life fuels our desires and gives the hope and drive necessary to achieve future success. Achievements are like food for the soul, nourishing our desires and spurring us on to further greatness.

While achievements build confidence and fuel desires, they also encourage dreaming. From the success of the speech competition, I dreamed of speaking to large crowds, of a career as a teacher or speaker or professor. I dreamed that I could even be president, speaking my mind to the world. The confidence and desire established by achievement give wings to our hopes and free our minds to dream. Achievement gives us new ideas and expands our horizons. We can dream with abandon of all that is possible in the future and all we might someday accomplish. Dreaming is the first blueprint for life's grandest future castles of success.

Achievements are the springboards for success. I am proud of all I've done since that speech competition, developing my skills and doing things I never thought possible. It is all thanks to the power of achievements. They build our confidence, allowing us to believe in ourselves. They fuel our desires, allowing us to yearn for future accomplishment. Lastly, they encourage our dreaming, allowing us to envision the vast possibilities that the future holds. Achievements give us permission to be our best, opening doors to success and all that life can hold.

TEKS Standard §110.31(b)(18)(A)

39. D: Charles schulz should be changed to Charles Schulz.

TEKS Standard §110.31(b)(15)(A)(iii)

40. B: Sentence 5 functions as the thesis statement for this composition. It briefly tells the reader what he'll learn in the piece, in much more depth. It reveals the author's main points.

TEKS Standard §110.31(b)(13)(C)

41. A: Changing "inert" to "inept" corrects the meaning of sentence, because inert is not the correct word choice here. It means motionless, unable to move, barely moving, etc., while "inept" means unskilled. It's much more likely that the author meant to say that Charles Schulz was unskilled at sports, rather than saying that he just stood motionless while engaged in athletic endeavors.

TEKS Standard § 110.31(b)(13)(D) and (18)(B)

42. C: Sentence 10 is a comma splice with two independent clauses, which is incorrect. Two independent clauses should be joined by a semicolon, not a comma.

TEKS Standard §110.31(b)(13)

43. A: Swapping sentences 13 and 14 will improve the organization and flow of paragraph 3, because they are out of chronological order as written. This is jarring and confusing to the reader.

TEKS Standard §110.31(b)(13)(D) and (19)

44. C: The word "appreciated" is a misspelling; the correct spelling is "appreciated."

TEKS Standard §110.31(b)(13)(D) and (18)(B)

45. B: A colon is the correct punctuation in sentence 17, not a semicolon.

TEKS Standard §110.31(b)(18)(B)

46. A: Sentence 18 is correct as written.

TEKS Standard §110.31(b)(15)(A)(ii)

47. D: The author has been talking about Sparky's struggles to succeed, and the history of the Peanuts strip, and in the final paragraph he demonstrates just how successful Sparky became, all thanks to the popularity of Peanuts. Sentence 21 serves as a transitional sentence between these two aspects of the article.

TEKS Standard §110.31(b)(13)(C)

48. B: The word "appeared" is the correct word to replace the misused word "appointed."

TEKS Standard §110.31(b)(13)(D) and (19)

49. B: The word "stiffling" is a misspelling; it should be "stifling. "

TEKS Standard §110.31(b)(16)(A)

50. C: Sentence 5 functions as the thesis statement for this essay. It's a brief summation of what the author intends to demonstrate in the entire article. Demonstrating that summer is the best season by giving three reasons is the author's main purpose in writing this piece.

TEKS Standard §110.31(b)(18)(A)

51. D: In normal usage, the names of the seasons should not be capitalized, so "Summer" should be "summer."

TEKS Standard §110.31(b)(13)(D) and (17)(A)(i)

52. A is correct because both verbs are now in the present tense. As written, the first verb in the sentence, "were" is in past tense, while the second verb, "roll", is in present tense. This is unacceptable. The article is written using the present tense for every other verb, so both verbs in this sentence should also be in present tense.

TEKS Standard §110.31(b)(17)

53. B: The word "simpler" is the correct comparative form of "simple." The phrase "more simple" would also be acceptable here, in order to match the construction of "more relaxed", but "more simpler" is never acceptable.

TEKS Standard §110.31(b)(17)

54. A: No change is necessary; sentence 11 is correct as written.

TEKS Standard §110.31(b)(13)(D) and (19)

55. B: The word "hamocks" is a misspelling; it should be "hammocks."

TEKS Standard §110.31(b)(18)(B)(ii)

56. D: A comma should follow the word "relaxation" in order to separate the introductory phrase from the main clause of the sentence.

TEKS Standard §110.31(b)(17)(A)(i)

57. C: Sentence 22 is written with passive construction, which is very awkward sounding. It should be written in the active voice: "I love the long, lazy, school-free days."

TEKS Standard §110.31(b)(18)(B)

58. A: Sentence 25 is correct as written.

TEKS Standard §110.31(b)(13)(C)

59. C: The word "accepted" is the proper word to use in this sentence. The author has either badly misspelled it, or has misunderstood the meaning of "excepted", which means "not included."

TEKS Standard §110.31(b)(15)(A)(iii)

60. B: Sentence 6 functions as the thesis statement in the essay. When the author begins her adventure, she assumes it will be very easy, but by the end of her day, she has learned that helping out on a fishing field trip was much more difficult than she had anticipated. That is the main point, or thesis, of this short essay.

TEKS Standard §110.31(b)(18)(A)

61. C: The word "kindergartners" should not be capitalized.

TEKS Standard §110.31(b)(13)(C)

62. C: In sentence 13, changing "read" to "red" is correct. The word "read" is a verb meaning "having looked at and understood"; "red" is a color.

TEKS Standard §110.31(b)(13)

63. D: The proper position for sentence 19 is after sentence 21. As written, the sentences in this paragraph are not in proper order, which is confusing for readers.

TEKS Standard §110.31(b)(13) and (17)

64. A: Sentence 22 is correct as written.

TEKS Standard §110.31(b)(18)(B)

65. B: The comma in sentence 23 is unnecessary.

TEKS Standard §110.31(b)(13)(D) and (19)

66. B: The word "kindergarden" is a misspelling; it should be "kindergarten."

TEKS Standard §110.31(b)(13) and (17)

67. A: Sentence 28 is correct as it is written.

TEKS Standard §110.31(b)(17)(A)

68. D: The reflexive pronoun "myself" is misused in sentence 33. It should be replace with "I."

STAAR Practice Test #2

Questions 1 -5 pertain to the following passage:

Caged

(1) I am caged.

(2) Dim, dark, dank,

(3) Depressing metal bars

(4) Are my home,

(5) My window on the world.

(6) But for one hour each day—

(7) Sixty precious, priceless minutes—

(8) I am led from the dungeon

(9) Into the bright, blinding light.

(10) That is my sanctuary,

(11) Wrapped in chain link

(12) And barbed wire.

(13) The air is sweeter,

(14) Tinged with freedom

(15) And fragranced with memories

(16) Of a lifetime so long ago

(17) It has almost been forgotten.

(18) I bathe in the welcome warmth,

(19) Cleanse my soul in the newborn breeze.

(20) I confess my sins

(21) In the brazen light of day,

(22) And hope springs eternal once again.

(23) But then they come.

(24) My time is up.

(25) Another hour of life has expired.

(26) And I return to the depths

(27) Of despair, discouragement, defeat.

(28) Freedom, forgiveness, and faith are forgotten.

(29) I am caged.

1. What is the connotation of the word "dungeon" in line 8?

a. The narrator lives in the basement of a castle
b. This poem is set in medieval times
c. The narrator's life is dark and unrelenting
d. The narrator is uncomfortable with life

2. What is the setting for this poem?

a. A prison
b. A farm
c. A house
d. A school

3. Which literary device is used throughout this poem to underscore the repetitive nature of the narrator's life?

a. Simile
b. Paradox
c. Onomatopoeia
d. Alliteration

4. What point of view is used in this poem?

a. First person
b. Second person
c. Third person
d. All of the above

5. What do lines 18-22 reference?

a. The narrator's love of sunny days
b. The narrator's desire for a fresh start
c. The narrator's anger at the circumstances
d. The narrator's memories of a normal life

Questions 6 – 10 pertain to the following short story:

Freedom Run

(1) The rattle of the key fumbling in the lock sent a shudder down her spine. He was home. Megan gulped down her emotions and fixed her face into a plastic smile. With a sigh, she clicked off the late show. The door swung open, and he stumbled inside.

(2) "There'sh my little Meggie-May," he crooned, slurring his words into one jumbled strand. "Howsh it goin'? What you up to tonight, little one?"

(3) He staggered toward her, arms outstretched. She stood, numb and motionless, like an observer in an overplayed scene. The same dialogue. The same motions. Rehearsed every night for some unscheduled performance. It was familiar. Too familiar.

(4) He tripped on a chair leg as he passed the dining table. The pleasant face instantly darkened as the shadow of impending rage fell. He swore loudly and turned on Megan.

(5) Why don't you clean up this pigsty," he yelled, the words clearer, colder, chilling.

(6) In two long strides, he crossed to where she still stood, rooted to the floor. She had learned long ago that backing away only prolonged the misery. His hand fell heavy across her cheek.

(7) "Lazy, good-for-nothing child," he screamed. He swore again, throwing her into the wall. "Ungrateful!"

(8) She no longer cringed as the blows landed. When he knocked her to the ground, she instinctively curled around herself, forming a tight little ball of misery. His feet crashed clumsily into her body, and she waited for it to end. In a while, it would be over. It never lasted forever.

(9) When the blows stopped, Megan struggled to her feet. She could taste the tang of blood on her split lip. She could feel the swelling in her eye. She watched him watching her. Then his face crumpled into a broken sob. He pulled her to his chest and stroked her hair.

(10) "I'm so sorry, Meggie-May. I don't mean to hurt you, darling." He sobbed louder. "Please forgive me, my little Meggie-May. I just get so mad sometimes. I won't do it again. Promise."

(11) Megan held him awkwardly, half-heartedly patting his back. "I know, Daddy," she murmured, her voice hollow. "It's okay."

(12) She led him gently to the couch and helped him sit. He clicked on the late show and settled into a subdued stupor. Megan crept upstairs and washed her battered face. She changed into a clean t-shirt and shorts and went back to the living room.

(13) "I'm going running," she announced, grabbing her house key from the table.

(14) He nodded silently. Then he glanced up. "Do me a favor before you go, Meggie-May?"

(15) "What do you need, Daddy?" she asked, knowing what he would ask for.

(16) "Bring me a beer, darling," he said with a wink.

(17) She brought him a frosty can, drowning in condensation. He took it and thanked her. Then he was lost in the eerie glow of the TV again, and Megan slipped out into the night.

(18) The cool summer breeze assaulted her senses, clearing the fog of pain and fear and anger and guilt. Her feet pattered, then pounded, then pummeled the pavement. She left the crumbling brownstone—and her crumbling life—far behind.

(19) She ran with the wind in her face and reality at her back. Running was freedom. Her aching, throbbing body loosened. Tears stung her eyes, and she submitted to the solace of sorrow. The empty streets embraced her. This was her escape.

(20) She ran for miles, past tall tenements that stretched concrete fingers toward the moon. She ran across a rust-speckled bridge, glancing down at the silent, slumbering, still depths of the river below. Across the river, larger houses sprawled on the banks. A few windows still glowed, but most were blank with darkness.

(21) It was time to go home. She knew it, even as every fiber of her body resisted. Winding her way back through silent neighborhoods, she pushed her body harder, gasping for air and aching for rest. As the streets grew darker and narrower, reality began to close again around her heart. The freedom and release gave way to fear, and she climbed the brownstone's dirty steps.

(22) Inside, the air was stale and thick. Megan's eyes adjusted to the glare of the TV, and she saw him, sprawled on the couch. She picked up the empty beer can that dangled from his limp fingers and took it to the kitchen. When she came back, she pulled a blanket loosely over him. He stirred in his sleep, nestling into the blanket. His eyes opened halfway.

(23) "Night, Meggie-May," he murmured, turning over to face the couch.

(24) Megan turned off the TV and started up the stairs. Halfway up, she stopped and looked down. Shadows danced across his features. He looked peaceful, helpless, deceptively harmless. She loved him and hated him in one tangled surge of emotion.

(25) "Goodnight, Daddy," she whispered to the darkness. Then she turned and went upstairs.

6. What do the misspelled words in paragraph 2 indicate?

a. The author's ignorance
b. The unusual dialect
c. A misprint in the text
d. The father's intoxication

7. Which of the following paragraphs clearly indicates that the physical abuse by Megan's father is a common occurrence?

a. Paragraph 6
b. Paragraph 7
c. Paragraph 9
d. Paragraph 10

8. Why is this story set late at night in dark settings?

a. People generally drink more at night
b. Running at night is safer
c. It illustrates the darkness of Megan's life
d. The setting is coincidental

9. Why does paragraph 21 say "every fiber of her body resisted" going home?

a. She enjoyed running and wanted to run more
b. Running was a freedom from her troubled life
c. She was afraid her father might be asleep
d. The route back home was mostly uphill

10. Which paragraph best describes Megan's feelings toward her father?

a. Paragraph 11
b. Paragraph 18
c. Paragraph 21
d. Paragraph 24

Questions 11 – 14 pertain to both "Caged" and "Freedom Run":

11. What symbol of depression and trouble is used in both of these pieces?

a. Metal bars
b. Physical abuse
c. Darkness
d. Dungeons

12. What strong desire do Megan and the narrator of "Caged" have in common?

a. Strength
b. Freedom
c. Light
d. Companionship

13. Which of the following emotions best describes the state of mind of Megan and the narrator of "Caged" at the end of the passages?

a. Hopelessness
b. Confidence
c. Joy
d. Anger

14. Which of the following is the key difference between Megan and the narrator of "Caged"?

a. Megan is a female; the narrator is a male
b. Megan is young; the narrator is old
c. Megan is hopeless; the narrator is hopeful
d. Megan is a victim; the narrator is a product of choices

Short Answer Question #1

What point of view is used in these passages? How does the point of view affect the power and meaning of each of these passages? Support your answer from the texts.

Questions 15 – 26 pertain to the following story:

The Top Five Reasons Video Games Are Good for Your Health

(1) Too many people think video games are just time-wasters. They say video games are for weak-minded imbeciles. They insist that no good can come from this electronic entertainment. In contrast to these common theories, I believe video games offer

numerous benefits. Let me share with you the top five reasons that video games are good for your health.

(2) First, video games improve overall coordination. Response times are quicker, attention is more focused, and awareness is heightened. When I play video games, I find myself focused and intent on my mission. Since I began playing video games, my coordination—particularly my hand-eye coordination—has improved immensely. The results are obvious in many areas of my life, from cooking to driving to sports. Even my handwriting has improved! The advent of motion sensor systems (such as Nintendo's Wii, Microsoft's Xbox 360 Kinect, and Sony's PlayStation 3 Move) has further enhanced users' coordination and reaction times.

(3) In addition to improving coordination and reaction times, many games also enhance logic and reasoning abilities. Most games employ some sort of strategy, whether in sporting competitions, driving pursuits, fantasy quests, or military battles. Winning a game—even just playing a game—requires a plan and the ability to adjust that plan and adapt to changing conditions. The ability to use logic and reason to solve problems leads to the ability to think on your feet. These are all important life skills, making video games beneficial for personal development.

(4) Sometimes, however, you are not concerned about developing new skills—you just want to have fun. Video games are a great way to fill empty hours productively. They focus mental energies and allow unbridled relaxation. They entertain small children and keep older ones out of trouble. Finally, video games allow safe and fun experimentation in a variety of environments, with a plethora of tools, at a relatively low cost.

(5) Beyond creating skills and filling the hours with fun, video games also create a sense of passion and excitement. They encourage goal setting and persistence. They develop a healthy spirit of competition. When you play a game often, you develop a deep desire to accomplish a little more or go a little further each time you play. This breeds excitement, anticipation, and a constant hope for success. Setting incremental goals and working passionately toward those goals leads to achievement in video games and in life.

(6) Finally, the skills and attitudes gained playing video games often open the door for development of deep social bonds. There is a unique camaraderie among those who play games together, almost as if they were teammates. These bonds tend to be strongest when a common game is played or when individuals are members of an online community. Even without these commonalities, however, the shared universe of video games provides the foundation for social interaction, conversation, and friendship.

(7) Are video games without pitfalls? Certainly not. But many games offer life-improving benefits that are often overlooked. They improve coordination and response time. They enhance logic and reasoning. They fill empty hours productively and create a sense of passion and excitement. Lastly, video games foster a variety of social bonds among players of all types, skill levels, and backgrounds. With so many positive aspects, video games are worth checking out. Try them—you might find you like them!

15. Which of the following is the best synonym for the word "imbecile" as it is used in paragraph 1?

a. Expert
b. Student
c. Fool
d. Child

16. Which of the following is not listed in this article as a primary benefit of video games?

a. They develop coordination
b. They enhance literacy
c. They create a sense of passion
d. They build social connections

17. What does the word "plethora" mean in paragraph 4?

a. A wide variety
b. A whole lot
c. Positive and negative
d. A few

18. What genre best describes this article?

a. Fiction
b. Memoir
c. Informational
d. Persuasive

19. Which paragraph presents personal examples to help illustrate the main idea of the paragraph?

a. Paragraph 1
b. Paragraph 2
c. Paragraph 5
d. Paragraph 6

20. What is the greatest weakness of the argument in this article?

a. It is poorly written
b. It is too brief
c. It is illogical
d. It offers no facts or statistics

21. What is the main idea of paragraph 4?

a. Video games fill empty hours with fun
b. Video games create a sense of passion
c. Video games help develop new skills
d. Video games develop social bonds

22. What does the author say has further enhanced users' coordination and reaction times?

a. More complex games
b. More complex controllers
c. Motion sensor systems
d. Increased game variety

23. What is the overall theme of this article?

a. Video games offer their users a number of benefits
b. Video games are powerful social tools
c. Many people think video games are time-wasters
d. Video games are not without pitfalls

24. Which of the following is a critique rather than a summary of this article?

a. This article takes a look at the benefits of video games
b. This piece identifies five positive effects of video games
c. With a sarcastic tone, this article ineffectively champions video games
d. Through opinion and experience, the author discusses video games

25. What is the most likely reason the author chose to list coordination development as the first benefit in this article?

a. It was the first benefit the author thought of
b. The author felt it would be the most persuasive thought
c. The benefits are listed in alphabetical order
d. There is no reason the author put that benefit first

26. Which of the following best summarizes paragraph 7?

a. Video games are good for everyone
b. Video games have a number of pitfalls
c. Social bonds are one of the greatest benefits of video games
d. Despite the pitfalls, video games are worth trying

Questions 27 – 38 pertain to the following story:

Hurricane

(1) The gentle winds that had toyed with the summer leaves were angrier by afternoon, going from playful to punishing. The cotton-ball clouds gathered into a slate-colored blanket, giving the world a dim, bluish cast. Hot, humid air hung heavily on branches and rooftops and hillsides. Breathing was a task; walking was a chore.

(2) Despite the impending storm, the little city center was alive with frantic bustle. Store shelves were cleared. Propane tanks were emptied in an army of cylinders. Cars were top-heavy with plywood and corrugated zinc. Restaurants and shops boarded their windows and locked their doors. The hurricane would roll in by nightfall, and no one wanted to be caught unprepared.

(3) Overlooking a deep gully two miles out of town, a little blue concrete house perched on a hilltop. Activity swirled around the house with the strengthening wind and gathering dusk. The house had seen many hurricanes in its long years on the hill, but none as broad and strong as this one was forecast to be.

(4) "Careful nuh, Adrian," Mimi called to her older brother. "Mi nah want yu fi fall."

(5) Adrian grinned down at her. He swung his lithe, lanky body across the rooftop, pausing to add another nail to the rickety zinc.

(6) "Mi nah gwine fall, Mimi," he promised. "Mi holding to dis yah roof like a likkle lizard."

(7) Mimi laughed and hurried back inside. Mama had dinner on the stove and she was busy stuffing the cracks around the kitchen window with old towels and scraps of cloth. The wooden slat windows around the house were all cranked shut, making the rooms dark and stale. In the front room and bedroom, Fitzroy moved beds and chairs away from the closed windows. The little boys had gone for water from the spring. Each member of the family knew exactly what to do.

(8) Mimi stirred the stewed beef and red peas bubbling on the old gas stove. Then she went to help Fitzroy. When the boys came back with the water and Adrian came down from the roof, they gathered for dinner. Plates of steaming beans and rice nearly covered the small, splintered tabletop. In the center, the flame of the kerosene lamp flickered and danced, casting unstable shadows around the room. From the shelf in the corner, a battery-powered radio squawked the latest news: the leading edge of the storm had already hit the southeastern tip of the island.

(9) An hour later, when the dishes were done and the zinc began to lift and shudder, the radio station was knocked off the air. A steady rain was falling, drumming evenly on the roof. Curious, Fitzroy opened the front door a crack and peered out. In the moonless night, the coconut palms were barely visible, bobbing and weaving like ghostly shadows in the brutal winds.

(10) "Fitzroy, shut di door, mon! Yu crazy?" Adrian pulled Fitzroy away from the door and shut it securely.

(11) They lounged on the beds and in chairs around the big room, reading or drawing or daydreaming in the dim light. The little boys played dominoes on the floor. The drumming of rain became a steady thunder and then a deafening roar. Wind slammed into the house, tearing at the straining roof panels and driving rain through the nail holes and window cracks. Each time a new leak appeared, they rearranged the furniture in a feeble attempt to keep things dry.

(12) Late in the night, Mama herded them to their beds and blew out the lamp. The boys piled noisily into the beds in their room. Mimi and Mama settled into the big bed in the front room. Inside, the house was silent, restful; but outside, the storm howled and raged like a petulant child, furiously flinging debris at the little blue house. Mimi was sure she could not and would not sleep. But she must have fallen asleep in spite of her fears, because she was awakened in the wee morning hours by the startling splash of water pelting her cheeks.

(13) Mimi sat up, groggy and disoriented. Mama was gone. Mimi could hear her in the bedroom, rousing the older boys to help move the big bed away from a gaping hole in the roof. Mimi slipped from bed and began pulling off the soggy blankets. The rain was lighter now, and the wind was just a whisper. A few beams of wayward moonlight drifted through the open roof. Mama came back with the big boys and lit the lamp.

(14) Adrian was dressed. He helped move the bed, then opened the front door. The air was thick and nearly still. Adrian disappeared into the darkness. Minutes later, he reappeared in the empty space above them. When he grinned, his teeth gleamed in the lamplight.

(15) "Be careful nuh, Adrian," Mama warned. "It mus' be slick up der. Hurry with di work before di storm starts up again."

(16) Adrian nodded and disappeared again. A new piece of zinc crashed down over the hole, and Adrian pounded a handful of nails into the crosspieces.

(17) "Di storm not over, Mama?" Mimi asked. "It seems so nice an' calm."

(18) "Only di first half over," Mama explained. "Di second half will start soon. An' dat one der is mos' times di stronger part."

(19) Mimi shuddered and swallowed hard as her heart sank. She wished for daylight, for sunshine, for real calm. She wished the second half of the storm could pass them by. She hated the darkness, the wind, the rain, the fear. She hated the uncertainty and the waiting. She hated the hurricane.

(20) Mimi sat stiffly in a cane-back chair as Adrian finished the roof. When he was done, he came back in, wet and weary. The boys went back to bed and Mama stood beside Mimi.

(21) "Yu best come back to bed," Mama said gently, placing her hand on Mimi's shoulder. "Di eye of di storm won't last long. We mus' rest while we can."

(22) Mama blew out the lamp and plunged the room back into darkness. She led Mimi reluctantly back to the big bed. They settled into the fresh, dry blankets. Moments later, Mama was sleeping, her light, wheezing snore coming regularly through the ebony silence. Mimi resisted sleep. Her eyelids were heavy, but her mind was buzzing with fear. What if the whole roof came off? What if the hillside beneath them slid into the gully, carrying the little blue house with it? What if the royal palms behind the house fell on them? What if . . .?

(23) The fear remained unfinished as sleep claimed her. And as her psyche submitted to slumber, the winds began to whip around the little house once more.

27. What is the connotation of the metaphor "cotton-ball clouds" in paragraph 1?

a. Small and round
b. Thin and stringy
c. White and fluffy
d. Fuzzy around the edges

28. Which paragraph indicates that this story is set on an island?

a. Paragraph 2
b. Paragraph 8
c. Paragraph 9
d. Paragraph 11

29. What is the implication in paragraph 9 when the author writes "the zinc began to lift and shudder"?

a. Someone was on the roof
b. The zinc was too loose
c. Zinc is a poor roofing material
d. The winds were picking up

30. Why does the author use dialect in this piece?

a. It enhances the cultural setting of the story
b. The author doesn't know how to spell properly
c. It is a requirement for strong literary pieces
d. It enhances the historical setting of the story

31. What point of view is used in this story?

a. First person
b. Second person
c. Third person
d. A and C

32. In paragraph 11, what literary devices are used?

a. Personification
b. Simile and paradox
c. Personification and irony
d. Simile

33. What word best describes the setting depicted in paragraph 2?

a. Relaxed
b. Excited
c. Angry
d. Busy

34. Why does the author use personification and metaphor in paragraph 1?

a. These devices add literary flair
b. These devices energize the setting descriptions
c. There is no particular reason
d. There is no other way to describe things

35. What is Mimi's attitude toward the second half of the hurricane?

a. Excitement
b. Indifference
c. Anxiety
d. Fatigue

36. Based on the information presented in this story, what is the eye of a hurricane?

a. The center
b. The leading edge
c. The back edge
d. The worst part

37. Based on the story, how would you describe Adrian's role in the family?

a. He shies away from work
b. He cares for the family
c. He is the youngest brother
d. He is a prankster

38. Considering the dialect, setting descriptions, and other clues in the text, where does this story most likely take place?

a. A coastal country in Africa
b. An island in the South Pacific
c. A coastal country in South America
d. An island in the Caribbean

SHORT ANSWER QUESTION #2

Choose one character from this story and describe him or her in detail, focusing on two or three key character traits. Use evidence from the text to support your ideas.

Writing Test

Composition Prompt #1 – Expository Composition

Choose a current social problem about which you feel strongly. How would you resolve this social issue? Identify a specific potential solution and explain your solution in a well-developed essay.

Composition Prompt #2 – Literary Composition

Imagine you are receiving an award at an international symposium. What award are you receiving? Why? What are the presenters saying about your work? Tell about your experience.

Questions 39 – 48 pertain to the following procedural essay:

How to Bake Beautiful Brownies

(1) Who doesn't love brownies. (2) For decades, this decadent dessert has been a favorite. (3) While some cooks still craft brownies from starch, there are many mixes available that produce perfect, chewy, chocolaty brownies. (4) In fact, with the help of a mix, you can bake beautiful brownies in three simple steps.

(5) The first step in baking beautiful brownies is preparing your tools and ingredients. (6) You will need a large mixing bowl, a sturdy mixing spoon, and a properly-sized baking pan. (7) You will also need cooking spray and, of course, the brownie mix and the ingredients listed on the package. (8) Spray the bottom of the baking pan with the cooking spray, and preheat the oven to 350 degrees Fahrenheit. (9) When you have assembled and prepared everything, your ready to start mixing.

(10) The second step in baking beautiful brownies is making the batter. (11) Next, add the oil, water, and eggs as directed on the package. (12) Dump the brownie mix into your mixing bowl. (13) Using the sturdy spoon, mix the batter approximately 50 strokes, or until everything is well-moistened. (14) When the batter is ready, pour it into the pan, smoothing the top with the back of the mixing spoon. (15) Finally, your brownies are ready to go into the oven.

(16) The last step in baking beautiful brownies is the actual baking. (17) Place the pan in the oven and set a timer for the appropriate time listed on the brownie mix packaging. (18) It is a good idea to check the brownies too or three minutes before the baking time is up to prevent over-baking. (19) When a toothpick inserted two inches from the edge of the pan comes out with moist crumbs on it the brownies are done. (20) Remove the brownies from the oven, and place them on a rack to cool.

(21) When the brownies are cool, cute them to the desired size. (22) Using a plastic knife to cut the brownies. (23) This will prevent tearing and create smooth cut lines. (24) Now, there's only one thing left to do—enjoy your beautifully-baked brownies. (25) You deserve them!

39. In sentence 1, what change, if any, needs to be made?

a. No change is needed.
b. Change the period to a question mark
c. Change the period to an exclamation point
d. Change the period to a comma

40. What change, if any, is necessary to improve the meaning and clarity of sentence 3?

a. No change is necessary.
b. Remove the comma after starch
c. Change craft to crave
d. Change starch to scratch

41. Which sentence functions as the thesis of this essay?

a. Sentence 2
b. Sentence 3
c. Sentence 4
d. Sentence 5

42. What change, if any, needs to be made in sentence 6?

a. No change is necessary
b. Add a colon after need
c. Remove the comma after spoon
d. Insert a comma between sturdy and mixing

43. What is the problem with sentence 9?

a. Have should be had
b. Your should be you're
c. There should not be a comma after everything
d. Everything should be every thing

44. How could the sentence order be improved in the third paragraph?

a. Switch sentences 11 and 12
b. Switch sentences 13 and 14
c. Switch sentences 12 and 13
d. Switch sentences 14 and 15

45. What change, if any, is needed in sentence 18?

a. No change is needed.
b. Change too to two
c. Change three to 3
d. Insert a comma after up

46. What punctuation change is most appropriate in sentence 19?

a. No change is needed.
b. Insert a comma after out and a comma after it
c. Insert a comma after it
d. Replace the period with an exclamation point

47. What change, if any, is needed in sentence 21?

a. No change is needed.
b. Remove the comma after cool
c. Change to to into
d. Change cute to cut

48. How would you classify the problem with sentence 22?

a. It is a gerund phrase, not a sentence
b. It is an infinitive phrase, not a sentence
c. It is a comma splice, not a sentence
d. There is no error in sentence 22

Questions 49 – 58 pertain to the following essay:

Road Trip

(1) Nothing says Summer like a family road trip. (2) There's just something about the sweaty, sweltering hours in a crowded car that makes each road trip seem like a memorable—if misguided—adventure. (3) I've been on several roadtrips in my life, and each one had its own special charm. (4) Above all other road trips, however, I will always remember my family trip to the Grand Canyon when I was twelve years old.

(5) The day we left was bright and cloudless. (6) I squeezed into the backseat between my little brother, Ronnie, and my big sister, Rebecca. (7) We piled the ingredients of a successful road trip around us, sodas, snacks, music, and games. (8) By the time we hit the freeway—a mere seven miles from our house—Ronnie and I had each already downed a whole soda and were starting on a second one, we were also halfway through a bag of chips. (9) What can I say? (10) We were growing boys. (11) Needless to say, we begged to stop at every rest area along the route, driving my father crazy.

(12) Another thing that drove my father memorably crazy was our road games. (13) Twenty minutes into our drive, Rebecca began the alphabet game. (14) We start with the letter A, and each time one of us saw the next letter of the alphabet, we shouted it out. (15) There were long periods of silence as we watched road signs and license plates intently. (16) Then, when a letter appeared, we would all burst out shouting, and my startled father would swerve in surprise and yell at us to keep the noise down. (17) The alphabet game was a source of grate amusement and a handful of fistfights during that never-ending trip.

(18) The trip wasn't all fun and games, however. (19) In fact, we had several disasters on our journey. (20) In retrospect, our challenges seem almost funny, but at the time, they seemed tragic. (21) We blue a tire on a lonely, dusty stretch of highway in triple-digit temperatures. (22) We caught some fish in a tiny, lakeside campground just across the Arizona border, but Mom turned our fish to charcoal over the campfire. (23) When we finally made it to the Grand Canyon, Rebecca fell on a rocky trail and broke her ankle. (24) We spent the rest of the trip in a dimly-lit hotel room, playing cards and watching movies so Rebecca wouldn't feel left out.

(25) Looking back, I'm sure it wasn't the trip my parents had planned for it to be. (26) But it was a trip I will never forget. (27) It was the imperfections that made the trip so memorable. (28) By the time we got home, we all hated each other a little and loved each other a lot.

49. What change, if any, needs to be made in sentence 1?

a. No change is needed.
b. Change says to say
c. Change Summer to summer
d. Change road trip to roadtrip

50. In sentence 3, what change is most appropriate?

a. Change roadtrips to road trips
b. Change been to being
c. Change had to has
d. Sentence 3 is correct as it is written.

51. Which sentence in paragraph 1 functions as the thesis of this essay?

a. Sentence 1
b. Sentence 2
c. Sentence 3
d. Sentence 4

52. How can the punctuation error in sentence 7 be corrected?

a. Insert commas after ingredients and trip
b. Change the comma after us to a colon
c. Change the comma after us to a semicolon
d. Remove the comma after music

53. What is the problem with sentence 8?

a. There is no problem with sentence 8
b. Sentence 8 is a sentence fragment
c. Sentence 8 is a comma splice
d. Sentence 8 has a misused infinitive phrase

54. What correction, if any, is needed in sentence 14?

a. No correction is needed
b. Change start to started
c. Change saw to see
d. Change shouted to shout

55. In sentence 17, what change is most appropriate?

a. Change grate to great
b. Change handful to hand full
c. Change fistfights to fist fights
d. Change never-ending to never ending

56. What change, if any, should be made in sentence 21?

a. No change is necessary.
b. Change blue to blew
c. Change highway to high-way
d. Change triple-digit to triple digit

57. In sentence 23, which of the following is the most appropriate correction?

a. Remove the comma after Canyon
b. Insert a comma after trail
c. Insert a comma after it
d. Sentence 23 is correct as it is written

58. Which of the following sentences would make the best concluding sentence for this essay?

a. The alphabet game was the best part of all
b. In the end, it would have been more enjoyable if we had not blown a tire and Rebecca had not broken her ankle
c. The challenges we faced and the unexpected experiences made our Grand Canyon adventure the most memorable trip ever
d. I feel blessed to have such an adventurous family

Questions 59 – 68 pertain to the following essay:

A Brief History of Basketball

(1) Basketball is, arguably, one of the most popular and most exciting sports of our time. (2) Behind this fast-paced sport, however, is a rich history. (3) There has been many changes made to the game over the years, but the essence remains the same. (4) From it's humble beginnings in 1891, basketball has grown to have worldwide appeal.

(5) One thing that sets the history of basketball apart from other major sports is the fact that it was created by just one man. (6) In 1891, Dr. James Naismith, a teacher and Presbyterian Minister, needed an indoor game to keep college students at the Springfield, Massachusetts YMCA Training School busy during long winter days. (7) This need prompted the creation of basketball, which was originally played by tossing a soccer ball into an empty peach basket nailed to the gym wall. (8) There was two teams, but only one basket in the original game.

(9) Dr. Naismith's YMCA game became so popular that teams began to form throughout the New England region. (10) Early games among these teams were rough and rowdy. (11) In fact, the games were generally played in steel or chicken-wire cages players often became injured when they crashed into these cages. (12) Over time, the metal cages were replaced by rope-mesh cages, reducing injuries and making basketball a more enjoyable game for the players.

(13) Just as the equipment for the game of basketball has changed over time the rules have changed as well. (14) The original game, as it was invented by Dr. Naismith, had only 13 rules written on two pages. (15) In contrast, the modern rulebook has more than 60 pages of rules! (16) Despite the increase in rules, the basics of basketball have not changed in more than a century, making it relatively simple to learn and play.

(17) Because of the simplicity of basketball, the game had spread across the nation within 30 years of its invention in Massachusetts. (18) As more teams formed, the need for a league became apparent. (19) The smaller National Basketball League (NBL) formed soon after. (20) On June 6, 1946, the Basketball Association of

America (BAA) was formed. (21) In 1948, the BAA absconded the NBL, and the National Basketball Association (NBA) was born. (22) The NBA played its first full season in 1948-49 and is still going strong today.

(23) Though much has changed in our world since 1891, the popularity of the sport of basketball has remained strong. (24) From it's humble start in a YMCA gym to the multi-million-dollar empire it is today, the simple fun of the sport has endured. (25) Although many changes have been made over the years, the essence of basketball has remained constant. (26) Its rich history and simplicity ensure that basketball will always be a popular sport around the world.

59. What correction, if any, needs to be made in sentence 1?

a. No correction is needed.
b. Remove the comma after arguably
c. Remove both commas
d. Insert a comma after popular

60. In sentence 3, what change is most appropriate?

a. Remove the comma
b. Change has to have
c. Change been to being
d. Sentence 3 is correct as it is written

61. How would you correct sentence 4 in this essay?

a. Change beginnings to beginning
b. Change worldwide to world-wide
c. Change has to had
d. Change it's to its

62. What type of error is found in sentence 6?

a. Punctuation error
b. Wording error
c. Capitalization error
d. There is not an error in sentence 6

63. What correction, if any, is necessary in sentence 8?

a. No correction is necessary
b. Change was to were
c. Write the numbers as numerals instead of words
d. Remove the comma

64. What is the problem with sentence 11?

a. It is a run-on sentence
b. It is a comma splice
c. It is a sentence fragment
d. Sentence 11 is correct as it is written

65. What change, if any, is needed in sentence 13?

a. No change is needed
b. Insert a comma after equipment
c. Insert a comma after time
d. Insert a comma after changed

66. Which of the following changes would most improve the organization and clarity of paragraph 5 of this essay?

a. The paragraph is correct as it is written
b. Move sentence 18 to the beginning of the paragraph
c. Switch sentences 19 and 20
d. Switch sentences 21 and 22

67. Which of the following words would best replace the misused word absconded in sentence 21?

a. Appropriated
b. Ascended
c. Aborted
d. Absorbed

68. What change, if any, is needed in sentence 24?

a. No change is needed
b. Change it's to its
c. Remove the hyphens from multi-million-dollar
d. Remove the comma after today

Answer Key and Explanations

TEKS Standard §110.31(b)(1)(B)

1. C: is the best choice because the connotation of the word "dungeon" is that the narrator's life is dark and unrelenting. The reason A is wrong is that the other details in the poem that precede line 8 (being caged, and surrounded by metal bars, having only one hour of being outdoors a day), wouldn't apply to someone living in the basement of a castle.

TEKS Standard §110.31(b)(3)

2. A: "Caged" is set in a prison. Although this fact is never explicitly stated anywhere in the poem, no other interpretation is possible. The author is caged, surrounded by metal bars, led around by authority figures, and allowed outdoors only once a day. Even when he is outdoors, he is still surrounded by chain link fences and barbed wired, and he is filled with despair and hopelessness.

TEKS Standard §110.31(b)(3)

3. D: Alliteration is used throughout the poem to underscore the repetitive nature of the narrator's life. Alliteration involves using words that share the same beginning sounds. Examples of this in the poem can be found in lines 2, 7, 9, 18, 27, and 28.

TEKS Standard §110.31(b)(3) and (5)(C)

4. A: is the best choice because this poem is written using first-person point of view. That is, the story is told from the point of view of the subject, the prisoner. Had the second person point of view been used, instead of "I", the author would have used "you" to refer to the subject of the poem. Had it been written in the third person, the subject of the poem would be "he" or "the prisoner", or the prisoner's name.

TEKS Standard §110.31(b)(3)(A) and (7)

5. B: is the best choice because lines 18-22 reference the narrator's desire for a fresh start. He talks about being "cleansed", or putting his past and his bad deeds behind him, and says that every time he comes outside hope wells up inside him, only to be dashed when the guards come to take him back to his cell.

TEKS Standard §110.31(b)(5)(B) and Figure: 19 TAC §110.30(b)(110.31)(B)

6. D: The misspelled words in paragraph 2 indicate slurred speech caused by the father's intoxication.

TEKS Standard §110.31(b)(5)(A) and Figure: 19 TAC §110.30(b)(110.31)(B)

7. A: Paragraph 6 clearly shows that the physical abuse by Megan's father is a common occurrence with this sentence: "She had learned long ago that backing away only prolonged the misery."

TEKS Standard §110.31(b)(5) and Figure: 19 TAC §110.30(b)(110.31)(B)

8. C: "Freedom Run" is set late at night in dark settings to illustrate the darkness that her father's drunkenness and physical abuse creates in Megan's life.

TEKS Standard §110.31(b)(5) and Figure: 19 TAC §110.30(b)(110.31)(B)

9. B: is the best choice because paragraph 21 is meant to indicate that Megan did not want to go home because running represents freedom from her troubled life.

TEKS Standard §110.31(b)(5) and Figure: 19 TAC §110.30(b)(110.31)(B)

10. D: Paragraph 24 is the portion of the story that best describes Megan's feelings toward her father. The author makes it clear that the abuse has caused Megan to develop a love/hate relationship with her father.

TEKS Standard §110.31(b)(7)

11. C: Darkness is the symbol of depression and trouble that is used in both pieces.

TEKS Standard §110.31(b)(2)

12. B: Megan and the narrator of "Caged" both strongly desire freedom, one from incarceration, and the other from physical abuse at the hands of her drunken father.

TEKS Standard §110.31(b)(2)

13. A: Both Megan and the narrator of "Caged" demonstrate a sense of hopelessness at the end. With the unnamed prisoner, this is expressed explicitly. His hopes for a new beginning are crushed every day when the guards return him to his prison cell, where he will face 23 more hours of despair. Megan's hopelessness is not as clear, but by not showing any indication of real change on the part of her father, the author clearly implies that Megan's life will be much the same tomorrow night, and every night for the foreseeable future.

TEKS Standard §110.31(b)(5)

14. D: Megan is a victim through no fault of her own. She has done nothing to deserve the violent physical attacks by her father, while the man in the poem is suffering in prison because of his own actions in the past.

SAMPLE SHORT ANSWER #1

"Caged" is written in first-person point of view. This gives the reader an inside perspective on what the narrator is thinking and feeling. With the use of the first-person pronoun "I," the reader feels intimately connected to the narrator, increasing the power of the passage.

In contrast to "Caged," "Freedom Run" is written in third-person point of view. This gives the reader a broad perspective on Megan's life and her situation. It also allows the author to include details that could not be included in first-person writing. This increases the power of the writing by making it more objective.

TEKS Standard §110.31(b)(1)(A)

15. C: The word "imbecile" is used as an insult; it means a very stupid person. The word "fool" means pretty much the same thing.

TEKS Standard §110.31(b)(10)(A)

16. B: The article does not list enhanced literacy as a benefit of video games, but it does list all the benefits found in the other answer choices.

TEKS Standard §110.31(b)(1)(A)

17. A: The noun "plethora" means "a wide variety."

TEKS Standard §110.31(b)(10) and (2)

18. D: This essay falls into the persuasive genre. The author is trying to persuade the reader that video games are actually good for one's health, contrary to widespread popular opinion.

TEKS Standard §110.31(b)(10)

19. B: Paragraphs 1, 5, and 6 do not use personal examples to illustrate the main ideas. Only Paragraph 2 does.

TEKS Standard §110.31(b)(10)(A)

20. D: The greatest weakness of this article is that it does not present facts or statistics to support its claims. A, B, and C do not reflect true weaknesses of the article. The article is lengthy enough for what it's trying to do, it's logical, and it's well written.

TEKS Standard §110.31(b)(10)

21. A: The main idea of paragraph 4 is that video games fill empty hours with fun. B, C, and D are not the best choices because they do not accurately represent the main idea of paragraph 4.

TEKS Standard §110.31(b)(10)

22. C: In paragraph 2, the author says that motion sensor systems have further enhanced users' coordination and reaction times.

TEKS Standard §110.31(b)(10) and (2)

23. A: The overall theme of the article is that video games offer a number of benefits.

TEKS Standard §110.31(b)(9)(A)

24. C offers an opinion-based critique of the article rather than a fact-based summary of the article. A, B, and D are all fact-based summaries rather than opinion-based critiques of the article.

TEKS Standard §110.31(b)(10)(A)

25. B most accurately reflects the reason that coordination development was listed as the first benefit in this article. The author says he is going to list the "top five" reasons video games are good for a person's health. Out of his five reasons, his first one, that video games improve coordination, is the most closely related to health. It's reasonable to assume that he therefore thinks it's the most important reason of the five.

TEKS Standard §110.31(b)(10)

26. D best summarizes the thoughts in paragraph 7, which is that video games are worth playing despite their pitfalls.

TEKS Standard §110.31(b)(1)(B)

27. C: Words can have both a denotation, which is their actual, literal meaning, and a connotation, which is the notion or feeling the word or phrase causes. "White and fluffy" are what most people would think of if they read the phrase "cotton ball clouds."

TEKS Standard §110.31(b)(5) and Figure: 19 TAC §110.30(b)(110.31)(B)

28. B: We know that this story takes place on an island, because it says so in paragraph 8: "the leading edge of the storm had already hit the southeastern tip of the island."

TEKS Standard §110.31(b)(1)(B)

29. D: The implication of "the zinc began to lift and shudder" in paragraph 9 is that the winds were picking up. The story indicates that people are using zinc to protect their homes from the winds, so when it begins to lift and shudder, it's a sign that the wind is getting even stronger.

TEKS Standard §110.31(b)(2)(C)

30. A: Dialect is used in this story to enhance the cultural setting of the story. By showing how the islanders actually speak, the author is adding authenticity to the story.

TEKS Standard §110.31(b)(5)

31. C: This story is written in third-person point of view. That means it's being told by a narrator, who does not have any part in the events. If it were written in the first-person, the story would be told by one of the main subjects, who would use personal pronouns such as "I", "we", "me", and "us."

TEKS Standard §110.31(b)(7)

32. A: When the author describes the rain as "drumming" in paragraph 11, this is an example of personification. Personification is attributing human actions or characteristics to inanimate things. Rain cannot play drums, but by employing this metaphor the author gives us an idea of how the rain sounded.

TEKS Standard §Figure: 19 TAC §110.30(b)(110.31)(B)

33. D: The setting depicted in paragraph 2 is best described as "busy." The opening sentence of the paragraph makes this clear: "Despite the impending storm, the little city center was alive with frantic bustle."

TEKS Standard §110.31(b)(7) and Figure: 19 TAC §110.30(b)(110.31)(B)

34. B: is the best choice because the personification and metaphor in paragraph 1 serve to energize the setting description; that is, they help bring the scene to life in the reader's mind.

TEKS Standard §110.31(b)(5) and Figure: 19 TAC §110.30(b)(110.31)(B)

35. C: Paragraph 19 makes it clear that Mimi's attitude toward the second half of the hurricane is anxiety.

TEKS Standard §110.31(b)(1)(B)

36. A: The text indicates that the eye of the hurricane is the center of the hurricane. It does so by showing the lull that develops between the first half of the hurricane, and the second half.

TEKS Standard §110.31(b)(5) and Figure: 19 TAC §110.30(b)(110.31)(B)

37. B: Throughout the story, Adrian works hard to help protect the family from the hurricane.

TEKS Standard §110.31(b)(7) and (2)(C)

38. D: Based on the dialect, setting, and other clues in the text, this story likely takes place on an island in the Caribbean.

Sample Short Answer #2

Mimi is nurturing, caring deeply for her family. Her nurturing tendencies are seen in paragraph 4, when she cautions Adrian not to fall, and in paragraph 8, when Mimi stirs the dinner without being asked and then goes to help her brother. These passages—and others—clearly demonstrate her desire to help and care for others.

In addition to her nurturing qualities, Mimi also exhibits a great deal of anxiety. In paragraph 12, she has trouble falling asleep because of the storm. In paragraph 20, Mimi sits "stiffly" even in the calm eye of the storm, while paragraph 19 discusses her fear in the face of the second half of the storm. Finally, in paragraph 22, Mimi is once again unable to sleep because of anxiety, reiterating the anxious nature of her personality.

Sample Composition #1 – Expository Composition:

Triumph Through Training Programs

In our current economy, unemployment is a pressing issue. The unemployment numbers for young people, however, are up to 50 percent higher than those for experienced workers. Most young people are not adequately equipped to compete in the work world. This problem can be tackled through training programs designed to help young workers identify their interests, develop skills, and build a professional network.

First, training programs can help unemployed young people identify their interests. Many young workers are clueless about their professional passions and natural aptitudes. Training programs can help them identify these things and find areas in which they should develop. This will help young and inexperienced workers develop passion and motivation for their job search.

Once interests have been identified, training programs can help young workers develop skills in those areas of interest. More practical and focused than college courses, training programs can hone in on specific traits and abilities necessary for particular jobs or industries. Developing these skills can give young workers both confidence and a competitive edge over other job candidates.

With a list of interests and a wealth of new skills, young workers can also use training programs to build a professional network. Industry contacts are more necessary than ever before when conducting a job search. The old adage, "It's not what you know; it's who you know," has proven true for many job seekers. Training programs can help young workers build a professional network of contacts through special speakers, job fairs, internships, and other avenues.

Searching for a job is always daunting, but it can be especially intimidating for workers with little or no experience. Training programs can help ease these fears. They can help workers identify interests, develop skills, and build a professional network of contacts. With these tools—gained through training programs—young workers will be equipped to beat the unemployment obstacles and go out and find the job of their dreams.

Sample Composition #2 – Literary Composition:

Humanitarian of the Year

The crowd hushed as the Master of Ceremonies stepped to the microphone. He began with the story of Peter, a sickly young boy who was cured by my dietary discovery. Then he spoke of Kayla, a mother of two, who was on her deathbed before using my serum. He invited the now-healthy Kayla, who was in attendance, to stand and wave. The audience smiled and applauded enthusiastically.

With a sideways glance at me, the Master of Ceremonies announced, "And now, please welcome our Humanitarian of the Year!"

As he called my name, the audience rose to their feet, and I slipped from my velvet-padded chair. I approached the podium and shook hands with the Master of Ceremonies. He gave me an award certificate and a plaque. We posed for a picture before the still-applauding crowd.

"Please, say a few words," he said, motioning to the microphone.

I nodded and stepped to the microphone as the audience took their seats. The room was warm and bright with soft lights and candles. Thick velvet drapes swathed the walls gracefully. Black-coated waiters floated among the well-dressed symposium attendees, refilling coffee and water and silently clearing finished plates. Nearly every eye was on me. This was my moment.

"Thank you for the honor of this award," I began. "The journey to this podium started five years ago when my mother became desperately ill."

I went on to tell them of my struggle to find a natural cure for her ills. From that struggle was born the dietary serum that had changed so many lives and helped so many people. I thanked my family, my research assistants, my sponsors, and my supporters. Then I took my seat.

Throughout the night, people approached me to share their stories. It seemed that everyone knew someone who had been affected by my discoveries. I listened to each story with an overwhelming mixture of awe and pride. I felt honored to be the Humanitarian of the Year, but I felt even more honored to have the opportunity to touch so many lives with my life's dream.

TEKS Standard §110.31(b)(18)(B)

39. B: Sentence 1 is a question and needs a question mark as the end punctuation.

TEKS Standard §110.31(b)(13)(C) and (D)

40. D: In this sentence, "scratch" is a better word choice than "starch." As written, that part of the sentence makes no sense, but it makes perfect sense if we replace "starch" with "scratch."

TEKS Standard §110.31(b)(15)(A)(iii)

41. C: Sentence 4 functions as the thesis statement for this essay, clearly presenting the main idea of the entire piece, which is how to bake beautiful brownies. Generally, the thesis sentence of an article will have much in common with the article's title.

TEKS Standard §110.31(b)(13)

42. A: Sentence 6 is correct as written; no change is necessary.

TEKS Standard §110.31(b)(13)(D) and (19)

43. B: Changing "your" into "you're" is the appropriate correction for sentence 9. "Your" is a possessive pronoun, while "you're" is a contraction of "you are", which is what the author intended to say here.

TEKS Standard §110.31(b)(13)

44. A: Switching sentences 11 and 12 improves the order and clarity of the third paragraph by organizing the steps more chronologically. B, C, and D would actually further disrupt the chronological order of the paragraph.

TEKS Standard §110.31(b)(13)(C) and (13)(D) and (19)

45. B: The word "two" is the correct word for sentence 18, as the concept referenced is a number. The word "too" means also, besides, in addition to, etc.

TEKS Standard §110.31(b)(18)(B)(ii)

46. A: Sentence 19 is correct as written; no change is needed.

TEKS Standard §110.31(b)(13)(C) and (13)(D)

47. D: The word "cute" is either a misspelling, or a typographical error; it should be "cut."

TEKS Standard §110.31(b)(17)(A)(i)

48. A: Sentence 22 is a sentence fragment consisting of nothing but a gerund phrase. It cannot stand alone as a sentence.

TEKS Standard §110.31(b)(18)(A)

49. C: The word "summer" has been improperly capitalized in sentence 1. In ordinary usage, the names of the seasons should not be capitalized.

TEKS Standard §110.31(b)(13)(D)

50. A: The phrase "road trip" should always be written as two words, not one. This holds true for the plural form of the phrase as well.

TEKS Standard §110.31(b)(15)(A)(iii)

51. D: Sentence 4 functions as the thesis in this essay. It introduces the main point of the article, which is to describe the author's memorable road trip to the Grand Canyon as a child.

TEKS Standard §110.31(b)(18)(B)

52. B: Changing the comma to a colon corrects the error in sentence 7 and prepares the reader for the list of items that follows.

TEKS Standard §110.31(b)(18)

53. C: Sentence 8 is a comma splice, which is a type of run-on sentence. A period should come after "one", and "we were also halfway through a bag of chips" should be converted into a complete sentence that stands alone.

TEKS Standard §110.31(b)(17)(A)(i)

54. B converts the verb "start" into the proper past tense, "started." This matches the tense of not only the rest of the sentence, but also the rest of the article.

TEKS Standard §110.31(b)(13)(C) and (13)(D) and (19)

55. A: The word "grate" is incorrect; it should be "great." Either the author made a spelling error, or he confused two words that sound exactly alike, but have two different meanings – "grate" and "great."

TEKS Standard §110.31(b)(13)(C) and (13)(D) and (19)

56. B: The word "blue"is a color. It should be replaced with the word "blew", which is a verb.

TEKS Standard §110.31(b)(13)

57. D: Sentence 19 is correct as written; no change is needed.

TEKS Standard §110.31(b)(13)

58. C: This is the best choice for a concluding sentence, because it's about the entire story. The other choices don't focus on the story as a whole, but only smaller parts of it.

TEKS Standard §110.31(b)(18)(B)(2)

59. A: Sentence 1 is correct as it is written.

TEKS Standard §110.31(b)(17)(A)

60. B: Sentence 3 needs a plural verb "have been" in this clause, in order to match the plural subject of the clause, which is "changes."

TEKS Standard §110.31(b)(17)(A) and (18)(B)

61. D: The word "it's" in this sentence is used incorrectly, because it is a contraction of "it is", which makes no sense. The word should be "its", which is a possessive pronoun.

TEKS Standard §110.31(b)(18)(A)

62. C: Sentence 6 contains a capitalization error. The word "minister" should not be capitalized unless it's part of a title. In this instance, it's not part of a title, but is used as a job description.

TEKS Standard §110.31(b)(17)(A)(i)

63. B: In the first clause of sentence 8, "teams" is plural, so it must have a plural verb to go with it. So "was" needs to be changed to "were."

TEKS Standard §110.31(b)(13)(D)

64. A: Sentence 11 is a run-on sentence. It should be corrected by adding a semicolon after "cages."

TEKS Standard §110.31(b)(18)(B)(ii)

65. C: Adding a comma after time separates the introductory clause from the main clause of the sentence.

TEKS Standard §110.31(b)(13)

66. C: Switching sentences 19 and 20 improves the organization and clarity of paragraph 5.

TEKS Standard §110.31(b)(13)(C)

67. D: The word "absconded" means "went away secretly and in a hurry"; it makes no sense in this sentence. The word "absorbed" should replace it, to show that the two entities combined to form a single organization.

TEKS Standard §110.31(b)(13)(C)

68. B: The word "its" in this sentence is used incorrectly, because it is actually a possessive pronoun. The word needed is "it's", which is a contraction of "it is."

Thank You

We at Mometrix would like to extend our heartfelt thanks to you, our friend and patron, for allowing us to play a part in your journey. It is a privilege to serve people from all walks of life who are unified in their commitment to building the best future they can for themselves.

The preparation you devote to these important testing milestones may be the most valuable educational opportunity you have for making a real difference in your life. We encourage you to put your heart into it—that feeling of succeeding, overcoming, and yes, conquering will be well worth the hours you've invested.

We want to hear your story, your struggles and your successes, and if you see any opportunities for us to improve our materials so we can help others even more effectively in the future, please share that with us as well. **The team at Mometrix would be absolutely thrilled to hear from you!** So please, send us an email (support@mometrix.com) and let's stay in touch.

If you'd like some additional help, check out these other resources we offer for your exam:

http://MometrixFlashcards.com/STAAR

Additional Bonus Material

Due to our efforts to try to keep this book to a manageable length, we've created a link that will give you access to all of your additional bonus material.

Please visit https://www.mometrix.com/bonus948/staareoceng1 to access the information.